MY
SEARCH
FOR PATTY HEARST

MY
SEARCH
FOR PATTY HEARST

BY STEVEN WEED
WITH SCOTT SWANTON

CROWN PUBLISHERS, INC.
NEW YORK

Library of Congress Cataloging in Publication Data

Weed, Steven.
  My search for Patty Hearst.

  1. Hearst, Patricia, 1954-   2. Weed, Steven.
3. Symbionese Liberation Army.   I. Swanton, Scott,
joint author.   II. Title.
F866.2.H42W4   1976   322.4'2'0924 [B]   75-44214
ISBN   0-517-52579-8

Fourth Printing, February, 1976

ACKNOWLEDGMENTS

If I can point to anything positive and affirming that emerged for me during the four months here described, February to June 1974, it would be the understanding, support, and friendship of the people below, to whom I would like to dedicate this book.

Joan Baez, Regis Debray, Bill and Patty Huett, Paul Jacobs, Tom Mathews, Jennetta Sagan, Hedy Sarney, Patrick Tobin, Jack Webb, and Colston Westbrook.

Political and social activists: Mark Dowie of Transitions To Freedom, Viela Garcia Hancock of the Vacaville Project, Willie Holder of The Prisoners Union, John Maher of Delancey Street, John McLean of the American Indian Movement, Eve Pell of the Prison Law Collective, Ron Silliman of the Committee for Prisoner Humanity and Justice, and Cecil Williams and Louis Sawyer of Glide Memorial Church.

Psychiatrists and scholars: Wes Davis, Frederick Hacker, Brian Jenkins, Robert Jay Lifton, and John Nardini.

Berkeley policemen: Steve Engler, Matt Perez, and Dan Wolke.

News people: Paul Avery, Skip Brown, Tim Findley, Bob Joffee, Carol Pogash, Richard Threlkeld, and Joe Russin.

Thanks also to researcher Mimi Swanton and editor Larry Freundlich.

And finally to Patty's and my friends, my parents, and attorneys Ellis Alden, Bob Lane, Murray Petersen, Ed Stow, and John Welles, without whom this book could never have been written.

And the end of all our exploring
Will be to arrive where we started
And know the place for the first time.
—T. S. ELIOT
Four Quartets

1

I AM WRITING this in a Berkeley apartment that I rented ten months after Patty was kidnapped. Stored in the garage below are some of her school books, which I packed in cartons when I moved out of our apartment on Benvenue Street. In the desk at which I am writing is one of her old student body cards from Santa Catalina, a Catholic boarding school she attended in the ninth and tenth grades. Her picture is on it, a fifteen-year-old girl with her hair in braids, smiling happily, carelessly. . . . It is still hard to believe that at this same moment, fifteen miles across the bay, Patty is sitting in a jail cell in Redwood City.

Yesterday I had a long talk with one of the four psychiatrists appointed by the court to examine Patty. A friendly, down-to-earth woman, she told me that, though reticent and withdrawn at first, Patty was now opening up and cooperating fully. The doctor could not discuss her conversations with Patty, nor her opinion of her mental state, but before leaving she hesitated and then showed me a picture Patty had drawn of a man and a woman as part of her examination. It shocked me. Crudely drawn with uneven lines, the bodies out of proportion and the faces unsmiling, the picture struck me as something that could have been produced by a six-year-old. "She worked on that for seven minutes," the doctor told me. "Don't underestimate what the last year and a half has been for her."

At this writing I have not yet seen Patty. The day she was captured, September 18, I called her attorney, Terrance Hallinan, and asked if I could visit her. "I think she'll pass on that," he said.

"You mean she doesn't want to see me."

"That's the feeling I get, Steve."

I was saddened by that, both hurt and a little resentful. Patty and I will see each other again—I've been told that her feelings are changing—but under what circumstances I cannot say. For now, my only contact with her is through some of our old friends.

Three days after my call to Hallinan, Mimi Swanton, Patty's and my closest friend in Berkeley, stepped into the jail's visiting room, a corridor divided by a wall of glass and a long table lined with telephones. Patty was waiting for her at the table, dressed in blue pants and a pale green prison smock.

"When I first came in she put both her hands up on the glass and I put mine up too," Mimi said. "We just held them there for a while. She looked pretty much the same, like the same old Patrish."

Because they knew their conversation was being recorded, they limited their talk to old friends and old times, the new permanent Mimi had gotten, that sort of thing. But then, toward the end of the visit, Patty tried to communicate something through the glass. "She was gesturing animatedly and trying to mouth out the words, but I couldn't get it," Mimi told me. She said that Patty took out a notebook, but was exasperated when she couldn't find a pen and sank back in her chair.

"I heard that you don't want to see Steve," Mimi said at one point.

"Not now . . . not in jail," Patty replied.

Mimi told me that Patty's eyes darkened with tears at that, but it was hard to know what she was feeling. "It's so weird," Patty kept saying. "It's all so weird, isn't it?"

A female guard moved up to her and informed her that her time was up.

Mimi said, "One of the things that was really tender: we put our hands up on the glass again, and then as we were leaving we were walking side by side on opposite sides of the glass. Just before she went in the door with the guard she turned and looked back at me, then smiled and waved. We were both on the verge of tears."

It is so weird, so entirely strange. Two years ago Patty and I were living quietly on Benvenue. Except for our friends and our families, no one knew us. Like most students' lives, ours were pleasantly routinized with our studies, movies on weekends, laundromat and grocery runs. We were just two people. We were in love and planning to be married. At nine o'clock on the night of February 4 all of that ended. Two men with carbines charged in our door, knocking me to the floor and yanking Patty into the kitchen. In those few seconds everything we had together and everything we looked forward to was destroyed.

I look around this room now, at the stacks of notes, the newspaper clippings, the books and photographs, and the reels of tape-recorded communiqués that document the months following that night. For all of it, though I have tried, I cannot summon up the rage and despair, the reality and the unreality of what those months were for me. And yet my memories of my days with Patty on Benvenue are clear and immediate. But they are not memorable just because those days ended so violently. Our time in Berkeley had a special character of its own, a warmth, an excitement, and a feeling of belonging that was new to us. We would have remembered them anyway. We knew that then and I know that now. Even as I write this I remember Patty walking up to me one day with an armful of books, her choppy, determined little step bouncing her along. "Guess what?" she said. "I had a huge Polish dog today, with sauerkraut and onions."

"You what?" I asked as though outraged that she had broken her latest diet. Patty was forever coming up with new diets, though she hardly needed them. "Well, I guess it's back to old Thunder Thighs," I said.

"And tomorrow I'm going to have *two* Polish dogs," she announced, trying to hide a smile. "And call me Tiny," she demanded.

Patty is tiny, small-boned and compact, almost childlike. She could go from feisty and impish—"I just *hate* chemistry," she'd say, tossing her book aside and crossing her arms obstinately—to elegant inside of ten minutes. We'd be out in the back gardening, for instance, Patty struggling with a sack of peat moss, and then she'd dust off her jeans and go inside. I would hear the shower running, hear it stop, and moments later she would appear in the patio in a simple dress and sandals, looking clean, fresh and, well, elegant. It was disconcerting.

And then leaning over her lunch tray afternoons on campus: "Do you love me? Come on, let me hear you say it!"

"Well maybe," I'd tease her. "But you're pretty short. You know, dubious genes."

In response Patty would quickly point out one of *my* "many imperfections," slightly webbed toes. "I can just see our kids," she would breathe out resignedly, "little four-foot-tall webbed-toed wonders."

And the times when I would remind her about her schoolwork—"Come on, stop messing around in the kitchen," I'd call in to her. "You know you've got that paper due."

"Yes, *dear*." She'd curtsy. Then she'd tilt her head to the side with a dopey look, stick out her tongue at me, and scamper upstairs out of reach.

When I remember moments like that and then think of Patty now, sitting in a jail cell, charged with armed robbery, kidnapping, and a dozen other felonies, it is almost incomprehensible. In spite of my attempts to understand what happened and why it happened, I still find myself shaking my head and asking myself a question that I have asked over and over again: How is it possible that everything between Patty and me has come to this? How is it possible? . . . I have been searching for a way to begin this and I guess that question is as good a starting place as any—to go back to those Berkeley years, to one day in particular that, in view of what was to happen later, now stands out in my memory.

It was a crisp October morning and Patty and I were walking to campus. I was still a bit sleepy and daydreaming, and Patty was nibbling on a graham cracker. The sky was clear and blue, the leaves were just starting to turn, and as we walked along I remember feeling almost perplexed that our lives were going so smoothly, so according to plan. It was one of those moments when your perspective widens lazily and you're pleased and grateful for what you have. There was no particular reason for it, no special occasion, we were just happy together.

Patty and I took our usual route to campus that morning, passing the ivy-covered brown shingle homes, the divinity school boarding house, and at the end of our street a beautifully designed Christian Science church—all weathered redwood, stained glass windows and ancient wisteria vines gnarled around the trellises. Directly across the street, and in sharp contrast to the church's age and grace, was People's Park. Once the scene of pitched battles between students and police, it was quiet now except for a few crashers shaking out their sleeping bags and talking under the trees. Two blocks down was Telegraph Avenue, and while Patty and I sometimes enjoyed that carnival scene, the handicraft booths, the pretzel vendors, the underground newspaper hawkers, and the evangelists singing out the praises of the Lord and slapping their dog-eared Bibles on the corner, we preferred Berkeley's quiet side —the little shops and cafes, the bookstores, and the students bustling off to their morning classes.

After kissing Patty good-bye and watching her duck through

the mist blowing off the Sproul Plaza fountain, I was heading toward Sather Gate when, out of the corner of my eye, I saw a young woman approaching me with a tape recorder. Behind her stood an expressionless fellow with two cameras hanging from his neck.

"Hello. We're from *Womens Wear Daily,*" she said brightly. I looked around to make certain she was talking to me. "Could we have a moment of your time?"

"Sure," I said, thinking she was going to ask me about fall fashions on campus or something like that. But no, she explained that she was conducting a survey on student activism. She wanted to hear my opinion on "the current Berkeley scene" ten years after the Free Speech Movement. She held up her microphone and the photographer began moving around us firing away with his Nikon.

At long last, fame.

"Well," I said, summoning up my best professorial tone, "I think the sort of political activism that took place in the sixties is pretty much dead."

"Oh?"

"Yes. You'd probably find more to write about if you were doing a story on the rebirth of fraternities and sororities."

"Hmmm. Then you don't foresee a rebirth of political activism?"

I told her no, that as far as I could tell radicalism and confrontation politics were on the downward swing of the cycle. She smiled and turned off her tape recorder. "Thank you so much," she said, then moved into the crowd in search of another interview with a "typical Berkeley student."

At the time I thought that I had given her a pretty fair assessment of the current scene. Although "Kill the Pigs!" would appear in spray paint on some empty wall and there might be a pipe-bomb discovered at a Bank of America construction site, these struck me as isolated incidents committed by isolated malcontents. The radical leaders of the sixties, principally Mario Savio and Jerry Rubin, were no longer in Berkeley, nor were they even considered radical anymore. From what I'd heard, Savio was down in Los Angeles somewhere finishing up his PhD, a family man with an eye to the future. Rubin was in San Francisco, wearing body shirts and dividing his time between hobnobbing with three-dot columnists and seeking higher consciousness. As for the masses of angry students that once gathered around the loudspeakers, raising their fists in militant salutes, many were now into communal living upcountry, displaying their handmade hookas down on Telegraph, meditating on the teachings of Zen, Jesus Christ, or Maharaj Ji, holding down straight jobs or whatever—just doing their thing.

But there was something else going on, a dark underside to the Berkeley scene that Patty and I were not aware of, or at least a side that was convenient to ignore. There were the latecomers— the embittered Vietnam vets, the angry young women, the drifters and dropouts who had come from all over because they had heard that Berkeley was the place to get your head together and work for the revolution, "funky Berkeley revolution," as Eldridge Cleaver had called it. "Death to the fascist insect that preys upon the life of the people," he had said. But after swatting flies in Algeria for two years, Cleaver had moved to Paris, and now he wanted to come home again. And although Huey was free, and Angela was free, and Bobby Seale was free, there was little talk of armed struggle, fighting in the streets, and revolution. Now it was "progressive legislation," food programs, lecture circuits, and Seale for mayor. To those who had come to Berkeley to struggle and fight, this was counterrevolutionary. It was copping out, compromising with the enemy, the pigs. There could be no compromise with the pigs. The time had come for action, not talk. The oppressors would "change or die by our guns!"

"Radicalism and confrontation politics are on the downward swing of the cycle," I told the reporter from *Womens Wear Daily,* then headed for my philosophy section.

Less than a month later, at seven o'clock on the night of November 6, 1973, Oakland school superintendent Marcus Foster, a highly respected black educator imported from Philadelphia, and his aide, Robert Blackburn, left an executive session of a school board meeting. They walked out the rear exit of the auditorium and down a narrow alley, passing two people who were leaning against the wall to their left. When they got to the car, Blackburn started to walk around it to unlock the passenger door for Foster, unaware that the two people had followed them. Before he got to it they began firing at Foster with pistols. One of the bullets hit Blackburn in the arm, then he was hit by a shotgun blast from a third assailant hiding in the shrubbery behind him. Both Foster and Blackburn went down. One of the assailants moved within point-blank range and shot Foster four or five more times before three of them fled. Blackburn managed to stand up and stagger to the school building, letting himself in the door before collapsing.

By the time they were taken to Highland Hospital, the odor of cyanide was noticed and grains of the chemical were found in Foster's wounds. He died en route. Blackburn was put in an intensive care unit and, though critically injured, he survived the attack.

The following morning, Berkeley's underground radio station KPFA received what was to be the first communiqué from a group calling itself the Symbionese Liberation Army. It stated that the "shoot on sight" order would stay in effect until all "political police" were removed from the Oakland schools and all forms of student identification were stopped. Incredible as it seemed, the statement appeared to be referring to a proposed "truancy team," which Foster had already removed from the school board's agenda as too controversial, and a student I.D. card program that was voluntary. That he had been shot to death in a parking lot for this stunned and confused the entire community.

A few days after Foster's assassination I remember my old Princeton roommate, Nate, and his girl friend, Gloria, dropping by our apartment and shaking their heads at the morning papers. "Looks like they're going to have to shoot all of us black folk to save us," Gloria said.

Like everyone else who had heard it on the six o'clock news or read it in the papers, Patty and I were upset by the death of Marcus Foster, but only temporarily. We were relatively new to Berkeley, and if we had heard of Marcus Foster before his death, we did not remember it. And although the scene of his assassination was only five miles from our apartment, it seemed far more distant than that, totally removed from our quiet life on Benvenue.

Patty and I had moved to Berkeley in the summer of 1972, or rather I had done the moving—lugging in the stereo, unpacking the pots and pans, negotiating the stairway with a box of books—while she toured through Europe, basking in the Mediterranean sun and absorbing the artistic magnificence of ancient Greece. "My Darling," she wrote on one of her postcards. "We went to some islands yesterday and spent the afternoon in the sun and sea. The water is so blue and warm, and it sparkles so. You'll really love Greece. I just wish you were here with me." So did I. While I was glad that she was having such a good time, I remember trying to shove a five-foot desk through a four-foot doorway and then resolving that she would be on the other end when it came time to shove the damn thing out again.

We had picked out the apartment together before she left —a two-bedroom unit in a modern, redwood-shingled fourplex with a patch of dirt in back for gardening—and I had bought her an inexpensive wedding band to wear when we signed the lease as Mr. and Mrs. Weed. A few weeks later, in mid-June, she took off on a tour with six other students led by Patrick Tobin, a rather erudite instructor from Menlo College who saw the trip as a cram course in art and culture. "I have to be carried through the Louvre on a litter, swooning," he told Patty, which was not far from the truth.

Still Patty enjoyed the tour, but then about halfway through it she wrote: "I hate to admit it, Sweetie, but I'm terribly homesick. . . . Venice is nice, but smelly. Rome is really beautiful, but I'm afraid to go out of the hotel alone—men don't just whistle here, they run at you and try to grab you! I am even getting tired of looking at all the uncircumcised penises on the statues around here! . . . I may never open another art book again. . . ."

But things improved. The high point of Patty's trip came in August, when she spent a week in the lush green countryside of Shropshire, England, visiting Heather, a lovely woman who had been her younger sisters' governess. She spent much of her time horseback riding, having heart-to-heart talks with Heather and looking after Heather's grandchild—all of which she loved—but she was still anxious to come home; and I was just as anxious to have her home. "I'm dying to get back and set up our little house," she wrote. "And I want Mexican food so badly I can taste it."

Patty's homecoming hardly lived up to her expectations, however. She had called collect from Chicago to remind me when she was arriving at the Oakland Airport, which was only a few hours later that same night, but she really just wanted to talk on the phone. We did talk awhile, but because I was disinclined to start off our life in Berkeley with a fifty-dollar phone bill, I was a little impatient with her. On the heels of this, when she got off the plane three hours later I was not there to greet her. I was cursing traffic in downtown Oakland, having taken the wrong freeway exit. When I finally arrived I was half an hour late.

The Oakland Airport is a small terminal that fills and empties with every flight. When I walked through the electric doors it was almost deserted, except for Patty. She was sitting forlornly on her backpack in the corner of the baggage department. She had been crying and looked like a wet dishrag. But she wasn't really mad at me for being late; she was just worried about us.

Despite Patty's self-confidence and the fact that we had rented an apartment together, there was an imbalance in our relationship at that point, and she knew it. We had met a year and a half before at Crystal Springs School for Girls. In those days she was an eleventh grader with a mind of her own and I was a second-year math teacher trying to keep such girls in their seats while explaining the mysteries of Euclidian geometry. I was twenty-three at the time; Patty was seventeen. Although we grew closer, finally falling in love and living together after Patty had graduated and enrolled in nearby Menlo College, the difference in our ages, in my "worldliness" and her inexperience, bothered her. Characteristically, she was bound and determined to catch up, which was one of the reasons she went to Europe in the first place. "Do you think I should go?" I remember her asking. I sensed that she wanted me to say no, but I told her I thought it would be a good idea. "You're right," she said matter-of-factly. "I'll go." And off she went, packing along a few pairs of jeans, some tee shirts, one dress, and my old Boy Scout shirt to knock around in. She had a good time, but, as I said, our reunion was not one of those spinning, slow motion embraces with violins enraptured. Her eyes were red and swollen, and she was sitting on a dirty knapsack.

"Oh, Patty, I'm sorry," I said, gathering her up.

"It's nothing," she sniffled. "It's stupid."

But it was not so stupid. After being separated for two months, the combination of my impatience on the phone and my late arrival had frightened her. Unlike our year in Menlo Park, which was a pleasant, but an experimental time for us, the move to Berkeley meant commitment, and for Patty her first real move away from home. In that sense we were really just starting out together.

One look at our new apartment and Patty called me a "poor, pathetic man." "What have you been living on?" she asked. Eggs, I told her. Scrambled eggs, boiled eggs, fried eggs, and egg salad sandwiches when I was feeling ambitious and there was some mayonnaise in the refrigerator.

Starting the next morning, and continuing well into the year, Patty and I began to set up our new home—buying some chairs and a coffee table, potting plants, refinishing an old dresser, framing prints, and stocking up the cupboards, the first on our list of priorities. In fact we worked from the kitchen outward, which quickly produced a natural division of labor. I did the outside work and house cleaning and doubled as a handyman when an upstairs faucet began to leak and soak a hole in the living room ceiling. Patty did most of the cooking and shopping, always dragging me along to the supermarket with her, then raising her eyes to heaven when I'd go sailing by on the back of our shopping cart, trying to pull a 360 at the end of the aisle.

At first Patty was a better shopper than she was a cook. I remember her buying a special omelet pan, carefully seasoning it, then burning her first omelet to a crisp. Another time I came in to find her sitting disappointedly on a chair, tapping a fork against the counter, and watching her first soufflé flatten out. But with the help of cookbooks, hints from friends, and determination, she soon became a competent cook. She had always been an excellent baker, making pies, cakes, cookies from "Grandma Weed's famous recipes," but sometimes, when time was short and the need great, she went to Duncan Hines, mixing the frosting while I lurked nearby.

Because most of Patty's and my friends were still living across the bay and we were busy with our new place, at first our only friend in Berkeley was Mimi, who had also taught at Crystal Springs. Mimi had moved to Berkeley shortly after we did, enrolling in the graduate folklore department, and we quickly became a threesome—checking out the local cafes and restaurants, going to a Charlie Chaplin film on campus, or just hanging around our apartment, laughing as Mimi regaled us with her misadventures in the Singles Scene, "singing for her supper," as Patty used to tease her. Our apartment was not the neatest place in the world— Patty's clothes piled on her dresser, books and papers cluttering the coffee table, *National Lampoon*s and *Sunset* magazines strewn here and there—but all in all it was "comfortably sloppy," as Mimi described it. It was also becoming a home.

By the time the fall quarter began, Patty and I were fairly well settled in. Each morning I would head for campus and Patty would drive to her job as a clerk at Capwell's department store. Although she could have entered U.C. immediately, Patty had never had a job before and insisted upon going to work. "It'll be really good experience for me," she said, and it was. Of course after a forty-hour week in the greeting card department, she looked forward to puttering around the garden, visiting Mimi, who would fill her in on the latest tragedy on "The Young and the Restless" —a TV soap opera they were both addicted to because it was "so straightforwardly stupid"—or having some of our friends over for dinner on the weekends.

Since Patty rarely saw her old classmates, many of whom were away at college, it was usually my friends who came to visit. Naturally they were Patty's friends as well, but most of them were also at least ten years her senior. Two of them, Diana and Stu Olson, had known Patty as a student at Crystal, where Diana taught, and then at Menlo College where Stu taught biology. So while they were extremely fond of Patty, the image of her in her checkered Crystal uniform, or as a pretty seventeen-year-old freshman at Menlo still lingered. Moreover, because all of us had known each other before I met Patty, we had developed the usual conversational shortcuts and in jokes and would often lock horns over old scores that sometimes went over Patty's head. But if this bothered her she didn't show it. While she was generally rather quiet during these gatherings, she had a sort of presence, a self-assurance that made itself felt in any conversation whether she was speaking or not. "At her age I would have been a little cowed in the company of my thirty-year-old ex-teachers," I remember Stu telling me once, "but Patty's definitely not cowed. She's got some kind of momentum going for her. I don't know if she gets it from her family, her private school upbringing and all of that, but it's there, a kind of quiet authority." Wherever Patty got it, she was amazingly self-possessed, confident, and good-humored.

"Oh, good," I remember her saying one afternoon, "Nate and Gloria are coming over so I'll have somebody to smoke grass with."

This was the opening line of a game Patty and I would repeatedly act out about the perils and illegality of smoking marijuana. Although we had half a shoebox of grass in the apartment, most of which I prided myself on having grown hydroponically in Menlo Park, I was only a social smoker at best, having put in my time in that pursuit during my days at Princeton. Patty, on the other hand, had smoked it for the first time only after she had graduated from Crystal. It was still new to her, and she enjoyed the giggles, the fascination with a section of orange, and the meandering conversations it brought on.

"I'll have none of that," I would say, wagging my finger at her. "This is a respectable household."

Thus began what amounted to our Virginia Slims' "You've-come-a-long-way-Baby" scenario. Gloria and I and whoever would be talking downstairs when we would hear Patty and Nate and whoever laughing from the bedroom. At that I would march up-stairs and catch her red-handed, hiding a joint behind her back. "Okay, what's going on up here?" I'd demand. Patty would look appropriately aghast, caught smoking in the gazebo, as it were. Then, "Steve's such a drag," she'd say and pass the joint to Nate.

As I look back on it there was a lot of teasing in our relation-ship and it went both ways. For instance, whenever she had time for breakfast before her morning classes, Patty would sit primly at the table and chip away at a single egg placed neatly in a dainty eggcup. For some unknown reason, and to Patty's delight, this distracted and bugged the hell out of me or at least it was my part to pretend it did. "What are you doing with that thing?" I'd ask impatiently. "Just irritating you." She'd smile coyly and then continue chipping away. What irritated her was my monthly routine with the *Reader's Digest*. Every year since my college days my father had insisted upon getting me a subscription to the maga-zine, and after failing to dissuade him of what was more a habit than anything else, I was finally reduced to sneaking it into the trash whenever it appeared in our mailbox. But like as not a few days later Patty would discover it there. "Steven!" she would scold me, then dutifully fish it out and place it on the coffee table where it would sit a respectable amount of time before returning to the trash.

Both of my parents were much taken with Patty the moment they met her, though my mother did take me aside after the first introduction and ask rather nervously if Patty was at least old enough to have a driver's license. My father thought she was a wonderful girl, better than I deserved. We did not see much of my parents, however, as they had divorced when I was sixteen and were living a hundred miles apart with their new spouses. Every so often we would drive down to Palo Alto, where Patty would enjoy watching my father run me all over the tennis court, or visit my mother and her husband for dinner in Santa Rosa, but that was about all.

We saw even less of Patty's parents during those first few months in Berkeley, and when we did, usually driving to Hillsborough for dinner, it was always a bit uncomfortable. The south side of Berkeley and the stately homes of Hillsborough were worlds apart. During these visits I would always be seated to Mrs. Hearst's left in the dining room, a large silver chandelier overhead and concealed beneath the carpet under the table a buzzer which I would invariably step on, accidentally summoning the family cook, a plump, friendly German woman named Emmy Brubach. "It's all right, Emmy," Mrs. Hearst would say. "It's just Steven." Then the talk would continue—with some difficulty, however, as Mrs. Hearst was distracted by and trying to avoid looking at the food caught in my moustache.

It was usually Mr. Hearst who would carry on most of the conversation, talking about his newspaper, the *Examiner,* almost as if it were a hobby, and asking us questions about it—what did we think of the new format, the new type being used, the latest headlines? Patty and I would nod politely and try to show some interest, but since we did not take the *Examiner* we were hard put to engage him in a conversation about it.

For her part, Mrs. Hearst's conversation would range from astronomy to the War of the Roses, and since she rarely provided any connections between her choice of topics, but sort of cast them out randomly—as well as an occasional conversation stopper such as, "McGovern was just a coward in World War II" —it was always rather difficult to follow. Because of this I generally tried to turn the talk to things at hand—their collection of ancient Greek vases, the rare books that lined their library, or Mrs. Hearst's plans to have the gardens relandscaped. But I was not always successful. As one of the more conservative members of the U.C. Board of Regents, Mrs. Hearst would sometimes decry "the deteriorating state of the university," the blame for which, in her eyes, fell primarily on permissive professors who never went to class. At this I would listen and nod, then politely disagree. But I can remember one occasion when she stated that "Governor Reagan is the only man in the state trying to save our schools." Again I was about to politely disagree when Patty blurted out, "Oh, Reagan's a jerk." There was a rather tense exchange between Patty and her mother, which was nothing new to either of them, then an awkward silence. After a moment I asked Mrs. Hearst how her plans for the garden were coming along.

Although Mr. and Mrs. Hearst were always pleasant and remarkably polite about Patty's and my living arrangement, they did not approve. Moreover, I was hardly the kind of man they would have chosen for their daughter. There were plenty of boys in Hillsborough who had been clamoring after Patty for years, and the Hearsts were dismayed that she had shown no more than a friendly interest in them. Still, Mr. Hearst was somewhat philosophical. "I don't know what she sees in the guy," he told one of Patty's friends, "but she's got a sparkle in her eye and a bounce in her step. She seems happy enough, so it's okay with me."

Mrs. Hearst, however, was not so philosophical. Later that year, when Patty joined her in Atlanta to have a specialist examine a bad knee that had been giving her problems since childhood, Mrs. Hearst insisted upon setting her up with the son of one of her old beaus. After going out with the fellow Patty called me at one in the morning. "I'm so lonely," she said, "and I'm so drunk. My mother's got me going out with this boy and he's nice, but I just want to get home."

It was shortly after Patty returned from Europe that she began talking about getting engaged, or rather worked into it gradually. At first she would talk about other people's marriages, which would generally lead into a discussion of the institution itself. Patty used to joke about not wanting "three kids, a collie, a station wagon, and membership in the garden club," and yet she genuinely wanted to be married. I used the word "genuinely" because marriage for her was neither a solution, an escape, nor a white lace dream out of *The Bride's Magazine*. Rather, she fully expected to work, to pursue a career, and be a "full person" as well as a married one. She also wanted children, preferably boys. "I think Jed is a nice name, don't you?" she'd ask. Or, "I'm not really sure about natural childbirth, but I do think it's important that the husband be in the delivery room . . . don't you?" I'd smile and nod to these questions and others like them, but it was always Patty who carried the conversation when the topic was marriage.

This is not to say that I had reservations about marrying Patty and having children with her. Far from it. I loved her and knew she would make a wonderful wife and mother. She was extremely good with kids and had that perfect combination of firmness, warmth, and understanding with them. Once I remember her marching outside after catching sight of two boys who had cornered one of our cats and were teasing it. "You boys stop that this instant," she commanded, and the boys stopped dead in their tracks, though she wasn't much taller than either of them. Patty then softened, explaining why they shouldn't frighten animals and making friends out of a couple of little hellions who had been terrorizing the neighborhood since we moved in. "They're nice kids really," Patty said later. "It's just that their parents let them run wild."

Despite all of this, since we had been in Berkeley for only a few months, the idea of getting formally engaged made me feel not entirely comfortable. Not so for Patty. "I saw this really beautiful ring set in Carmel," she told me one afternoon. "You'd really like them and they only cost a hundred dollars." And then other times she would tug me over to a jewelry store window to look at rings on the way home from campus. These hints continued without much response from me into the fall, and then, right around Christmas vacation, Patty dug in her heels. "If he doesn't give me a ring," she told Mimi, "not a fancy ring, but some kind of ring, I'm leaving and taking all my stuff with me."

When Mimi relayed this to me—"She's really fixed on it," Mimi said—I was not so sure that Patty was bluffing. Then, on Christmas Eve, it became suddenly and painfully clear that Patty had dismissed my pooh-poohing of the engagement idea as "typical Weed," fully expecting to get a ring as a present. She was sitting next to a little Christmas tree she had bought and decorated the day before—over my feigned objections—under it a few presents we had gotten for each other. "I'll just open one," she said, then picked up the smallest present and tore it open. I can't recall what it was, but it was not a ring and although Patty pretended to be pleased, she was obviously disappointed. After waiting for her to go to bed and making sure she was asleep, I went into the workroom and gift-wrapped a wicker basket with a note inside—"Good for one ring."

The next day Patty and I did not rush out and buy her a "fancy ring," but shopped around, finally picking out an unusual one with a cabochon-cut tourmaline. While she was excited about the ring and pleased when people would compliment her on it, it was really the commitment that meant most to Patty. We were living together; we loved each other; and it was simply time we acknowledged it by getting engaged.

With the end of Christmas vacation, Patty's job at Capwell's had also come to an end, and she enrolled as a science major at U.C. She had always loved animals and hoped to be a veterinarian, but she soon discovered that the simple love of animals was not enough to see her through beginning calculus and biochemistry. Three weeks into the quarter and the sciences were killing her. And although I would sometimes help her with her problems, Patty preferred to walk all the way to campus to attend nightly review sessions, wary of falling back into the teacher/student roles of our days at Crystal Springs. In short, she was determined to make it on her own.

Whereas Patty did most of her studying during the day, I was a night worker, sometimes staying up until 3:00 or 4:00 A.M. Many of those nights Patty would bring in a blanket and sleep in the easy chair next to my desk just to keep me company. When I had had as much Kantian schematism as I could stand, I would wake her gently and she would shuffle sleepily into the bedroom and collapse into bed. Other nights I would bring my books and papers to bed with me, studying with a tensor lamp hanging over my shoulder. "Give me a leg," Patty would say, then snuggle down in the covers and go to sleep with her hands wrapped around my knee.

Patty and I must have spent at least half our time in that bed. After a late night it was not unusual for me to sleep until noon. When the alarm would go off, Patty would grumble, stagger out of bed, dress, and go off to her morning classes, then return and climb back in bed with me. It was almost a daily ritual. When we were hungry we would often bring up some cheese and crackers, or some "treats" she had baked, and sit up against the headboard eating, talking, phoning friends, studying, or finding excuses not to.

There was little we could find to argue about, and, when a conflict did arise, it was usually more comical than serious. Once I remember her driving off in a snit over something I had said, but when she returned an hour later her temper had cooled and she felt a little foolish. "Why don't you just hold me when I get like that?" she asked. And then another time she became angry because I wasn't saying anything at all. We were having dinner and I was preoccupied with something, probably a paper that was due; perhaps I was reading. Anyway, Patty said something, I mumbled something back, and the next thing I knew she had flicked a spoonful of soup in my face. If she wanted attention, she got it. I saw absolute red, picked her up bodily, put her kicking and swinging out the front door in her bathrobe, and locked it. Then I went back to the table. "You let me in!" she shouted angrily, and I ignored her. A moment, then, "Come on . . . let me in. . . ." I did and a few minutes later we were back to normal. That is the closest thing to a real fight that I can remember. Of course there were other times when we would become irritated with each other and things would cool between us, but by and large these moods passed rather quickly, prompting Mimi to inquire, "Don't you guys ever fight? You're like some old married couple. It's disgusting."

"We just get stubborn with each other," Patty told her, which was a good way to put it.

At that point Mimi was rapidly tiring of the "Dating Game" scene, and although she would laugh about it with us, she longed for something less frivolous. Then one night in May of that year, with the encouragement and then some gentle prodding from Patty, Mimi found something more permanent.

The three of us had met in our usual laundromat on the north side of campus, which had to be the seediest laundromat in Alameda County. It was called "The Wash House," appropriately enough as the place was always awash with muddy water on the floors and, if you were particularly unlucky, dirty water in one of the broken washing machines into which you had just thrown your clothes. Sometimes people got violent in there and would kick one of the machines, while others evidently got sleepy and would sometimes climb *into* one of the machines. Loaded down with wet clothes, I once found a rumpled guy snoozing peacefully in a dryer. On another occasion Patty and I were entertained by a fellow sitting in full lotus position and booming out Gregorian chants at the top of his lungs.

That was the thing about Berkeley, and especially the north side of campus which was a microcosm of Berkeley—just when you thought you'd seen it all a fellow in a gold lamé jumpsuit would come walking around the corner wearing antlers. Because of this we never knew just what we'd see, or experience, either in the Wash House or around it. Next door was The Espresso Cafe —known as the Depresso—which was always filled with existential types, professors, and students. On the other side was Rather Ripped Records and up the street LaVal's Beer Gardens, Swenson's Ice Cream Parlor, and Northside Books, a "clean, well-lighted place" open to all manner of late night refugees who'd had enough beer, existential despair, or ice cream. It was for all of this, the whole scene, the entire spectrum, that Patty, Mimi, and I would meet at the Wash House, punch our quarters into the washers, and take our chances.

But on that particular night things were pretty quiet. Local characters like "Earthquake McGoon," "Oliver Twist," and poor old "Lice" were nowhere to be seen. A couple of beery fraternity men on the corner were arguing about whether or not the Raiders were bound for the Super Bowl, but that was about it. The three of us went into Northside Books, which was really more of a newsstand/candy store, and started browsing around. I remember Patty was over at the magazine rack flipping through a *Cosmo-*

politan, and I was chewing on a licorice whip, when Mimi nudged Patty and nodded toward the cashier, a thirtyish fellow with a large moustache and rimless glasses.

"I want that man," Mimi said half-jokingly.

Patty looked at the fellow, who was standing on a platform behind the cash register surrounded by candy, cigars, and cigarettes, then nodded. "Just write down your name and phone number," she said, "and put it on the counter in front of him."

Mimi said something to the effect that she couldn't possibly do that, but Patty insisted that she certainly could. "I would if I were you," she said, and she probably would have. Patty was never one to suffer from a lack of confidence, but was unable to foster the same spirit in Mimi. After returning to the laundromat and putting our clothes in the dryer, Patty insisted we go back to the bookstore and then, as Mimi bought some chocolate, she stood to the side and tried to urge her on. "I knew you'd chicken out," Patty teased her when we were back out on the sidewalk. Then, just as we were walking away, Mimi glanced back to catch the cashier looking through the window at her. Although none of us knew it, that night marked the end of our threesome and the beginning of a foursome: Patty and I, and Mimi and Scott Swanton, the cashier at Northside Books.

Because Mimi was busy getting to know Scott, and then setting up house with him, we saw much less of her that spring. "Maybe she doesn't like us anymore," I remember Patty worrying. But it was quite the opposite. Once Mimi and Scott were settled in, she and Patty became much closer, each of them having a man to contend with and get away from for an afternoon. They'd have coffee in their favorite outdoor cafes, go shopping together, hang around one of our apartments, or meet for lunch on campus after their classes.

As a friend Patty was utterly dependable. She was always there when you needed her, which Mimi did when she went to Planned Parenthood to be fitted with an IUD. I remember Mimi later remarking that "it hurt like hell" and how glad she was to have Patty there "to sort of hang on to." That was precisely how

I felt when I came down with a bad case of the flu that year. Patty sat up with me all night, which was hardly pleasant as I spent half that night in the bathroom, unable to keep even a bowl of soup down. She was beside herself with worry about me. "Maybe I should call a doctor," she said, putting her hand on my forehead. "You're burning up." I told her no, but asked her to take my temperature. She rushed to the medicine chest, but was so upset her hands were shaking when she took out the thermometer. I heard it shatter in the sink, heard her cry "Oh no!" and the next thing I knew she had thrown a coat over her nightgown and had hurried off to an all-night drugstore to buy another one. Then, just before dawn, she went out again to get me some 7-Up when I mentioned that I might be able to hold it down. She was like that, caring, concerned and there when you needed her.

But on the other hand, if Patty got it in her head that you did not deserve her sympathy, she could be cool, indignant, or outright rude. Whenever a magazine salesman or a recruiter for Jehovah's Witnesses would appear at our door, I always sent Patty to handle them. Like as not I would hear that door close pretty quickly. Patty could also look right through you, her jaw firmly set, if you were a panhandler on Telegraph or a union picket at Safeway. Mimi once remarked that Patty was a typical double-natured Pisces and, although I have never had one scintilla of faith in the stars, I have to admit there is some truth in that. Patty *was* somewhat double natured, at one moment warm and caring, and the next moment scathingly sarcastic. "Oh, Dad went on and on about his 'Little Brown Brothers' thing," she would say wearily of her father's concern with the plight of Mexican-Americans, or "Where did Ed pick up *that?*" she once said about a friend of mine's date.

Moreover, it was not uncommon for Patty to suddenly come 180 degrees and support something that she had been arguing against a few days before. She had a tendency to react to things immediately, to take a stand on some issue often depending solely upon her mood at the time, the opinion of someone she respected, but most typically, on her strong, but often inconsistent sense of what was right and fair, and what was wrong and unfair. For example, if I was irritated by the union pickets' "Hey man" approach, Patty took it one step further, sometimes shopping at Safeway just for the pleasure of marching through the picket lines. "They have no *right* to bother people like that," she would fume. And yet at the same time I'm quite certain that she would have supported any effort to unionize the clerks at Capwell's, many of whom were kept "off the clock," which made them ineligible for medical and retirement benefits. "It's not fair that they're treated like that," I remember Patty saying earnestly one night after work. Her sympathies were always strongly with the underdog when she could see that an individual or group *was* an underdog, but her feelings were not regulated by generalities such as "unions are good" or "unions are bad." She judged things as they arose in the concrete, not along any systematic lines of principle, and it's therefore not surprising that her interest in politics expressed itself more in the form of the nonpartisan wisecrack than anything else —Richard Nixon and D'Army Bailey (a local radical politico) receiving equal shares of her sarcasm.

But for the most part these willful inconsistencies were not apparent. And if she occasionally got herself into a snit of moral indignation over something—the neighbors who had started to use *our* parking place, for example—I'd smile amusedly at her and soon she'd catch herself and laugh too. She was generally calm, practical, and quite happy. An avid photographer, she would spend hours in the darkroom on campus or lazy afternoons sitting on the couch making a macramé plant holder. And while she was disappointed in herself for doing badly in the sciences, and realized a change of majors was in order, she was encouraged by an "A" in an art history class and looked forward to enrolling in that department the following fall. I looked forward to being a teaching assistant for one of the undergraduate philosophy courses and having a regular paycheck to supplement student loans. In short, by the end of the spring quarter everything was falling into place for Patty and me. Although she would sometimes complain to Mimi that I wasn't affectionate enough—"Hugs and kisses," she would demand with her arms outstretched—or that I couldn't, and therefore wouldn't, dance, she was no longer worried about us.

We were no longer just starting out together. Our first Berkeley year had been a good one, and we were into our first real summer together.

Patty and I were in and out of Berkeley that summer, but with Mimi to water our plants and our next-door neighbor Suz to feed our cats, we were mostly out—at a friend's cabin on Tomales Bay, visiting friends in Palo Alto, and on a few occasions packing up Patty's MG and driving down the coast to her grandfather's castle at San Simeon.

William Randolph Hearst's "$30 million cathedral of American capitalism," as it is rightly called, is, of course, incredible. A towering white structure set in the foothills overlooking the Pacific, old "W.R." had filled it with priceless works of art and chunks of history—marble statues from ancient Greece and Rome, Renaissance paintings, medieval tapestries, Egyptian stonework, pieces from all over the world, much of it inlaid with gold. That's the image I have of it, a castle dripping with gold. But by then, twenty years after his death, it was also filled with long lines of tourists from all over the country. "Can't you just imagine William Randolph Hearst entertaining two hundred of Hollywood's elite at a cost of six thousand dollars a day," the tour guide would say. "Can't you just imagine Clark Gable and Carole Lombard here on their honeymoon closing these velvet curtains and wrapping themselves in a cocoon of darkness!"

Although Patty and I wondered how the tour guide managed this sort of enthusiasm day after day, it was fun to imagine such things—the enormous, star-studded masquerade balls held there and presided over by old W.R., the statesmen, matinee idols, and captains of industry lounging around the Neptune pool, and the carefree tennis games between Marion Davies and her Hollywood friends. Still, Patty did not like to be associated with all of this. Once, when a guide learned that she was William Randolph Hearst's granddaughter, she asked if Patty would mind being so introduced to her charges. "Yes, I would mind," Patty said politely, but rather firmly.

Usually when Patty and I visited San Simeon we were given

private tours, and while we thoroughly enjoyed them, it was when the tourists had departed and the place was quiet that we had the most fun. At times like that the castle would lose its sanctity as a historical monument and become, as Patty once called it, "my grandfather's old place," where we could rummage around, explore, and perhaps sneak down to the cellars to make off with a few old bottles of wine.

But the real summer for us, our best times, were our trips to what had been W.R.'s mountain retreat, a cluster of Bavarian mansions, as well as another castle, he had built along the McCloud River in northern California. The place is called Wyntoon and is a hundred square miles of the most beautiful country I have ever seen.

When Patty and I would drive down the eight-mile private road through the pines and enter that glade by the river it was like stepping into another world, discovering the most fantastic ghost town imaginable. Except for a caretaker and his wife, "The Village" was absolutely deserted, drifts of pine needles covering the old tennis courts, the two swimming pools now cracked and empty, and the Black Forest mansions silent except for the chittering of swallows nesting in the eaves and the constant rush of the river. We had it all to ourselves and going there was always a bit like a dream.

Patty and I would usually stay in one of the huge bedrooms of the "Cinderella House," which, like the "Brown Bear House" and the "Angel House," was decorated on the outside with intricate hand-painted fairytale murals, while inside furnished with an amazing assortment of medieval and Renaissance antiques, oriental rugs and a wide variety of artwork. With a Hearst Corporation catalogue in hand, we would spend hours just trying to locate and identify various pieces, from Albrecht Dürer woodcuts to pre-delft tankards. However, the original interior of the third mansion, the Angel House, had been torn out simply because it did not strike W.R.'s fancy and was now stacked with crates of furnishings. Although it was to be the showpiece of the Village, for some reason Angel House was never completed, and forty years later Patty and I were nosing around in the dark with flashlights, prying open the crates and peering at the treasures inside. In one we found piles of W.R.'s personal effects—papers, scrapbooks, awards, and things like a baseball signed "1923, Babe Ruth"—that his sons had evidently collected together to donate to a museum. But by then all it was collecting was an even layer of bat guano deposited by hundreds of the creatures hanging from the darkened ceiling. One afternoon, one of them came winging down right out of a Dracula movie and bounced off Patty's head. She let out a blood-curdling scream, and with that we decided to go for a hike along the river.

That was the beauty of the place. One moment we could be flipping through one of W.R.'s note pads on which he had scribbled his initials over and over like a bored schoolboy, listening to his scratchy voice on an ancient dictaphone, or looking through the library at the stone castle, and the next we might be trying our hand at panning for gold or searching for arrowheads. When it was hot we would go rafting down the icy river and then step into a large, tiled sunken tub and look out at the river until the leaded windows steamed up. In all, it was a wonderful place to be decadent in for a weekend.

But Patty and I did not just limit ourselves to the Village. The surrounding forests were laced with fire and logging roads, and we would often take long, rugged jeep rides up into the mountains. Once, at the top of a barren granite peak, we came across a fire lookout and startled a woman who stayed up there for five months at a time, "playing solitaire mostly," she told us. She said her only complaint with the job was the thunderstorms that would sometimes roll in.

"Whenever we get storms up here," she said, "the lightning hits this roof. And whenever it starts hitting this roof I stand on a stool in the middle of the floor and just put my hands over my ears." Patty and I laughed at the story, but as luck would have it a few weeks later we got caught in a thunderstorm ourselves.

We were sitting peacefully in a meadow along the river with a knapsack of sandwiches and a joint of extremely good grass, which we were passing back and forth. It was a beautiful day, the sun baking down, the meadow glittering with butterflies, and then just as the grass was beginning to make them glitter all the more we were suddenly jolted by a deafening clap of thunder. Within seconds the sky clouded up, lightning forking directly above us and the earth shaking with the tremendous ka-booms. I thought it was the end of the world, and Patty thought that, even if it wasn't, we would either be split down the middle by lightning or consumed by a raging forest fire she was certain she saw starting on the ridge across from us. It turned out to be low-hanging clouds. Anyway, by the time we got back to the house we were soaking wet and shivering, but not for long. It was back into the hot tub, this time a bubble bath, with two large slices of water-melon.

On our last visit to Wyntoon that summer, Patty and I decided to put aside our raft for water skis. It was a first for me and I felt like a real champion, rising out of the water and going the length of Lake Wyntoon on the first try. Pride goeth before a fall, as they say. Patty said, or rather yelled, "Take off your glasses!" "I can't see without them!" I yelled back and waved her on. I was up, was boldly cutting across the wake, and then I was airborne. Patty motored up beside me and asked if I was okay. I told her I lost my glasses.

I heard a lot about my glasses on the three-hundred-mile drive back to Berkeley, Patty behind the wheel and me squinting at the blur of highway ahead. But all in all she was very good-natured about it, teasing me as I would have her. It had really been a wonderful summer, and although we were sad to see it pass it was the perfect ending to our first year in Berkeley together. By then our once empty apartment had become a comfortable home full of potted plants and books, the walls covered with prints and some of Patty's photographs, our small back patio area thick with pumpkin and tomato vines, and our two cats forever curled up on the couch. We had a history now, two-and-a-half good years that we had shared together.

In the fall of that year Mimi and Scott were married, and

spurred on by this, perhaps, Patty decided it was time to tell her parents of our engagement. She was really coming into her own by then, maturing and getting along with them better than ever before. But in spite of this, and in typical fashion, Patty's announcement of our engagement was somewhat unconventional. Whereas her older sister Gina's husband, Jay, had very formally asked for Gina's hand in marriage and had engaged Mr. Hearst in a rather awkward man-to-man talk, Patty seized a moment when I was off in the bathroom to break the news. But it didn't matter. Both of her parents were glad that our living arrangement was finally and formally to be legitimized.

The day of the "public" announcement, December 19, I had my hair cut, trimmed my moustache, put on my best sports coat and presented myself to Patty for inspection. She said I looked "vaguely presentable." When we arrived in Hillsborough, however, her mother and Emmy said that I had never looked better. Both of them were pleased that I had had a bout with the scissors, though I'm certain they wished they had been more victorious. After a photographer from the *Examiner* posed us under a painting of Patty's grandmother, Millicent Hearst, and followed us as we took a walk through the gardens, we sat down to a dinner with her parents and her sisters, Vicky and Anne, and were toasted with champagne.

It was the beginning of Christmas vacation by then, and after a quick run to the Wash House, where we were shyly congratulated by a girl holding an open copy of the *Examiner* and nodding at our engagement picture—Patty blushed, but was pleased—we joined the family for a weekend at their lodge at Sugar Bowl, a ski resort near Lake Tahoe. Those two days at Sugar Bowl were the closest thing to a warm, homey scene I had witnessed with the Hearsts. There was always someone in the kitchen fixing snacks, always someone clattering in with their skis, always a fire going on the hearth, and hot chocolate on the stove. Although Patty couldn't ski because of her bad knee, she thoroughly enjoyed herself. I would come back exhausted from the day's skiing to find her reading, feeding dabs of peanut butter to blue jays out on the terrace, or just relaxing by the fire.

In the evening after dinner, we might go for a walk, crunching along the snow-packed roads, or play a game of Anti-Monopoly —a Christmas gift from Patty to her father—or just sit and talk until we were sleepy. But when it came time to turn in, Jay and I would march dutifully to our room, Patty and Gina to theirs. The arrangement struck us both as silly at first, especially since it meant that Jay and Gina could not have a room to themselves, but in the end it turned out to be a very good thing. For the first time in years Patty and Gina, who had been rivals of sorts, "were really able to talk," as Patty told me later. This, I suspect, was due in no small part to the fact that Patty was no longer just the younger sister, but was soon to become a married woman herself.

From what I gathered, much of their late night conversations were centered around marriage, children, and their hopes and plans for the future. After growing up in a family of five girls, Patty definitely wanted boys, as I said earlier. Gina, however, did not want children, and the eldest of the sisters, Catherine, a childhood polio victim, couldn't have them. That left Patty. Her parents, of course, were delighted at the prospect of having grandchildren. Once Patty asked her father if he could get her a beautiful antique cradle from Wyntoon. He broke into a broad smile and promised to deliver it personally when it was needed.

On our last night in Sugar Bowl, all of us went down to the main lodge for a turkey dinner and afterward piled into a huge sleigh drawn by four plow horses for a long ride.

"Wouldn't it have been wonderful to have been marooned this Christmas?" I remember Patty saying. "Winter weddings are so beautiful . . . everyone gets married in June. But I guess you're right, summer is a better time for us. . . ."

The next morning we said our good-byes, loaded our gear into her MG, and headed back to Berkeley. With the end of Christmas vacation the winter quarter at school loomed ahead of us. Our only real concern that quarter was my upcoming comprehensive exams, which were a source of considerable worry, but an equal amount of teasing. "I wonder if I've learned enough to pass them," I mused on the drive back. Then I launched into a graduate school horror story: "Last year nine students took them and only two passed—a fourteen-year-old prodigy and another guy who had a complete nervous breakdown."

"I'll leave you if you don't pass them," she threatened. Then, "No, I won't. But please pass them."

I told her that if things didn't work out I could always get a job delivering her father's newspapers.

"Terrific," she said.

On January 10 her father's newspapers, as well as newspapers all over the country, ran a story on the capture of two men, Joseph Remiro and Russell Little, charged with the murder of Marcus Foster. But again the news passed pretty much over our heads. The winter quarter was in full swing, and Patty and I were finding it difficult to get into gear after the holidays. But by February we had finally settled down to our studies, though we could not help looking forward to our wedding and we hoped a summer of travel in Europe. Nineteen seventy-three had been a very good year for us, and we had no reason to believe that it would not be so this new year.

Friday, the first of February, marked the end of an uneventful week of studying and going to school. That night we put our books aside and went to an *Examiner*-sponsored indoor track meet with Mimi and Scott, then got up late the next morning and resumed our studies. We broke for dinner around nine o'clock and then, just as we were about to go back to our books, the doorbell rang. Both of us were somewhat startled.

Walking into the narrow entrance hall with Patty behind me, I could make out two figures through the translucent sliding glass door. I slid it open to find a rather dissipated young woman standing on our doorstep and behind her, hanging back in the shadows, a tall, thin, curly-haired figure. The woman was obviously nervous and began asking me questions about renting one of the apartments in the fourplex. She claimed to have tried renting one the summer before and mentioned the name of the realty company.

But there was something strange about the whole exchange. The woman listened to my answers, but did not appear to really hear them, while the person behind her nodded obsequiously every time I spoke. "I guess you know the rent here is two hundred and forty dollars a month," I remember saying. Yes, she knew the rent, she said, then thanked us and left with her friend.

"What do you think they wanted?" Patty asked me when I closed the door. I told her I didn't know, that because the porch light was burned out I couldn't even tell if the second figure was male or female. Male, Patty said and added that he looked "pretty creepy." I tried to assure her that they were nothing to worry about. "I could have knocked that guy over with one hand," I said.

But in spite of my bravado we were both a little unsettled by the incident. The area in which we lived had the highest crime rate in Berkeley, and only a few months before our apartment had been broken into by a burglar who was short on finesse, but very big with a crowbar, which he had used to shatter the glass rear door. But then maybe we were just being paranoid—some of our friends certainly considered us so, especially after I had installed a rather elaborate burglar alarm. In any case, by the time we went to bed that night both of us had sloughed off the two strange visitors entirely.

The next day, Sunday, we were back at our books, studying until well into the night. Patty called it quits around midnight while I continued reading in the workroom, finally turning in at 2:00 A.M. In view of this I was not in the best of moods when Nate knocked on our door at nine the next morning. He had come by to use my deck to record a KPFA interview with Anthony Braxton, a jazz musician, to be used in a Stanford literary magazine Nate was helping edit. I got up groggily, sort of felt my way downstairs, let him in, then felt my way back upstairs and flopped down on the bed trying to go back to sleep. But it was no use. After a few minutes I dressed, kissed Patty good-bye, and headed for campus. After I left she got up to make some tea and keep Nate company. When I returned a few hours later, I remember stopping short in the doorway at the sound of unfamiliar voices. They were from the Braxton interview Nate had recorded. I entered to find him sitting on a stool next to the battered, chartreuse piano a friend had given me. On top of it was the tape deck and Nate was laughing and shaking his head as Braxton said:

"Do it, you know?"

"Do what?" the puzzled interviewer asked.

" 'Do it' is defined as whatever you did, that's what you *dood*. Can you dig it?"

The interviewer apparently could not and went on to another question.

"Just what is going on here?" I asked, but Nate just kept on laughing. Patty looked up from her schoolwork and raised her eyes. "I know," she said. "It's been going on like this all morning." The two of us went into the kitchen and, while she cooked me an omelet, we made rude remarks about Nate, who was in earshot but chose to ignore us. After eating, I headed back to campus and Patty settled down with her art history books again. As I left, Nate was still cracking up and slapping his thighs. It didn't look as if Patty was going to get much work done.

When I returned to our apartment that evening Nate was gone and Patty was still reading. We talked awhile, lounged around, then I started going over some notes before dinner. We ate leisurely, watching an old rerun of "Mission Impossible," then "The Magician," before turning off the set and clearing the table in preparation for another night of studying. It was Monday night, February 4. The day had been ordinary, uneventful. The coming week promised more of the same.

At about 9:20 the doorbell rang.

Patty and I stepped into the entrance hall and looked toward the door. Through it we could see a single, ill-defined figure. We were both puzzled and a little apprehensive. "Who's that?" Patty asked. Even though the porch light was still out, we could tell it wasn't a friend.

I walked to the door, Patty behind me, sort of using me for protection, and pulled it open. The hall light fell across a young woman dressed rather shabbily—loose-fitting slacks, a baggy sweater, maybe a trench coat. There was something suspicious about her. It later occurred to me that she was obviously trying to avoid being seen face-on. She was turned almost sideways, her head downcast, her brown hair falling across her face.

"I've just had a car accident and I need some help," she said nervously. "Can I use your phone?" But she didn't even finish the sentence. Suddenly, two black men with carbines were pushing their way past her, crowding us back into the hallway and ordering us to get down. We were stunned. Our minds just stopped at the unreality of it. It was a military maneuver. Unlike a mugging or a robbery, I had the feeling that, given the slightest excuse, they might blow our heads off.

"Get down. Get your face on the floor!" the first man ordered, and I got down on one knee fairly quickly, but not quickly enough. He began kicking me, knocking my glasses off. I was ducking, was jolted by a couple of blows, then went face down in the hallway, my head toward the door, as the second man—DeFreeze—pushed Patty into the kitchen. The woman's feet came up beside me and I felt my hands being yanked behind my back as she wound a rope around my wrists and cinched it tight. She then stepped to the bookcase that lined the hallway, picked up my wallet and Patty's purse, and started digging through them.

"Keep it *down!*" the man above me said, then kicked me again. Although I was flat out on the floor he continued to kick me, not angrily, but as if he was kicking something he simply hated, something almost inanimate. But there was no pain, just a ringing pressure and the thud of his boot. I was in an altered state, a strange kind of high that made everything at once stark and real, and yet weirdly removed.

One of the kicks turned my head toward the kitchen and I could see DeFreeze's legs, flashes of Patty's blue bathrobe, and a rope trailing across the floor. "Stop struggling or I'll have to knock you out," I heard him tell her. I could not see Patty during this, nor did I ever see her again, but I could hear her pleading with him. "Please leave us alone. . . . Please. . . ."

"Just do what they say," I tried to call out to her, but I don't think she heard me. She started to whimper. She was utterly terrified. I was too, but my disorientation was just as strong as my fear. My mind was racing, trying to grasp what was happening and why. I looked through the open door and saw that the door of the apartment across the breezeway was also open. I thought I heard some movement outside. The only thing I could figure was that these people were raiding all the apartments. But it made no sense. Our assailants showed no interest in the valuables we had in plain sight—the color TV, the stereo. They hadn't even left the hallway and the kitchen. Just the woman stepping over as she dug through Patty's purse. Then she stepped over me again to the kitchen to watch Patty as DeFreeze went to the front door. I caught a glimpse of him holding his rifle across his chest and standing guard. His timing was propitious. A few seconds later one of our neighbors, a Japanese student named Steve Suenaga, stepped out of his apartment expecting his girl friend and spotted DeFreeze. DeFreeze saw him too and stepped outside pointing his rifle at him. "Oh, no, you don't," he said, then, "turn around."

All I heard was his voice, then a commotion as he grabbed Suenaga by the shirt and yanked him inside. There was a stumble of feet in the hallway. "Shut up and get down," DeFreeze said, then Suenaga's body thumped down half on top of me, head to feet.

"Who's that?" the man above me asked.

"I don't know. Tie him up," DeFreeze told the woman.

I heard Suenaga groan as he was struck with the butt of the man's rifle.

"Where's the money?" the man began asking me. "Where is it?"

"It's right there. My wallet's right there," I told him. "Take it. Take anything you want and leave us alone."

"Where's the safe?"

"We don't have a safe."

"Where is it? Is it upstairs?" He punctuated each question with another kick. He didn't care about my answers.

Aside from his questions, the three of them said almost

nothing during the assault, obviously having planned it out and rehearsed it beforehand. At first they had given each other short, whispered instructions: "Did you find it?" "Go check the kitchen." But once I was tied up there was only one more statement that I can remember.

The woman came out of the kitchen, then paused in the doorway. "They've seen our faces," she said; said it almost as if she was reading a line—halting, mechanically. "They've seen our faces. We have to get rid of them."

"Oh, my God, you're not going to . . ." Patty said, horrified.

Up to that point I had decided to comply, to be kicked in the head all night if that was what was required. But the pressure had been building. I had been waiting for something to happen, for a sign as to their intentions. The woman's statement was it. No explicit flashes or thoughts crossed my mind. There was just the sudden realization that they were going to execute us.

I heard what sounded like the click of a rifle bolt being cocked above me and was straining to look up when I was hit over the head with a bottle of wine the man had grabbed from the bookcase. Again there was no pain, just a tremendous thudding crash as my face hit the floor. He hit me three times and I was starting to black out. I could feel him winding up when he hit me and thought he was trying to knock me out. I slumped down feigning unconsciousness, there was a pause, then he hit me again, harder if that were possible. I then thought he was trying to kill me by knocking my head in. I knew he *would* kill me if I let him hit me anymore. I jackknifed and lurched to my feet, but was too dazed to really see anything. I must have crashed into him and then staggered back half-conscious. The open front door was only five feet behind him, but for some reason I went running into the living room, making myself an easy target. Yanking at the ropes that bound me, I was crashing around, knocking over plants and chairs and the coffee table, yelling as loudly as I could, hoping to alert our neighbor, Suz. And as strange as it sounds, I remember feeling a momentary flash of humiliation at having to do that—crash around in my own living room like a madman.

At some point during those seconds my hands came free and I was against the rear door trying to pull it open. It was double-locked with a floor bolt. I fumbled with it expecting shots at any moment, then pulled it free, yanked open the door and rushed out onto our patio. I rolled over the fence to the right, fell in a sprawl on the concrete, staggered a few steps and rolled over a second fence before I realized they weren't chasing me. A moment, then I went over the back fence, picked myself up and ran up the alley back past the rear of our apartment.

About thirty seconds had elapsed since I had jumped to my feet. Almost immediately the second man had dragged Patty out of our apartment as Suz and a visiting girl friend rushed to their door. "Let her go!" the friend had shouted, and Suz had pulled her back just as DeFreeze fired three shots at them, one bullet shattering our front door, another going through two walls and ending up in Suz's freezer. Patty had struggled and sobbed, "Oh, no! Not me! O God! Please let me go . . . !" and she had been hit in the face with the rifle butt and thrown into the trunk of the idling convertible. DeFreeze had let go another burst of gun-fire at three students who had run out on the porch of the Reagans' house next door, and the car had screeched out of our driveway onto Benvenue, turning right once again on Parker.

I did not hear any of the shots, but was dimly aware of the rush of cars as I came running out of the alley to Parker. There was a darkened house to my right and I stumbled up the stairs and started pounding on the door. "Call the police!" I kept yelling. It was horribly frustrating because I knew I was terrifying the people inside. I kept pounding on the door, then heard the squeal of brakes and turned to see a squad car roaring past me up Parker. I watched it, then half fell back down the stairs and ran around the corner to Benvenue.

A small crowd was already gathering in front of our apart-ment building. They were stunned and silent, then visibly shocked when I rushed up to them. One of our neighbors took me by the arm. "You're hurt, Steve," he said and tried to get me to lie down on the sidewalk. I pushed past him and ran up the steps to our apartment. A few more people were gathered in front of our door, the glass now shattered by the gunfire.

"Where's Patty?" I ran into the apartment. "Where's Patty?"

No one said anything for a moment, then someone said, "They took her with them."

"The police are coming," someone else said.

I stood there for a moment, and then I began to sink. A couple of people took me by the arms and eased me down onto the floor. Someone found a towel and placed it under my head to stop the bleeding. No one said anything after that. I just lay there, unfocused, staring up into space. It was the beginning of a lot of that.

2

I REMEMBER TWO AMBULANCE ATTENDANTS lifting me onto a stretcher and rolling me out the door, the sirens wailing, and then the hospital emergency room. I was at Herrick Hospital for two hours, but I remember very little of it.

As soon as they rolled me in, a woman knelt by the stretcher, asked my name, then handed me a release form to sign while a nurse behind me was saying, "We're going to have to shave some of your hair off, Mr. Weed." I scribbled my name across the bottom of the form, started to slump back, but was raised up again. I heard the buzz of the clippers as the nurse began shearing into my hair. From there I was wheeled into the X-ray room and lifted onto the table. I remember asking the doctor if my teeth were knocked out. I couldn't feel them. The doctor checked them and shook his head. "Just numb," he said. I was still on the table, being turned this way and that, when two cops entered the room. One of them asked who the "young lady" was.

"Patty Hearst," I said and told him he could reach her parents in Hillsborough . . . No, Washington. They were in Washington, D.C.

"Hearst." The cop wrote it down, then frowned. "Would that be the same Hearst family . . . the newspaper family?"

I told him yes and he hurried off to a phone in the corridor. Only then did it sink into me: Patty had not been taken hostage after an aborted robbery. She had been kidnapped.

I vaguely remember being told they were taking me to Cowell Hospital on the university campus. All I remember is suddenly being there, an English woman doctor gently probing my wounds and checking my eyes. "You're still a bit shocky, Steven," she said. "Did you black out?" I told her I didn't think so.

After some more X rays, I was wheeled to a room off what seemed to be a long, totally deserted corridor. A plainclothes guard holding a walkie-talkie was sitting on a folding chair next to the door. As two orderlies were lifting me into bed, Detective Steve Engler and another Berkeley policeman entered the room and introduced themselves. They waited for the orderlies to leave, then Engler pulled up a chair next to my bed.

A soft-spoken, athletic young man, Engler was extremely sympathetic. He told me that one of the three getaway cars had been discovered abandoned not far from our apartment, but that the department had pretty good descriptions of the other two. Then he paused. "Steve, I know what you're going through," he said quietly, then explained that only a few months before his wife had been beaten and strangled by a burglar who had fled, leaving her for dead. "But she came through it all right," he said. I nodded and he opened his notebook. "Can you talk?" he asked. I told him I could, but by then my jaw had frozen up, and I had difficulty getting the words out.

We talked for over an hour that night, Engler scribbling down notes, while I tried to come up with anything that might be helpful. Aside from physical descriptions, which were sketchy at best,

I tried to convey three of my strongest impressions of both the kidnapping and the kidnappers themselves: they were extremely militaristic; they had obviously planned the assault down to the smallest detail; and each of them performed a specific role which he played to the hilt, almost as if they were making a training film or had Vietnam battle experience. When I told him that the second man in the door (DeFreeze) definitely seemed to be in charge, Engler nodded. The first man sounded like a "hard case," he said, whose sole function was probably just to beat me up, to kick all the fight out of me, and make certain I was in no condition to put up any resistance when it came time to take Patty. In that he had succeeded eminently well.

"Did they say anything, mention any names that might help us?" Engler asked.

I told him I couldn't think of anything.

"What about identifying any of them?"

"Maybe one of the men," I said.

Before Engler left I asked him about the other person who had been tied up next to me. "A Japanese kid named Suenaga," he told me. "He took a few lumps, but he's okay." Engler closed his notebook and stood up. He said that the first squad car on the scene couldn't have been more than thirty seconds behind the kidnappers, shook his head at that, then told me to try to get some sleep. "We've got the whole department working on this," he said.

Engler had been investigating a burglary only five blocks from our apartment when the 207 calls began coming in over his walkie-talkie—possible kidnap in progress—shots being fired. He made hasty apologies to the burglary victims and ran to his car. When he pulled up in front of our apartment building less than a minute later, a crowd had already gathered out on the sidewalk. "A guy's been shot in one of the back apartments," someone told him. Engler found Suenaga first. He had been dragged back into his apartment by his roommates who were untying him. Engler then moved through the people standing around our door. When he saw the blood under my head he thought I *had* been shot and, from the looks of me, was either already dead or dying.

By the time a second officer, Larry Lindenau, arrived a few minutes later, Engler was trying to piece together a description of the getaway cars from witnesses. At first everyone was still too shaken to say much of anything, and Engler began to badger them. Then suddenly they were all talking at once—Patty had been thrown into the trunk of a white convertible. Three taillights. Maybe a Chevy, a '64. There was also a light-colored station wagon. Shots were fired from the rear window. And a blue Volkswagen bug. Two people in it. Engler sorted out the confusion and put it together. The convertible had pulled out first, then the station wagon, then the VW. Someone said they had seen the VW turn left on College Avenue and had told the first cops on the scene who had taken off after it.

But they lost it. The VW had turned left, as the witness had said, but the other two cars had turned right. Some twenty minutes later an off-duty patrolman had come across the abandoned convertible on fashionable Tanglewood Road, about eight blocks from our apartment. A check showed that it was registered to a Peter Benenson of Berkeley. On the front seat were lengths of rope and a shell casing from a .38 automatic, on the back seat two bags of groceries. It was assumed that Benenson's car had been commandeered and that he too had been kidnapped.

Engler was still questioning witnesses when Lindenau went upstairs. He returned with the *Examiner* clipping announcing our engagement that Patty had cut out and left on her dresser. "This one will be for ransom," he said. A few minutes later the ambulance arrived. Throughout all of this, I had just been lying there, the two officers stepping over me, our neighbors looking inside, whispering to each other, then moving out of the way as the ambulance attendants rolled in the stretcher.

After catching up with me at Cowell Hospital later that night, Engler had returned to headquarters for a 1:00 A.M. briefing. All the brass had been rousted out of bed, as well as representatives from the Berkeley and Oakland FBI offices, who were sitting in "unofficially." They would officially enter the case twenty-four hours later, when it could be assumed that the kidnappers might have crossed state lines. But their interest in the case was not limited to the kidnapping itself. They were currently investigating another crime that had similar trappings—the assassination of Marcus Foster.

The briefing that night lasted until 3:00 A.M., and much of the talk was already focusing on the possible, the likely involvement of the Symbionese Liberation Army. From my account of the paramilitary assault—the almost flamboyant wielding of carbines, the whispered orders, and combat boots; from other witnesses' descriptions of the well-coordinated escape—the three-vehicle convoy and the covering rifle fire from the rear of the station wagon; but, most importantly, from the wealth of evidence authorities already had in their possession, everything led to the conclusion that the abduction of Patty Hearst was right in line with another SLA "operation."

Authorities had been investigating the terrorist group for three long months, since Foster's death. But for the first two of those months they had had little to go on—vague descriptions of Foster's assassins, two communiqués, ballistic reports, but no solid leads. Then, through a series of almost happenstance occurrences in early January, the case broke wide open, with one man's hunch.

At two o'clock in the morning of January 10, a police sergeant named David Duge was working the night shift when he spotted two men in a van cruising slowly through a housing tract just outside of Concord, a suburban community some twenty miles east of Berkeley. Duge had recently taken a course on burglary prevention in which an ex-burglar mentioned how careful he had been to drive lawfully, as well as his preference for vans when casing a neighborhood. With this in mind Duge flipped off his lights, followed the van for five blocks, and then pulled it over. Appearing agitated, the driver identified himself as Robert Scalise and said he was looking for the Devoto residence on Sutherland Court. Duge went back to his car and called in a check. The department's cross-directory showed no such name on Sutherland Court. Unaware that there *was* a Devoto on that street, but that the house was listed under its landlord's name, Duge became increasingly suspicious. He approached the passenger's side of the van and ordered the second man to climb out. The man complied, but then suddenly reached for a pistol tucked under his belt. Duge ducked behind the van, ran back to his car as the man fired two shots at him, then turned and returned the fire. The man moved to the driver's side of the van and four more shots were exchanged, one of Duge's bullets going into the van and nicking the driver in the shoulder. With that the man sprinted off into the darkness, and the driver roared away only to be stopped by another squad car responding to Duge's call for help. Concord police and Contra Costa County sheriffs quickly converged on the area and sealed it off.

Three-and-a-half hours later another officer spotted a man crawling through some shrubbery near Sutherland Court and ordered him to halt. "I've had it," the man shouted. "I'm coming out!"

Meanwhile, a search of the van had turned up two more guns and a bundle of SLA flyers. Held in the Contra Costa County jail, the two men were identified as Joseph Remiro and Russell Little. Amazingly, though the rifling had been altered, the pistol Remiro had thrown out when arrested matched up almost perfectly with the weapon used to kill Marcus Foster. On the basis of this, both men were charged with his murder.

But this was only the beginning. At around seven the following evening, just before sunset, a few neighbors on Sutherland Court saw a man and a woman hurry out of a small three-bedroom house and load up a white Oldsmobile with boxes. The two then got in the car and screeched away, the rear bumper grinding the pavement as they swung out of the driveway, turned the corner, and disappeared. Moments later smoke began billowing out of the house they had abandoned, and firemen were quickly called to the scene. After extinguishing the flames and taking a look inside, the firemen called the police and the bomb squad team. With these came the FBI. If the SLA was considered a dangerously weird group of terrorists to begin with, after the discovery of the

Concord "safe house" they fulfilled every paranoid fantasy the FBI, or anybody else, ever had about left-wing revolutionary organizations.

Eerily illuminated by fire engine headlights, investigators moved into the house after it had been cleared of explosives. What they found in the wet, charred interior was, as one lawman put it, "something out of fiction." Aside from stacks of books on communist theory, pamphlets on urban guerrilla warfare, and boxes of ammunition, there was a device used to cap cyanide bullets and, assembled alphabetically in scrapbook form, a long list of prominent Bay Area businessmen upon whom these bullets might be used. Among the names appearing was that of Patty's uncle, William Randolph Hearst, Jr., whose neatly typed résumé, like the others, featured a magazine photograph of him that had been clipped from an advertisement and carefully pasted on the page—in this case a picture of him in the lobby of Washington, D.C.'s Mayflower Hotel. Also discovered in the house were bottles of acids and poisons, makeup kits and changes of wardrobe, a large collection of charts, topographical maps, hand-drawn escape routes, and—in case of a police assault—sophisticated two-canister gas masks and a tunnel, a second line of defense, that had been dug under the foundation.

But most valuable were the personal effects some of the SLA members had left behind. There was a notebook of a Nancy Ling Perry filled with grandiloquent scribblings on "The Theory Of The Ruling Class," as well as references to "Camilla's pad in Oakland," "Teamwork games," and numerous checklists such as the following:

Security Around The Pad
1. Watch shadows.
2. Watch all curtains—don't brush against them.
3. Radio or records should be on at all times when there is activity or discussion.
4. Keep your handgun with you at all times.
5. Always know where your shoes are.
6. Always know where your Molotovs are.

Another notebook contained still more checklists, names, and addresses, and a diagram of the Kaiser Building in Oakland under which was the notation—"One visible uniformed security guard, old man/ Company floor #18/ Parking lots all around." And still another, Joseph Remiro's notebook, listing his contacts in the United Prisoners Union, Vietnam Veterans Against The War (VVAW), and Venceremos, the group into which the most violent remnants of sixties radicalism had funneled, but that had formally disbanded a few months before. There was a library card made out to a Gary Atwood, letters from Clifford "Death Row" Jefferson, a well-known inmate at Vacaville State Prison Medical Facility, addressed to a Willie Wolfe at 5939 Chabot Road, Oakland, and more, much more.

With the arrest of Remiro and Little, and the discovery of the Concord house, the long drought was over, and the authorities were suddenly deluged with almost more evidence than they could handle. Although all the names and addresses were punched into police computers, it still took the FBI seven weeks just to microfilm and catalog the boxes of material carted out of the hideout, from cans of gunpowder all the way down to "a woman's handkerchief, slightly stained." And new leads and information kept pouring in. The white Oldsmobile was found abandoned in Berkeley, registered to a Dr. L. W. Wolfe, an anaesthesiologist in Pennsylvania. He had a son named Willie. Neighbors on Sutherland Court positively identified the woman they knew as Mrs. Devoto as Nancy Ling Perry. A check showed her to be a former student at U.C. whose parents hadn't seen or heard from her in months. The Oakland address Little had given after his arrest was cross-indexed against Department of Motor Vehicle records and found to be the same address used by a Jonathan Salamone and an Anna Lindenberg, aliases for a Bill and Emily Harris. The couple had recently moved to Berkeley from Bloomington, Indiana, and had a history of involvement in radical movements. Gary Atwood was found to be a student at Indiana University in Bloomington, having separated from his wife, Angela, the summer before. He told authorities that the last he had heard she was living in Oakland with their two old friends, Bill and Emily Harris. From all of this information a fantastic web of connections, aliases, and safe houses began to emerge, and investigators had just scratched the surface.

Paralleling the computerized aspects of the search for the identities of the SLA members, and beginning within hours of the discovery of the Concord hideout, was a series of raids by the FBI and the Oakland Police on other suspected safe houses. Two of the most important of these were on the Chabot Road house and the Harrises' apartment on Forty-first Street, both in Oakland. Although the Harrises had disappeared, aside from their rather expensive furnishings and clothes, their poster-lined apartment yielded more SLA documents, another list of "targets," another address book, and evidence that two other women had also lived there—Angela Atwood and a Robyn Steiner, Russell Little's girl friend who had come from Florida to Berkeley with him in 1972.

But it was the raid on the Chabot Road house—a political commune known as "Peking House"—that finally began to shed some light on the SLA's origins. Two important tenants of the house, Dave Gunnell and Jean Chan, were found to have participated in a visitors' program at Vacaville known as the Black Cultural Association (BCA). Originally designed to give inmates some contact with the surrounding community, thereby making their eventual transition to society an easier one, in reality the BCA had become something of a study group in radical politics. Among the hundred names on the BCA's visitors' list besides Gunnell and Chan were their friends, and sometimes roommates, Willie Wolfe, Joseph Remiro, and Russell Little, as well as Bill and Emily Harris and a number of other Berkeley/Oakland Maoists. Nancy Ling Perry had also applied, but was rejected by prison officials because she was already visiting two other inmates at the time, Clifford "Death Row" Jefferson and his friend Albert Taylor. Furthermore, one of the inmates who had been deeply involved in the BCA was a thirty-year-old black man, Donald David DeFreeze, who went by the "reborn" name Cinque Mtume.

Meanwhile, another source of information had opened up. Shortly after the raid on the Chabot Road house on January 11,

Chris Thompson, a twenty-eight-year-old black man who had been a member of the Black Panthers and a onetime resident of the Chabot Road house, contacted the Oakland FBI through his attorney. Fearing that a pistol he had sold to Russell Little might implicate him in the Foster assassination, Thompson wanted to tell his story and clear his name. What he did, however, was confirm the authorities' suspicions. The Chabot Road house and the BCA were indeed at the heart of the SLA's formation. Thompson described the various meetings and "armament classes" held at the house and at various Oakland-Venceremos communes, the political films that were shown, and the sense of urgency and excitement generated in Wolfe, Little and the others by their twice-weekly trips to the BCA meetings at Vacaville. Although Thompson claimed never to have met, or even heard of "Cinque DeFreeze," by then it was a moot point. DeFreeze's fingerprints had been discovered in the Concord house and one line in Nancy Ling Perry's notebook read, "Cin's room is our base." It all fit. In December of the year before, DeFreeze had been transferred from Vacaville to Soledad State Prison from which he escaped the following March, having been assigned to repair a boiler in a minimum security area. Up until the discovery of the Concord hideout, his whereabouts had been unknown.

In short, then, the FBI and Oakland Police had come a long way in their investigation of the SLA since the Foster assassination. By the end of January they had identified as members of the terrorist group DeFreeze, Wolfe, Perry, Remiro, Little, the Harrises, and Angela Atwood; in a few days they would add Mizmoon Soltysik's name to the list, in a few weeks Camilla Hall's. But despite their progress the last thing heard from the SLA was Nancy Ling Perry's January seventeenth "Letter to the People" in which she greeted her two captured comrades, Remiro and Little, and described the "Foster Operation" as a "specific response to the political police state programs." But her whereabouts, along with those of the other suspected SLA members, remained a total mystery. They had all dropped out of sight and, after three weeks of intensive investigation, their trail began to run cold. Then, on the night of February 4, the FBI was notified that there had been a kidnapping at 2603 Benvenue Street in Berkeley. The victim was Patricia Hearst, daughter of the newspaper publisher. The kidnappers were described as a mixed group of white men and women and two blacks. A preliminary search of the Benvenue apartment turned up a box of cyanide loaded bullets found under a bookcase in the entrance hall. It did indeed seem to be another SLA "operation."

At the briefing at Berkeley Police headquarters that night, FBI agents and police began putting together a photo lineup of twenty-five suspects that they would show me the following morning: photos of the eight "prime" suspects, as well as known associates from "Peking House," VVAW/WSO, Venceremos, and the United Prisoners Union. Unofficially the authorities knew almost everything about Patty's kidnappers—what they looked like, where they came from, how they met, and what kind of people they were—everything but where they were holding her. Officially, they knew nothing. They were starting from scratch, they said, which could produce nothing but fear and despair in those of us who loved her. . . . But it is not clear to this day if they were aware of, or had simply overlooked, three scribbled lines in one of the notebooks taken from the Concord house a month before: "At U.C.—Daughter of Hearst—That bitch's daughter—Junior art student. Patricia Campbell Hearst. On the night of the full moon, Jan. 7. Can you make up a teamwork game?"

The next full moon came into phase on February 4.

"Try to get some sleep," Engler had said. He went out and closed the door behind him.

Suddenly all the noise and confusion, the whirl of lights and faces stopped and I was alone. It was just darkness, silence, and loss. I turned my head and looked out the window. I knew that out there hundreds of men were working on the case, that roadblocks were going up and cars were being searched. But from where I was I couldn't even hear the sound of footsteps in the corridor. There was nothing I could do. I was beginning to hurt by then, but worse was the feeling that something had broken loose, that the fabric had torn and behind it there was nothing but blackness.

I remember thinking of the world going on, of friends and family who still did not know what happened . . . and then what had happened—the terror I had heard in Patty's voice, and the terror that must be continuing for her unless she were dead. There was just no way of coming to grips with what had happened to us.

I was still awake when a nurse entered my room at 8:00 A.M. carrying a breakfast tray. The tray sat untouched as two doctors examined me. Every few hours a nurse would come and run salt water over the eye that had swollen shut. Then came more X rays for possible skull fractures and a broken ankle. After the X rays, I asked for and received a small radio, but was told by the guard— a different one—that news of Patty's abduction had not broken yet. All the local media had agreed on a blackout in an attempt not to panic the kidnappers.

A few minutes later another nurse came in and began digging some thorns out of my hands—one of the fences I had gone over had been lined with rose bushes—when two men in suits entered the room. Addressing me as Steven, they introduced themselves and showed me their FBI identification, then stood quietly next to the window until the nurse had finished with my hands and left the room. Then the questioning began.

Although the two agents were also sympathetic and seemed genuinely concerned about Patty, unlike Engler there was a distance, a cool formality about them. Their questions were straightforward and matter-of-fact. Would I describe our assailants? I did. Had I ever seen any of them before? No. To my knowledge had Patty ever seen any of them before? No. Was I certain? Yes. I then told them about the suspicious couple who had come by our apartment the Saturday before. They listened attentively and scribbled down some notes, but I had the feeling that either they already knew about it or were after something else. I wanted to help them in the worst way—at that point the FBI seemed like my only hope of getting Patty back—but throughout the interview I kept getting the uncomfortable and frustrating feeling that I was giving them nothing they hadn't heard before. And then I began to wonder just how much they had heard, how much they knew. Period. But there was no way of telling. They did not volunteer a single fact and were impossible to read.

"Do you have any black friends, Steven?" one of them asked. I told them yes.

"Are they or have they ever been connected with a terrorist-type organization?"

"No."

"A radical organization like SDS, for example? Any connections whatsoever?"

"No."

Actually both Nate and I had had a passing acquaintance with some of the SDS leaders at Princeton, but that was four years ago and it was so tenuous that I didn't think it important enough to mention. As it turned out, however, the two agents had already been briefed on my background and knew of this, but did not press me on it—not then.

One of them brought out a large scrapbook of photographs. "Steven, we have some photographs we want you to look over," he said. "If any of them strikes you as even remotely familiar, we'd like to know."

Between going in and out for more tests, and having my bandages changed, I must have spent three hours going over and over the book of photographs, some of which were loose, the names on the back carefully covered with pieces of adhesive tape. By late afternoon I had almost committed to memory the face of every Weatherman and escaped convict in the country as well as the faces of the SLA, etc., that would filter into newspapers in the coming weeks. But there was only one photograph that really struck me as familiar. It was a six-by-eight of a young woman.

"If you took this woman, put her in Berkeley, and let her dissipate herself for three years," I told them, "she could be the one who came by our apartment that Saturday night."

The agents made a note of it, but said nothing.

There was another photograph that struck me, but not because the person looked familiar. Rather, he looked completely out of place among all the other dour faces. Moreover, his picture kept turning up, in snapshots, in what appeared to be a passport photo, and in one where he was leaning jauntily against a sports car—a clean-cut, good-looking young man wearing a moustache and smiling into the camera. "This guy almost looks like a prep student at Menlo College," I told the agents. Did I mean a prep student I had *seen* at Menlo, they asked. No, just the prep student type. There was a quick exchange of glances at this, but again the agents made no comment. But out of the hundreds of photographs I had been shown, I had hesitated at two—Bill and Emily Harris.

"Steven, thanks for the help," one of the agents said, closing the book at the end of the session. "We might have to get back to you a little later, if that's okay." I told him of course it was, but I could not see why. I didn't feel that I had been any help at all.

Later that afternoon I was visited by my mother and father. They came separately and stayed only a short while. My mother patted my hand and bravely tried to cheer both of us up, saying that when Patty was released one look at my puffy face and shaved head and she would want nothing more to do with me. My father tried to make sense of what had happened, then shook his head and sat in silence next to my bed.

After they left, two Berkeley policemen entered the room with their own book of photographs, and then Jay and Gina Bosworth came in. They were badly shaken, especially Gina. And while Jay tried to be rational and reassuring about the whole thing, acting as both a member of the family and a reporter for the *Examiner,* there was nothing to be reassured about and we all knew it. Like all the other visits I was to have by people who knew and loved Patty, it was impossible to say anything that did not sound hollow in the face of what had happened and what *was* happening to her at that very moment.

Jay and Gina were still there when a special FBI artist, who had been flown in from Washington, D.C., entered the room with a sketch pad and a book of facial types. Jay told me he would return the next day so that we could prepare something for the *Examiner,* then he and Gina said good-bye and left. The FBI artist showed me his identification, then pulled a chair up next to my bed and opened his book as two more agents entered the room. Just from the artist's appearance it was clear that he was from a different branch of the service. That is, he was the Bureau's version of an "artist"—a little older, a little shorter, and very bald. But like his fellow agents he was serious, efficient, and wore the same kind of suit, though it was a bit rumpled from his flight. "Okay," he said, putting the book on my lap, "let's see what we can come up with."

For over an hour we went through pages of eyes, lips, noses, hairlines, and facial types. Then he started putting them together, the other two agents looking curiously over his shoulder. Despite my vague recollections, he managed to come up with three composites that turned out to be somewhat accurate. They would go over the wires within the hour, he said, then thanked me for my cooperation and left with the other two agents.

There were a few quiet moments after that, then Steve Suenaga, who was occupying the room next to mine, came in still dressed in his hospital gown and still badly unnerved by the attack. He went over the details of the kidnapping from his point of view, which was almost identical to mine, then began pacing back and forth at the foot of my bed. He was particularly agitated at having picked out one of our assailants from the photo lineup he had been shown. "The guy by the door [DeFreeze]. It's the SLA for sure," he kept saying. I asked him how he knew and he said he had overheard two agents talking about them in the corridor. "Man, I'm getting out of here," he said. "I've got some relatives up in Reno. Maybe I'll go up there for a while." He paused at the door, said he was sorry about everything, then went out, almost bumping into the two agents who were on their way in.

Unlike the other agents I had met, these were younger and more nattily dressed. They showed me colored I.D. cards instead of black and whites. I later found out that they had joined the

Bureau after J. Edgar Hoover had died, the rigid gray-on-gray dress standards dying with him. But their manner was the same.

"Do you own a firearm, Steve?" one of them asked.

When I told him no, he reached into his pocket and took out a box of bullets. "We found these under the bookcase in your apartment." There was a pause, then, "They must have dropped them," he said flatly.

I asked them if they'd checked out the couple who had cased our apartment that Saturday. They said yes, they'd seen a report on it, but would go no further.

"We have something else they might have dropped," the second agent said and then pulled a Jimi Hendrix wide-brimmed felt hat out of a paper bag.

"That belongs to a friend of mine," I said disappointedly.

"Your black friend?"

"Yes." I did not know Nate had shown up early that morning and had been pounced on.

"To your knowledge is he or has he ever been connected with any kind of radical or terrorist organization?"

And so it went, and with much of it my confidence in the FBI. On one hand I was sunk with the feeling that they were getting nowhere and were reduced to a mechanical recitation of the same questions over and over again. On the other I was sure that they knew *something* about Patty's captors, but were not about to tell me what. Moreover, it seemed that once they were reasonably certain that I was not going to break down, go hysterical on them, and hamper the questioning, they could dispense with the sympathy and get down to being agents. Above anything else that's what they were. They looked like agents, walked and talked like agents, thought like agents, and after checking into my background they were not all that sure that I was just a victim, just a guy caught in the cross fire. That's the feeling I began to get. But I was too crushed, too blown out, to feel much more than a dull, aching frustration at this. I believed the FBI was our only hope; and when that hope began to fade, everything else did, my life, Patty's life, everything. There was no room for anger then, and when there was it was useless, just another emotion I had to keep under control if I was going to be of any help in getting Patty out.

It was dark by the time the agents left. The nurse changed my bandages and then brought in my dinner tray, but I was unable to eat. I sipped some orange juice, then turned on the radio to hear that the *Oakland Tribune* had broken the news embargo. "Patricia Hearst, daughter of Randolph and Catherine Hearst and heiress to one of America's largest fortunes, was kidnapped from her Berkeley apartment last night," the newsman said. He announced my "satisfactory condition" at Cowell Hospital, then went on to describe how Peter Benenson had called authorities from the Berkeley YMCA twelve hours after having been held prisoner while his Chevrolet convertible was used in the kidnapping. "There have been no breaks in the case at this point," he said, leaving "The Hearst Case" and picking up the latest on Watergate. I turned off the radio and lay back in the silence.

At around ten the next morning, Jay returned. At that point we still thought it possible that Patty might have been taken as a hostage, or as the only real witness to the attack. On the basis of that we tried to put together a story that would reassure her captors and yet pressure them. After working and reworking it for over an hour, Jay read me the crucial lines:

> Weed, twenty-six, was beaten viciously by at least one of the three armed abductors. He has given police descriptions of the two men and one woman. With his help, investigators believe they can identify the woman, who was white, and at least one of the black men if apprehended. . . . Despite the potentially useful evidence he holds, Weed vows he will not cooperate in the prosecution of his fiancée's abductors if she is released. . . . "If that happens I won't testify, make any identification of suspects or give any evidence, directly or indirectly," Weed said. . . .

It was our hope that this would reinforce Mr. and Mrs. Hearst's "Plea From Parents" as it would run in the next day's *Examiner*.

Mrs. Hearst and I pray to God that the men who took our daughter will show compassion and will return her unharmed. . . . We do not believe we are clutching at straws when we say there is evidence that the abductors are not senseless and brutal. They were heavily armed and could have eliminated all witnesses. They did not. . . . In short, there are witnesses who saw the men who took our daughter. Thus, Patricia is no more a threat to them than are the others. . . . We want our daughter back unharmed. If she is released we will not seek to imprison her abductors.

With the publication of these two stories there was nothing we could do but wait. And if there was a ray of hope in us, it was only because we were totally unaware that this pressure/promise tactic was to be the first in a long series of unsuccessful strategies to free Patty; totally unaware that it marked the beginning of a long, grueling exchange of desperate pleas through the media that would be answered by SLA communiqués demanding the impossible and denouncing the Hearst empire, the "fascist insect that preys upon the life of the people."

Sometime later that same afternoon I was visited by Charles Gould, a close friend of the Hearsts and publisher of the *Examiner,* and twenty-six-year-old Willie Hearst, one of Patty's favorite cousins. They could not have been a more unlikely pair. Dressed in his three-piece, blue serge suit with an American flag lapel pin, Mr. Gould was the perfect American business executive—deliberate, pragmatic, his bald head wrinkled with studious concern. Willie, on the other hand, looked straight off a soapbox in Berkeley—baggy corduroys, beat-up moccasins, unruly hair, a moustache, and eyes just like Patty's. In spite of their differences, they respected each other and both would play an important role in the weeks ahead.

Like my other visitors, Willie and Mr. Gould expressed their deep concern and sympathy, but found it difficult to say much more. At one point I remember Mr. Gould commending what he called my bravery for declaring that I could actually identify the kidnappers, that I was their most dangerous witness. In view of my twenty-four-hour police protection, I did not think it at all brave, but felt a bit better for his saying it all the same. At that stage, considerations of bravery, or the lack of it, had not even entered my mind. They had entered other people's minds, however. Shortly after Willie and Gould left a nurse came in with a large floral bouquet. The note attached read: "You're still a hero in our eyes, Steven. Get well soon. The Hearsts." The implication that I definitely was *not* a hero in other people's eyes went right over my head. I was just grateful for the flowers, sent at a time when I knew the Hearsts were in at least as much pain as I was.

Mr. and Mrs. Hearst had been in Washington, D.C., where they were attending the Hearst Foundation's Senate Youth Program, when they first received word of Patty's abduction. Earlier in the evening they had had dinner with Senator Charles Percy, then returned to their suite at the Mayflower Hotel. At about 1:15 A.M., the bedside telephone rang. It was Anne, Patty's younger sister, calling from Hillsborough. She told them what had happened. The police had just called and informed her that Patty had been kidnapped. There had been shots fired. Steve was injured, but she didn't know how seriously.

Anne, Emmy, and Vicky, the youngest of the sisters, had been fixing a snack in the kitchen when the police had telephoned. After hanging up they immediately called Jay and Gina, who locked up their apartment and went to a friend's house to spend the night. The next call went to Washington.

Stunned by the news, Mr. Hearst went straight to the top. He called Clarence Kelly, head of the FBI, who confirmed Anne's call, but said there was nothing new to report. Mr. Hearst then made a number of calls to the Berkeley Police, family members, and friends, before he and Mrs. Hearst began packing their things. At 5:00 A.M., a special breakfast was prepared for them, but it sat untouched as they endured a two-hour wait, then drove to Dulles International Airport and caught the first flight to California.

Meanwhile, Willie Hearst was sitting numbly in his San Francisco apartment watching the police install a telephone-monitoring device. Willie had been notified of his cousin's kidnapping at approximately 10:00 P.M. He had been arguing with his girl friend, when the San Francisco Police called, told him about Patty and said a Lieutenant Loller and two men from the Intelligence Division were on their way. "We'd like permission to monitor your calls," the officer said, "because your phone number's listed." Willie told them fine, anything. A few minutes later the police arrived and began hooking up the monitor. One of the first calls they recorded was from Charles Gould, who explained the news embargo. "If we get a ransom call we'll know it's legitimate," he told Willie.

There were no ransom calls, but Willie was up all night waiting for one. When Mr. and Mrs. Hearst arrived late the following morning, he was one of the first to call. He offered to drive down to Hillsborough and help out, do whatever he could. "No, that's okay, Willie," Mr. Hearst told him. Willie arrived in Hillsborough the next morning. For the first time in his life, the bright, energetic, and cynical young man was suddenly overwhelmed with a sense of Family and a need to band together. Other members of the family felt the same. Jack and Phoebe Cooke, Patty's older cousin and her husband, Gina and Jay, and the eldest of the sisters, Catherine, who flew in from Los Angeles, arrived shortly after Willie did.

By Thursday, three days after the kidnapping, Willie had moved in for the duration. The FBI already had their tape-recording equipment set up in the library, giving the house the feeling of a command post, a house under siege. Outside, a dozen members of the press were setting up their equipment on the chance that it might be a "big story." Twenty-four hours later, after the arrival of the first SLA communiqué, the ranks of the press gathered outside the Hillsborough home would swell to encampment proportions. The story was a big one.

That same afternoon a tall, balding man in a pin-striped suit entered my room and introduced himself as Professor Hardin

Jones, a friend of the Hearsts. Although he was very concerned and was trying to be helpful, Professor Jones was also the first in a long line of rather curious characters I would come to know in the next few months.

The professor taught physiology at U.C. and had been a colorful figure in the debates over marijuana that had taken place on campus the year before. His stand on the issue was quickly revealed when, after the usual inquiries about my health, he asked me to describe the two people who had cased our apartment before the kidnapping. When I explained that I hadn't really gotten a very good look at them, he asked me about their skin.

"Was it yellowish?" he inquired.

I told him I didn't quite understand his question.

"Chronic marijuana users can usually be identified by their sickly, yellowish complexion, Steve," he explained.

I was still stumbling over that one, when he moved closer and set a piece of paper before me.

"We know something about these people," he said quietly, then began pointing out what amounted to a flow chart complete with lines and arrows connecting boxes marked as "The War Council," "Combat Units," "Medical Teams," and "Intelligence Units." At the time I gave it as much credence as his Yellow Skin Theory. I had no idea that Professor Jones had sources within the FBI, that the paper I was holding was an SLA document taken from the Concord house.

The professor was still standing next to my bed, while I studied the chart as seriously as possible, when Scott and Mimi entered the room. On their first visit, the day before, they had been carefully screened and searched before being escorted to my room, but were still worried about my safety. I remember Scott going to the window and scanning the building across the way. He tried to shrug off his paranoia, but both he and Mimi were obviously concerned about possible snipers. "Hell, you're the only real witness around," Scott said, "and these people are off the wall." I told him there was nothing to worry about, that the guard had a shotgun hidden under a blanket on the gurney next to him. I did not, however, tell him the extent of my own paranoia, having almost bolted out of bed the night before when a black janitor walked into my room.

Professor Jones smiled and extended his hand as I introduced the Swantons to him. I told him they were Patty's and my closest friends in Berkeley.

"It's a terrible thing," the professor said sympathetically. "It's too bad we don't have the old counterinsurgency units anymore. Back in the fifties we'd send them out to take care of groups like this."

"What would they do?" Scott asked incredulously. "Kill them?"

"No, just rough them up a bit." The professor smiled. He took the chart from my hand, folded it up, and put it in his coat pocket. "It's a shame we had to meet under such circumstances," he told the Swantons. He patted my shoulder and assured me that they had some very good men working on the case, then left.

After he was gone there was a pause. Mimi started to ask if I was certain all the hospital entrances were being guarded, then suddenly stopped and fought back tears. She had an armful of the day's newspapers and set them in my lap. All of them featured large photographs of Patty smiling happily, her hair backlit in the sunlight. I put them aside for the moment.

The Swantons and I talked for about half an hour that afternoon. Then, just as they were leaving, Scott said something that had apparently been on his mind since he heard of Patty's kidnapping. "Try not to blame yourself for what happened, Steve," he said. "There was really nothing you could have done to stop them . . . nothing anyone could have done." I nodded, and he said they'd see me tomorrow.

After they left I began going through the papers. I was reading an article about Peter Benenson, a rather shadowy figure in the case who had refused to cooperate with authorities or to talk to newsmen, when I heard some activity in the corridor. The guard poked his head in the door and told me to turn on the radio to KPFA. "They've just got word," he said. I tuned in the station to hear Paul Fischer, the news director, reading a letter that had been sent along with one of Patty's credit cards. As I was listening, an FBI agent entered and handed me a copy of the letter.

SYMBIONESE LIBERATION ARMY
Western Regional Adult Unit

February 4, 1974

Communique #3*
Subject: Prisoner of War
Target: Patricia Campbell Hearst
      daughter of Randolph Hearst
      corporate enemy of the people

Warrant Order:
Arrest and protective custody and if resistance, execution

Warrant Issued by
The Court of the People

On the afore state date, combat elements of the United Federated Forces of the Symbionese Liberation Army with cyanide loaded weapons served an arrest warrant upon Patricia Campbell Hearst.

It is the order of this court that the subject be arrested by combat units and removed to a protective area of safety and only upon completion of this condition to notify Unit #4 to give communication of this action.

It is the directive of this court that during this action ONLY, no civilian elements be harmed if possible, and that warning shots be given. However, if any citizens attempt to aid authorities or interfere with the implementation of this order, they shall be executed immediately.

This court hereby notifies the public and directs all combat units in the future to shoot to kill any civilians who attempt to witness or interfere with any operation conducted by the people's forces against the fascist state.

*SLA communiqué #3 is the *first* communiqué received *after the kidnapping,* but the *third* sent by the SLA—the first two had to do with the Marcus Foster murder (see p. 8 above). When the author refers in his diary to the "third communiqué"

Should any attempts be made by authorities to rescue the prisoner, or to arrest or harm any S.L.A. elements, the prisoner is to be executed.

The prisoner is to be maintained in adequate physical and mental condition and unharmed as long as these conditions are adhered to. Protective custody shall be composed of combat and medical units to safeguard both the prisoner and her health.

All communications from this court MUST be published in full, in all newspapers and all forms of the media. Failure to do so will endanger the safety of the prisoner.

Further communications will follow.

S.L.A.

DEATH TO THE FASCIST INSECT THAT PREYS UPON THE LIFE OF THE PEOPLE

For three days I had been praying for the kidnappers to make a ransom demand, but I was not prepared for this. The words "shoot to kill," "executed immediately," and the description of the attack as having "served an arrest warrant" leapt out at me as totally insane, crushing my relief that Patty was apparently, and for the time being, still alive. I reread the communiqué, then lay back feeling nauseated.

The next morning, Friday the eighth, the papers were filled with speculation that the SLA would demand a prisoner exchange, Patty for Remiro and Little. The authorities' response to this was depressing, but anticipated. Charles Bates, FBI chief of the San Francisco bureau, was quoted as saying he knew of "no precedent in United States history for the exchange of prisoners in such circumstances," adding that such a decision would have to be made by the district attorney, the governor, or the attorney general. A spokesman for the Berkeley Police reacted to this:

No governor, no policeman is going to release these men. So they know they have to ask something that can be done. It would be unrealistic for them to believe that Remiro and Little can be released.

(see p. 127), he does so because it is the third relating to the kidnapping; though by the SLA's numbering it is rightfully communiqué #5.

At around one o'clock that afternoon, Scott and Mimi returned to find two FBI agents showing me another book of photographs. Mimi asked if they could see them, but was told it was "not policy." While I went through the book they stood out in the corridor talking with another agent. Scott suggested that the kidnapping appeared to have been patterned after *State of Siege,* an extremely popular film about the Tupamaro guerrillas in Uruguay that was currently being shown all over the Bay Area. The agent shrugged. He said he had never heard of either the film or the Tupamaros. A few minutes later the two agents left my room and the Swantons entered.

"I cannot believe it," Mimi said, looking back toward the door.

Scott asked if she meant the agent's not having heard of the Tupamaros.

"No, that book of photographs they were showing Steve. You know what the label said? Hersnatch."

I told them that sadly enough that was the first sign of any imagination I had seen in the FBI since I was admitted, then added that I was being released the next day, Saturday. The Bureau had arranged for an escort to Hillsborough. Earlier in the week Mr. Hearst had called and suggested that it might be a good idea for me to join the family after I was released, "for all of us to stick together during this thing," he said. I agreed and he made arrangements with the FBI.

My last night in the hospital was almost as bad as my first. When I was admitted, I was dazed and sick with dread. Four days later, with the arrival of the communiqué, my worst fears had been realized. Patty was in the hands of people who had murdered Marcus Foster in cold blood and would not hesitate to murder again, people who had vanished without a trace, leaving the authorities to show me page after page of photographs and ask me about my friends.

That night I remember starting to read a reprint of Nancy Ling Perry's January "Letter to the People" in one of the newspapers Mimi had brought me. I was searching for some sign of compassion and, if not that, at least an indication that she and her fellow SLA members had some grasp on reality. But it was all "the Foster Operation," and "pig agents," and "I have learned that there is no flight to freedom except that of an armed projectile." I couldn't even finish it.

A couple of hours before my release the following morning, I was interviewed by Carol Pogash, a young, no-nonsense reporter for the *Examiner*. As we walked down the empty corridors—me trying to get my legs back after lying in bed for five days—she told me that she had been covering the SLA since the Foster assassination. The minute she had heard about Patty's kidnapping she feared it was the SLA. "They're a very weird group," she told me. "After digging around Berkeley for sources close to them it got to the point where I was afraid to go home at night. . . . A couple of times I *didn't* go home. I stayed with friends."

While Carol and I were talking, scores of newspeople were busy setting up their cameras outside both exits, crowding around the doorways and jockeying for position. After the interview, I received another call from Mr. Hearst. I told him I was stopping by our apartment to pick up some clothes and arrange for the care of our two cats. He asked me to bring something of Patty's along, something personal. I thought, I hoped, that maybe he knew something that I didn't and asked him why.

"Never mind, Steve," he said, "just bring something."

Because I was still pretty wobbly on my feet two FBI agents helped me down the corridor and into the elevator. "Brace yourself for a mob scene," one of them said as we reached the first floor. The doors slid open and we were blinded by flashbulbs. Surging around the elevator were at least twenty-five newspeople, half of whom were crowding forward and pushing their microphones into my face. Like some surreal cinema verité, my vision was jostled and blurred as the two agents formed a wedge in front of me and pushed through the crowd. The reporters backpedaled down the hall, shooting and reloading and shouting questions. One of them stumbled over a camera cord and went sprawling, but the others merely stepped over him in their frantic attempt to get in a question. We finally pushed our way out the door and down the steps toward a waiting car. When we ducked inside my hands were shaking. The shouted questions, the pushing and shoving had triggered images of the assault that Monday night before.

"Ever see anything like that?" one of the agents said. The other breathed out and shook his head.

As we pulled away, all I could see out the side windows were legs, cameras, and equipment as the reporters ran alongside trying to get that one last shot. Looking back and seeing them hurry to their cars, I was unaware that this was a scene that would be played over and over again.

3

WHEN WE TURNED RIGHT on to tree-lined Santa Inez Avenue
and drove up toward the Hearst home I felt something close to
déjà vu—a feeling of having, and yet not having, done this before. The differences were great between the first time I had
driven up that street to meet Patty's parents and driving up it now
to stay with them under these circumstances. And yet both times
there was the same anxiety at not knowing what to expect.

In some two years between these times, the Hearsts and I
had gradually come to know each other, our differences glossed
over simply because we both loved Patty. She was the link between us. But what I could not know as we now approached her
parents' home was that in the coming weeks, with Patty gone and
the pressure and despair building steadily, the differences between
the Hearsts and me would reemerge, would affect what we tried

to do to help Patty, and in the end would finally divide us all. Because of this I think that it is important to stop here and go back to the spring of 1971 when I first met Patty at Crystal Springs School for Girls. To really tell the story of the first few weeks of the kidnapping requires a deeper understanding of Patty and her family and of how I came to have a place in all of this.

Crystal Springs is probably the closest equivalent to an exclusive East Coast finishing school that California can offer. Set on ten acres of land in Hillsborough, some intelligent remodeling has turned what was once the massive Crocker mansion into a comfortable secondary school attended by two hundred girls from some of San Francisco's most prominent families—the Roths, Gettys, and the Hearsts, among others. A large ballroom in the main house has been converted into an assembly hall, the upstairs wood-paneled bedrooms into classrooms, and the old lawns and gardens into playing fields. Where the Crocker family once entertained their guests and led their privileged lives, now the girls, dressed in their blue blazers and pleated skirts, attend classes, chat in the halls, and play field hockey on the wide lawns. But the estate's exclusive atmosphere remains. Situated in the middle of an upper-class residential area, Crystal Springs is physically sheltered from the outside world.

I was fresh out of Princeton, age twenty-two, when I was hired as a mathematics instructor at Crystal in the fall of 1969. My salary was $600 a month and my hiring, I suspect, was part of a conscious effort to increase the diversity of backgrounds on a teaching staff that was dominated by women in their late forties and fifties. There were eight new teachers hired that year, and five of them were men, four of them young men. If the Crystal administrators wanted innovation and change, they got it. There was Michael Koepf, a burly Ken Kesey look-alike, who pounded tables, was proud of his radical politics and was, ironically, in the midst of writing a novel in which a radical teacher plots the kidnapping of one of the school's rich students. He was fired after his first year. There was Pat Cunningham, naive, enthusiastic, and disarmingly straightforward. After a large blowup over a urine test for schizophrenia he proposed to run on his chemistry students, Pat too was sacked after his first year. There was Ron Jensen, a good-looking physical education teacher—too "informal" with his students, who used to pelt him with erasers. The sack again. The sole survivors of that year were Harry Nugent and me. Harry survived because he was forty-five, polite, and unassuming. I survived by doing my work, keeping my opinions to myself, and in general shuffling through the year as quietly as possible.

Even though I continued to maintain this "low profile" during my second year at Crystal, it was not unusual for me to get phone calls from students, sometimes as late as two or three in the morning, which generally consisted of a great deal of giggling or long, deadly serious, but deadly boring conversations about family problems—problems I had heard over and over again. These calls usually came from a particular group of students, a small following I had attracted my first year there. They were basically awkward girls who would gather around me at Crystal dances, using me as a buffer and urging me toward the boys who were lined up against the wall on the far side of the dance floor. It was my function to break the ice, then beat a hasty retreat. Without fail, a few days later my phone would ring and I would be treated to a detailed description of the girl's success or failure or why their parents hadn't even let them attend the dance in the first place.

But Patty Hearst was definitely not a member of this group. She was new at Crystal that year, and it wasn't too long before everyone was well aware that she was not, and would not be, a member of any group. Rather, Patty was determined to be an individual, to stand apart from the crowd. And she did stand out. Scanning a group of uniformed students in the hallways between classes, your eyes would stop on her, the girl in the blue tights and two-inch clogs, her long blond hair swinging across a sweater coat that concealed her checkered uniform. And then there were the simple earrings and the thin gold bracelet she wore, all the stylish little touches of "that Hearst girl." Once I remember overhearing two students complaining about another girl who was getting away with driving her new MG roadster to school each day. It was Patty, naturally.

By choice rather than circumstance Patty made only a few close friends that year who, like her, were known for their individualism and general displeasure with Crystal Springs. One of them, a tall, good-looking girl named Chris Johnson, had been in my geometry class the year before. At the time she was captivated by Crystal's resident radical, Michael Koepf, and would sometimes come bustling in the door all smiles and write revolutionary slogans on my blackboard or suggest that the class forget about geometry and talk about Abbie Hoffman. When she and Patty met the following year, they found that they were kindred spirits. They would often sneak off campus for a quick enchilada at Celia's, a nearby Mexican restaurant, or a bowl of pea soup at Doc Carter's, another local hangout. On weekends the two of them and another friend, Kate, would sometimes go up to the Fillmore auditorium in San Francisco to hear various rock groups or just rumble around in what Patty called "The Duckmobile"— a mud-spattered old junker her father used for duck hunting.

In any event, though Patty was not a member of my little following, I had no desire to see the membership increased and therefore was not particularly sympathetic—in fact I was a bit irritated—when she called me the first time. She was not in any of my classes so at that point I knew her only in passing, although I was aware of some of her first attempts to get to know me. Earlier in the semester I remember amusedly telling my girl friend Garnett, with whom I was living at the time, that "there's this funny little girl who keeps following me around school." Some weeks later that "funny little girl" dropped into a guitar workshop I was teaching, but then dropped out after a couple of sessions. I later learned that she had decided that strumming "Wabash Cannonball" with a half-dozen other girls was not a promising avenue of approach.

After that there were a few brief, rather awkward conversations in the halls between class, usually about geometry problems, and then in early February she called. As I remember it Patty asked me about yet another geometry problem she was supposedly having difficulty with and I told her how to solve it. "Oh," she said. There was a long pause and a couple of false starts as she tried to move the conversation out of the realm of isosceles triangles and into something personal. Then somebody else picked up one of the extensions in the Hearst home.

"Hello? Is somebody on the line? Vicky, is that you?" asked a woman's voice.

"I'm making a call, Mother," Patty said. "Will you please get . . ."

Another extension was picked up. Her father. "Hello? Hello?"

"Randy?" her mother asked.

"Catherine, is that you?"

"I'm using the phone," Patty cut in. I could feel her face reddening with embarrassment and anger. "Will both of you please get off the line?"

"Is that you, Vicky?" her father asked.

"It's *Patty.*"

"Oh, sorry, honey."

Both extensions hung up, thus ending my first encounter with Mr. and Mrs. Hearst. When Patty apologized it seemed not so much for her parents' interruption, but for the embarrassing fact that she actually *had* parents. I told her there was no need to apologize, that I wasn't much good on the phone anyway. Neither was she, she said, and asked if she could come over sometime, for help with her geometry. I told her that would be all right.

Although I didn't give much thought to Patty's dropping by, I certainly didn't mind the prospect of having some company. At the time I was living in a large, two-bedroom house in Menlo Park that was shaded by oak trees and recently vacated by Garnett. An extremely volatile person, after living with me for a year and a half, Garnett gave me an ultimatum that dealt a death blow to what had been an affectionate but stormy relationship: marriage by Christmas. Three weeks later I was knocking around an empty house and tending a pregnant Siamese she had left. She had taken our male cat and promptly had him neutered, an act that some of my friends found symbolic.

Anyway, I think it was only a few days after Patty called, perhaps the very next day, that she came by unannounced. As luck would have it, Nate and his girl friend were visiting for a few days and had brought along another girl, making it a foursome. Patty was introduced and then, contrary to what you would expect from most schoolgirls—awkwardness, an apology for intruding, then an equally awkward good-bye—she sat down on the couch and made a great show of puzzling over her geometry. Patty knew exactly what she was doing. So did my "date" for the evening and was not amused.

But I admired Patty's persistence. There was none of that naive innocence or guile common to most girls her age. She was straightforward and proper, always addressing me as "Mr. Weed." And yet it was quite clear that she was determined to advance our relationship beyond the student and teacher level.

Student flirtations were hardly new to me or any other single male on the staff. The school was filled with young girls becoming young women who were filling out, breaking away from home, dating, experimenting, and smiling at male teachers in that innocent, come-hither way. While I enjoyed calling their bluffs, flirting back with mock lasciviousness, actual involvement, if not unthinkable, hardly seemed appropriate. The girls were good to look at, fun to tease, but often pouty, sometimes insecure, and invariably adolescent. But almost from the first moment I met her it was clear to me that there was something different about Patty. She seemed as much a woman as a seventeen-year-old girl. She had determination and a sense of what she wanted.

The day after our first "tutoring" session I returned home from school to find Patty's blue MG parked in front of my house. She was waiting for me in the backyard, resting comfortably against the gnarled trunk of a large oak tree, and it was really the start of things. In the following weeks Patty's visits almost became a matter of routine. Soon she was skipping her afternoon ballet classes, choosing instead to drop by with a bag of groceries for me. It is a poignant detail, I think, of how Patty was standing between the worlds of adolescence and womanhood that she would always drive the twelve miles back to her parents in Hillsborough in order to have dinner with them. After having satisfied that superficial commitment to propriety, she would drive the twelve miles back to our place. Soon she would drag out her geometry book and we would go over a few problems. But as we became more relaxed with each other, these tutoring sessions were often cut short by talk, an ice cream run, or going to the movies. On one occasion, after seeing the surrealistic film *Orpheus* at Stanford, I remember our returning home to discover that my cat, Melissa, had given birth to five kittens. Patty made a note of the date, March first, as we huddled over the kittens, petting them and congratulating their mother.

Although Patty was "scared" of me during these early days, as she said later, I wasn't particularly aware of it. Nor was I exactly certain what she had in mind. But the way I saw it, she was bright, remarkably mature and self-possessed, and it was pretty much her game. Patty saw it the same way and went about that game with a funny kind of formality; I was always "Mr. Weed." In fact it wasn't until after we had slept together for the first time that Patty felt comfortable enough to call me Steve. But if she felt somewhat awkward because of the difference in our ages, she held her own that evening by surprising me with the statement that I didn't have to worry, she was taking birth control pills. She said this very matter-of-factly, acting as if it was the most natural thing in the world, but I could tell she was pleased to startle me a little. Afterward, lingering at the front door, she hugged me and said, "I wish I didn't have to go back." She didn't say "home." In the following days I came to depend upon arriving home to find her MG now parked neatly to one side of the driveway, leaving a spot for me.

So Patty's and my relationship began with her quiet persistence and my usual nonchalance about letting things lead where they may. It was an odd way to start a love affair. Despite our growing feelings for each other, we had nothing in common at first, except the excitement and adventure of our secret affair. Patty was seventeen and felt inexperienced, while I was all of twenty-two and, in her eyes, had been around. "You've done all those things, been to all those places," I remember her telling me. "It's not fair." This attitude was reflected in our conversations. When we would talk about our pasts it was almost always *my* past she wanted to hear about—my trip to Europe, my years at Princeton, the crazy incidents, the odd characters I'd met here and there. The present was pretty much her domain—primarily talk of Crystal and her family. But because she was trying to be an adult, trying to disassociate herself from these things, much of her talk took the form of complaints: the time her mother mortified her by insisting on hiring a chauffeured limousine to take her and an old boyfriend into San Francisco to see *Hair;* how her younger sister, Anne, had worn one of her new sweaters for a quick dip in the Pacific; the way her father sometimes blew up at the breakfast table over Vicky's "forgetting" to keep her orthodontist appointment; her older sister Gina's irritating "air of superiority," and so on. A year or two later she would laugh to me about "Silly Billy," one of her cousins who was forever complaining about how hard it was "to be a Hearst," and yet during our first few months together Patty was doing pretty much the same thing, even to the extent of considering changing her name.

Although I could understand some of her problems, being a Hearst did not sound all that terrible to me, especially after having grown up as a Weed. I couldn't help thinking that while she had had a limousine summoned for her, not to mention having been presented with a new MG when she was sixteen, at that age I was riding a balloon tire bicycle to school and taking a bus to see my girl friend. By the same token, while she was being brought up by a series of nannies and governesses, I was bent over my school books and doing my weekly chores around the house. In short, the differences in our backgrounds made it somewhat difficult for me to appreciate many of Patty's problems and concerns.

Raised in a middle-class neighborhood of Palo Alto, I had attended public schools that were a far cry from Crystal Springs— schools of academic rather than social prestige. In high school I was an overachiever who thrived on day-to-day assignments and, unlike Patty, cherished my frequent role as teacher's pet. In 1965 I graduated as class valedictorian and National Merit Scholar, and Stanford and the Ivy League schools offered scholarships. For a time I thought seriously about going to Harvard. But everybody from Palo Alto High School who could went to Harvard, so just to be contrary I in the end decided on Princeton.

I expected to take Princeton by storm. I entered in the top 2 percent of the class as a "university scholar," with no formal class or examination requirements. Four years later, and considerably more humble, I graduated dead in the middle of the class and was lucky at that. But aside from my comeuppance as a student, what was most difficult to adjust to were the cold, gray days, the bleak atmosphere, and the strange East Coast social rituals. Imprinted in my memory is the day my new friends tried to cheer me up by dragging me along to a campus mixer—known as a "cattle drive" by veteran Princeton men—that was being held in the gymnasium. While we waited in front, stamping the cold out of our feet, four busloads of girls from Briarcliff were hustled in the rear doors of the gym and led up to the balcony. Then the big moment. The front doors were unlocked and three hundred Princeton men stampeded across the basketball court and charged up the balcony stairs.

"Unbelievable," I said to a friend who had also hung back.

"Well, it beats 'street meat.' " He shrugged and headed for the pandemonium taking place in the balcony.

Next came what are called the "eating clubs," which have traditionally dominated Princeton's social life. There were thirteen of them, rigidly stratified from the most prestigious, catering to Princeton's elite, to the least prestigious, whose membership consisted of what in Princetonese were described as "wonks," "wienies," and "lunchmeats." Against my better judgment and the sound advice of my roommate and track team friend Nate,

I decided to make the eating club rounds. A few days later I received my bid. I was cordially invited to dine with the "wonks," "wienies," and "lunchmeats" of Key and Seal eating club. I hadn't seriously been interested in the eating clubs anyway, I told Nate, who found the whole episode exceedingly amusing.

"Deciding" against the eating clubs, the following year Nate and I moved into Wilson College, a group of dormitories and cafeterias that was rapidly becoming the center of Princeton's "counterculture." For Princeton too, like most other colleges and universities in the sixties, was undergoing marked changes. The influence of the eating clubs was waning; mixers were giving way to political rallies, and beer at the local rathskeller to grass in poster-covered rooms that shook with the Jefferson Airplane. The new scene was a refreshing change. I grew a beard, painted my walls in Day-Glo, and started to play the guitar. Doug Seaton, president of Princeton's SDS chapter, was a roommate, and our suite was always bustling with meetings, planning sessions, and the comings and goings of campus ne'er-do-wells.

But toward the end of my junior year my interest in this sort of "social alternative" peaked, then began to fade. Nate and I played as ringers for the SDS in a much-heralded football victory over the combined forces of Princeton's ROTC—complete with television coverage, high school pom-pon girls, and a hailstorm. Still, it was clear to everyone—except perhaps Princeton's track coach, who, upon reading in the papers of me, his bearded team captain, cavorting on a football field with a crew of anarchists, decided that it was time to leave coaching—that I could not take "politics" any more seriously than I could the eating clubs. Seaton and his friends finally gave up the attempt to recruit me and, instead, contented themselves with giving me a nickname: "Brownshirt."

Increasingly, I was finding everything hard to take seriously. I dropped my original plan to major in mathematics and changed to the philosophy department. And while I enjoyed the courses Princeton's excellent instructors gave, it began to take enormous acts of willpower to keep up with my work. I was tired of the long winters, the muddy slush, the damp mufflers, and steamed windows. I was weary of dorm food, "big weekends," and Che Guevara posters. I wanted out, but I wasn't sure where.

In view of this it is not surprising that my senior year was not a good one. In the fall I came down with bronchial pneumonia and was more or less incapacitated for two months. By the time the year came to a close I was so far behind that I had to work day and night for two weeks to finish my senior thesis, barely managing to submit it in time to get my graduation papers processed. It was then, with no prospects in sight, that I sent off some last-minute letters of application to several private high schools in California. Shortly after graduation the headmistress at Crystal Springs, Francena Hancock, wrote back inviting me to stop by for an interview when I could.

At about the time I was walking through the June New Jersey heat to receive my diploma with the rest of the graduating class, Patty was finishing the ninth grade at Santa Catalina, the sixth private school she had attended since kindergarten. For as one of her closest friends there remarked, "Patty changed schools whenever she decided that the school or the people running it, or attending it, were all wrong somehow." Whether these decisions were left to her, or just influenced by her discontent—I suspect the latter—the move from Sacred Heart in Menlo Park to Santa Catalina in Monterey proved to be one that she would soon regret.

Modeled after the Spanish missions that graced California's coast a hundred years before—red tiled roofs, white plaster walls, and tiled floors—and situated in the pine-covered Pebble Beach area, Santa Catalina reflected the old and new in an unfortunate way. While its students were modern teenage girls, its educational approach was almost medieval. Under the firm, unswerving hand of the headmistress, Sister Mary Carlotta, the school's policies were so severe and the discipline so strict that Patty likened it to reliving the Inquisition. Every Friday there was an assembly where, one by one, each student stood at attention on the stage to hear her merits and demerits for the week read off to the assembly by a nun. Merits for such things as good grooming and tidy rooms— demerits for such breaches as whispering in the library, being late for meals, or having "poor attitudes."

During her two years at Santa Catalina, Patty stayed in what was known as "the lower hall." This consisted of a long, tiled corridor lined with rooms that were partitioned off by seven-foot makeshift dividers and closed by curtains. The slightest whisper carried from one end of the hall to the nun's room at the other end. After the lights went out, the girls would shine their flashlights on the ceiling and play silent games of tag with the girls in the next room. Of course there were demerits for this as well.

In view of this it is something of a miracle that Patty lasted as long at Santa Catalina as she did. I have no idea if Mr. Hearst was angered or disappointed by his daughter's desire to change schools again, but he must have felt a sort of historical fatalism about the Hearst family's lack of success at formal education, which went all the way back to his father, William Randolph Hearst. In his famous biography of Patty's grandfather, *Citizen Hearst,* W. A. Swanberg describes "Willie's" first year at Harvard:

> An indifferent student, Willie enjoyed the theater and never missed an opportunity to go by carriage with a group of cronies to presentations in Boston. On one such occasion they carried custard pies into their box at the Howard Atheneum and pelted the performers with them. On another, Hearst and Lent returned from Boston in a hack, hurling oranges at policemen they passed en route. Hearst somewhere acquired a small alligator, which he christened Champagne Charlie, occasionally making calls with the reptile in tow.

Patty's father "Randy," the youngest of William Randolph Hearst's five sons, attended a number of East Coast boarding schools, but fared no better than his father. In a letter to his estranged wife—he was living with actress Marion Davies at the time—William Randolph Hearst wrote of Randy and his twin brother David's problems at school:

Dear Millicent:

I have read the headmaster's letter about Randolph and I suppose David, too. There is nothing very surprising in this. These boys are simply behaving as the others did. We may not approve of their behavior, but this is characteristic of the clan.

They do not take kindly to education. This is probably a defect, but as Brisbane says, "It takes a good mind to resist education." Anyway, a certain kind of good mind does resist education. . . .*

The "Old Man" was not quite so philosophical with the boys themselves, however. He wrote the following to them while they were attending Lawrenceville School in New Jersey:

You have had a good time at Palm Beach and we try to give you a good time as often as possible; but you cannot always be merely having a good time, and your mother and I expect something more of you than to be playboys. This is not a good period in the world's history for playboys. Things are too serious. Situations are too dangerous, and I want you two boys, who are now getting to be men, to begin to take a man's view of life. You will have to work, and work hard. You might as well be learning how to work now. You have got to get an education that will make you able to take care of yourselves. No one knows whether you will inherit anything or not; but if you are not able to make money, you will not be able to keep money. If you are not trained for the contest that is ahead of you, you are likely to bring up the rear of the procession.**

Sound advice, but not followed. Enrolled at Harvard in 1933, Randy quickly proved a better swimmer than a student. Shortly after breaking the university's fifty-yard freestyle record he was "given the boot" because of pranks and poor grades. So much for his formal education. Like his brothers before him,

* *William Randolph Hearst* by Edmond D. Coblentz (New York: Simon and Schuster, 1952), pp. 78-79.
** Ibid.

Randy moved out of school and into one of the many Hearst enterprises, taking a job as an assistant to the editor of the *Atlanta Georgian.*

It was in Atlanta that Randy, one of the town's most eligible bachelors, met Catherine Campbell, a telephone company executive's daughter, who had just made her debut at the age of sixteen. They began dating steadily and soon announced their engagement. After Catherine completed her senior year at Atlanta's Washington Seminary, and Randy had passed his catechism classes—which he later attributed more to a lenient priest than to his admittedly sketchy knowledge of the Baltimore Catechism—they were married at Sacred Heart Church on January 12, 1938.

After serving his apprenticeship on the *Atlanta Georgian,* Randolph Hearst, then twenty-three, and his eighteen-year-old bride moved to San Francisco where he became assistant to the publisher of the *Call-Bulletin.* Their first child, Catherine, was born in 1939. As the senior Hearst had pointed out in his letter some years before, the world situation was indeed dangerous. Later that same year, in early September of 1939, England and France declared war on the Third Reich. Two years later Randy moved his family to Texas where he was stationed as a captain in the Air Transport Command, ferrying planes to England.

When the war ended the Hearsts returned to the Bay Area and moved into a large house in suburban Burlingame. These were busy years, especially for Randy who began working his way up the corporate ladder, while his wife, freed from domestic chores by a staff of servants, painted, read, and involved herself in charity work. It wasn't until 1949, ten years after Catherine was born, that Mrs. Hearst gave birth to her second child, Gina. Patty was born in 1954, followed in successive years by Anne and Vicky.

To grow up in the Hearst household was to hear stories about famous people and sometimes to meet them—President Kennedy, Prince Philip of England, the Shah of Iran, and even the budding recluse Howard Hughes, whom Mrs. Hearst nearly drove to apoplexy on one occasion. The Hearsts had invited him to attend a small dinner party with them in Palm Beach, and at Randy's urgings he reluctantly agreed to accompany them. But when they arrived at his hotel, he was not, to their surprise, waiting for them in the lobby. Mrs. Hearst told Randy to wait and went up to the front desk. The hotel's speakers crackled, then, "Paging Mr. Howard Hughes. Paging Mr. Howard Hughes," a voice echoed through the halls. Dripping with shaving cream and horrified, Hughes came charging out of the first-floor men's room frantically waving his arms for the clerk to get off the microphone. "Silly man," Mrs. Hearst whispered to her husband. But with the help of a pair of dark glasses Hughes soon recovered, and the three were off to the party.

During these years it was a series of servants who took care of the Hearst girls. When asked about her childhood, Patty often remarked that "I didn't know my parents until I was ten." If she didn't know them, Patty apparently didn't miss them that much. From all accounts she was a happy, cheerful girl. But if overstated for effect, her statement is probably close to the truth. Instead of strong memories of her mother and father, Patty remembered the servants, Aggie, the kindly Irish nursemaid, and a husband and wife team that served as butler and cook. There were also the odd characters: Mrs. Jones, the alcoholic nannie who really had it in for Patty and was eventually fired; a rather exotic Indian mulatto cook; and a German housekeeper who was rumored to have been a part of Hitler Youth.

Patty's memories of her mother in those early days are especially vague. This is not to say that Mrs. Hearst neglected her children, but rather that the maternal role did not come naturally to her and was not particularly encouraged. Steeped in the traditions and proprieties of a good Atlanta family of the twenties and thirties, she was raised and continued to live in a world totally apart from that of her daughters. I remember Patty and me watching a television production of F. Scott Fitzgerald's *The Last of the Belles*. Afterward she said that the heroine reminded her of her mother. Patty could be scathing in her criticism of her mother, but at its core was always her frustration that her mother could have been more than a predictable Hillsborough matron. Her mother's role, Patty thought, had been thrust upon her as much as she had created it. Her mother was intelligent, had demonstrated considerable talent in painting, and had won a college scholarship in the days when higher learning was usually denied socially acceptable young women. But she was also married at eighteen and gave birth to her first child a year later. During their first year of marriage Mr. Hearst once came home from the paper to find his wife trying to hem her first pair of curtains. "Don't bother, dear," he told her. "We'll buy some nice ones." So the curtains were bought, the nannies, servants, cooks and housekeepers were hired, leaving Mrs. Hearst to continue her primary role as the attractive wife of Randolph Hearst, instead of evolving, growing into an attentive mother who ran her own home and raised her children.

Of course Mrs. Hearst did not leave the children's upbringing entirely to the nannies and nursemaids. She often read the girls bedtime stories, including a selection of Little Black Sambo stories she had saved from her own childhood—which Patty showed me one time with some amusement—and a book called *The Singing Tree,* which Patty loved and hoped to read to her own children someday. Mrs. Hearst was also fond of taking the girls shopping for dolls and helping them stage little plays such as *Cinderella,* the girls changing scenes by moving from room to room in the large house. According to one of Patty's childhood friends these were happy occasions—barring minor tiffs between the sisters over who got the best roles—but they were also rare. While Mrs. Hearst made many plans to be with her daughters, more often than not she would be too busy with charity matters, or her new duties as a Regent of the University of California, to see them through. So, by the time Patty was ten it was Heather, the English governess Mr. Hearst had hired for Vicky and Anne, who would accompany them on various outings.

Arriving in 1964, Heather remembers Patty as the most precocious and independent of the four daughters living at home. "At first I thought she was impossible," she said, "until I took her aside one day and explained to her that I was Anne and Vicky's governess and that all I expected from her was cooperation in allowing me to do my job." After that she never had a bit of trouble with Patty. "The key thing with Patty," she observed, "was winning her respect; then you could count on her absolute loyalty." As another friend put it, "Patty hated to be treated like a child." And yet this is precisely what Mrs. Hearst did. When Patty reached the age where she wanted a chemistry set and Beatles records for Christmas, her mother gave her dolls, stuffed animals, and dainty blouses. When Patty was twelve and preoccupied with typical adolescent concerns, revealed in the little lists she and her friends used to compile—How to Use Makeup, How to Get Boys, et cetera—her mother would try to engage her in rambling conversations about medieval history.

As Patty lived through her adolescence, it appeared that she and her mother acted on one another like the same poles of a magnet. Patty's predilections seemed consciously to be molded in contradistinction to her mother's. Mrs. Hearst did not like to drive cars; Patty felt compelled to become an excellent driver. Mrs. Hearst's friends seemed to Patty to be shaped by the same cookie cutter; Patty's friends tended to have a specialness—intelligence, grace, talent—many were older than she, but all had a sense of their own difference. Patty at first refused to try marijuana because she disapproved of her mother's overreliance on prescribed drugs. The constant tension between them escalated tiny irritations into substantial annoyances, and, what's more, both Patty and her mother seemed to seek out one another's sore points, almost as if they measured their identities by their incompatibility with each other. I still feel that the obverse side of their hostility was a deep attachment that had not found a healthy way to find expression. Compounding their problems were Mrs. Hearst's deep religious convictions. In spite of Patty's strict Catholic upbringing, she never went through a serious religious period. In this Patty was like her father, who liked to sleep late on Sundays. But Mrs. Hearst would have none of this from her daughters. Every Sunday morning she would get out their mantillas and bundle the girls off to Mass— this at a time when Patty and her friends were up to such things as secretly sending away to Fredricks of Hollywood for sexy lingerie catalogues.

While Mr. Hearst could not even be called a Sunday attender, religion dominated Mrs. Hearst's approach to almost everything. Combined with her insular upbringing, this only served to increase her inability to come to grips with an increasingly secular world. Though a member of the Board of Regents, no one could have been less well suited to deal with and understand the problems at Berkeley. The moving spirit of the university in the sixties was 180 degrees from what drove Mrs. Hearst, and Patty felt this acutely. She used to complain that her mother had no right to sit on the Board of Regents because "she never even *went* to college." But what Patty really meant was that her mother was almost by nature, and certainly by upbringing, at a total loss to understand why anyone would want to change anything about "The System" —especially the educational system from which he benefited. To Mrs. Hearst's mind the free speech movement, the emerging counterculture and the antiwar demonstrations were not explainable social phenomena that had to be reckoned with, but rather conscious acts of subversion that had to be stopped. In short, her world view was diametrically opposed to the forces that were molding and changing colleges and universities all across the country—the world for that matter.

But then this was the outside world, against which Mrs. Hearst tried to protect her daughters. From the Catholic Church and the various parochial schools the girls would learn the importance of tradition. With a fine home in Hillsborough and membership in the Burlingame Country Club, they would mingle with the "right sort" of young people. And with her guidance and encouragement, they would learn to value what she herself valued above all things—good carriage, good breeding, and God.

But things did not quite work out this way. Rather than adopting their mother's values, the girls often rebelled against them, especially Patty. Aside from the minor transgressions at Santa Catalina, she was restricted to campus for two weeks for skipping

Mass. And although she was an excellent tennis player and a competitive swimmer—a natural athlete as friends described her—she stopped going to the country club because she disliked its stuffy image. And finally the crowning blow: at the age of fourteen she announced that she would make her own arrangements for attending church, the result being that she rarely went at all. Considering Mr. Hearst's spotty attendance, I imagine he was caught in the cross fire over this one. But in the end Patty got her way. As her sister, Anne, put it, "By the age of fourteen you couldn't tell Patty what to do." You could reason with her as an adult and she might defer to your judgment, but treat her like a child, as her mother often did, and you were up against a brick wall. On the other hand, blow up at her at the dinner table, as her father often did, and she would sit there silently, sometimes blowing bubbles in her milk. She simply refused to be punished. You could scold her, restrict her, send her up to her room, and she would go quietly, showing no signs of remorse, and wait for the anger to subside. But like as not things would never reach this point. She was a master at sidestepping authority.

"Patty, where are you going?" her father would call downstairs.

"Out. I'll be home around ten."

"Goddamn it," he'd yell, "where are you going?"

Silence.

Patty could depend on her father's next move. He'd grumble to himself, then come downstairs and apologize for shouting at her. And off she would go . . . wherever she was going.

If Patty sounds like the typical brat in this, it is important to remember what Heather pointed out—that she "reacted well to discipline, *when* she respected you." But Mr. Hearst was an inconsistent disciplinarian and in this he did not command her respect. One of the first things Patty ever told me about her father was about how he was always losing his temper. Digging through one of my desk drawers, I came across a cassette tape she had sent to her sister Anne, which illustrates the sort of complaints I used to hear from Patty early on. In it she talks about her father's latest explosion at Vicky, who had demanded to know why she always had to get up from the dinner table to call the cook:

> So Dad gets really mad and goes, "Well, Goddamn it, you must be pretty stupid if you don't know the reason why! It's because you're the youngest and lowest on the seniority list. . . ." So that argument lasted awhile. I mean we had to have an argument of course because Dad had been away for a couple of days, and as you know, he can't come home for dinner without having an argument the first night he gets back. . . .

But while her father would suddenly blow up at the girls, he would deflate almost as quickly. "Dad can never stay mad for very long," Patty used to tell me. For this reason, though she did resent her father's temper and was even more irritated by the apologies that always followed, in a sense Patty took neither very seriously. Nor did the family servants, it seems. Heather said that the Hearsts were the best employers she ever had. They were generous, they gave lovely gifts, loaned money, and paid for the wedding dress for the daughter of one of their servants. Even when some of their employees took advantage of their generosity by stealing silverware, drinking, and pushing their duties on the others, Mr. Hearst apparently could not bring himself to dismiss them. "My Dad can't stand to fire anyone," Patty once told me, "not even some of those old fogies at the paper." She did not say this with any malice, but rather shook her head at her father's soft-heartedness.

Overall, it is safe to say that Patty felt a good deal closer to her father than her mother. A friend remembers her once looking at a picture of him when he was a little boy, remarking how pleased she was to take after him. On another occasion I remember her telling me that her grandmother, Millicent, loved her because "I look so much like Randy."

Despite his chairmanship of the Hearst Corporation, with all the pressures and responsibilities that are part of such a position, Mr. Hearst was a surprisingly easygoing man. While his wife treasured her privacy, he loved to take his daughters out to the movies, along with him on business trips to Washington, D.C., or New York, or down to La Paz, Mexico, where they would stay at the vacation home of their Hillsborough neighbor Bing Crosby. Mrs. Hearst, however, was never particularly keen about these excursions south of the border. "Mexico," she once explained, "is not a country. It's a disease."

By the time Patty was in high school, Mr. Hearst was in a position to work at the *Examiner* when and if the spirit moved him. When it did, he would rise at 5:30 A.M., drive to the office, and work well into the night. When it didn't he would sometimes stay in bed until 11:00 in the morning. Once, when a maid cracked open the door and asked if she could slip in and clean the room, he replied, "It's fine with me if you can get this mattress off my back." On these occasions he would lounge around the house in his pajamas, perusing the latest sampling of paperbacks from the Corporation's Avon Books division, or sometimes discharging his business responsibilities by telephone—"Trading his orange groves for an elephant," as Mrs. Hearst joked to a friend. Then, without warning, he would be up at 5:30 A.M. again and rushing off to the office.

In spite of their social position, Mr. and Mrs. Hearst led quiet lives, spending most of their evenings at home, rarely entertaining except for an occasional dinner party for a few close friends. Although they were often invited, they seldom attended social gatherings. On one occasion I remember both of them going upstairs to dress for a debutante party of one of Anne's friends, a major event of the season. Anne had left earlier with friends, and they were to join her later. But as soon as Mr. Hearst donned his formal attire his enthusiasm for the affair began to fade. After a few minutes he plopped down on the couch next to Patty and me and spent the rest of the evening watching television in his tuxedo, Mrs. Hearst joining us later.

Vacations, however, were quite another matter. In an attempt to find some new place or possession which the whole family would enjoy, Mr. Hearst had bought, in succession, a ranch in

Grass Valley, a twin-engine airplane, a beach house in La Jolla, a penthouse condominium in Honolulu, and a sailboat. None of them went over very well. But with the purchase of the condominium at Sugar Bowl he scored a tremendous hit with everyone . . . except himself. After a few days on the slopes, Mr. Hearst discovered that he didn't really like skiing at all. Patty, on the other hand, enjoyed Sugar Bowl but, as mentioned earlier, was unable to ski because of cartilage problems in her knees. This was not the first time Patty had had trouble with her legs. When she was eight years old she somehow got a severe infection in her calf and nearly died. Then, at fourteen she gave her parents another scare: doctors found a bone tumor near her right knee which had to be removed.

By the time of this operation Patty was enrolled at Santa Catalina in Monterey. In spite of her aloofness, the boys at the neighboring Robert Louis Stevenson prep school vied for her attention, kidding each other about which one of them would "marry the Hearst." Among these boys was a sixteen-year-old named Stanley Dollar with whom she exchanged letters. Much has been made of their puppy love relationship, but in actuality it seems to have been primarily a pen pal affair. Patty was more interested in another boy, perhaps because he was the *only* boy available at Santa Catalina—Bob, the school handyman and part-time student at a nearby college. He was a shy boy who, as one of her friends remembers, "followed her around like a puppy dog." Patty was considerably more precocious sexually than Bob, having slept with a seventeen-year-old boy the summer after her ninth grade. It was an awkward experience and she later told me she was "just glad to get it over with." It was no less awkward with Bob. After the first time they slept together the following year, he was filled with remorse and apologized profusely. Patty found this embarrassing and unnecessary and lovemaking disappointing again.

Her tenth-grade year at Santa Catalina was an especially difficult one. Because she was stubborn and independent, her name was always on the demerit list. As one of her classmates said: "A bunch of girls would get so mad at a teacher that they would all decide they were going to refuse to take a test. But when it came

down to it, Patty was the only one who would *not* take the test."
So while the other girls were strolling around the lawns or engaged in free reading, Patty would be restricted to her room or stacking folding chairs in the assembly hall.

Aside from a handful of close friends, if there was one ray of light in Patty's two years at Santa Catalina it was the school handyman, Othello. He was a middle-aged Venezuelan, bright, guileless, and so well liked that one of the senior classes made him a gift of an airplane ticket back to his native country for the summer. Othello lived in a small cottage on the school grounds and was often visited by students after school. His quiet wisdom, his interest in archaeology, and his sympathy and understanding must have made his cottage seem like an oasis in the rigid atmosphere of Santa Catalina. Not surprisingly, Patty sought him out and pursued his friendship more than the rest of the girls. On one of her last visits Othello gave her a box of tea as a going-away present. It was the kind of gesture she never forgot.

Nor did Patty forget the great scandal that descended upon the school her last year there, when a small group of senior girls thought they'd take the opportunity of an off-campus party to smoke pot. Somehow the school authorities caught wind of this, so to speak, and the Inquisition was on. Every girl in the school was called into the office and grilled relentlessly. Many broke down in tears and one of them simply walked off one night and caught a bus home, telling her parents, "I'm never going back there." The mood on campus was fraught with tension and suspicion during these days. Girls would return from class to discover that their possessions had been gone through. Soon the incident began to take on the proportions of a witch hunt—whispering campaigns, rumors, accusations, and fear. While Patty was against smoking grass and thought anyone who did was "stupid," she was angered by the administration's handling of the matter. It was at this point that she came home and told her father that she'd had it with Santa Catalina, even though it meant leaving her three closest friends. Whatever Mr. Hearst's reaction, Patty was enrolled at Crystal Springs the following semester, the beginning of her junior year.

Like me, Patty was something of an outsider when she arrived at Crystal that fall of 1970. But unlike the other two hundred girls who filed into the converted ballroom the first day to be introduced to the staff, she wasn't concerned about making new friends or even doing well in her classes. She had attended too many first-day assemblies in new schools, had heard too many speeches about the advantages of a private education, the importance of learning good study habits, and the excellent staff the school had to offer. It was just another school year to get through.

Francena Hancock, the headmistress at Crystal, called my name and I stood up in one of my father's hand-me-down business suits. "Mr. Weed has been with us for a year now and has done a fine job," she announced to the girls. "He will be teaching algebra and geometry. Thank you, Mr. Weed."

Two years later Patty would tell Mimi that she remembered looking at me and thinking, "Uh-oh, I'm going to get in trouble again this year."

We did not get into trouble that year. While a number of teachers were aware of our developing relationship, none of them suspected how far it had gone. Not so some of Patty's fellow classmates. A senior caught us shopping together at the Co-op supermarket one afternoon and spread the word. Fortunately she was not considered a reliable witness and the word died out, but not before Patty's youngest sister, Vicky, buttonholed me in the hall one morning. "Are you having an affair with my sister?" she asked matter-of-factly with studied nonchalance. I leaned close so as not to be overheard and told her no, that actually my paramour was the head of the math department, a very large woman in her late forties who always wore billowing mumus and had long since established herself as the bane of my Crystal existence. Vicky seemed satisfied.

Patty was amazingly circumspect and self-controlled about our affair, even when it came to her closest Crystal friend, Chris Johnson. Only after we had been seeing each other for months did she

My grandmother's snapshot of Patty and me in Monterey, California. May 1972.
(*Mrs. R. E. Weed*)

In front of "La Casa Grande," San Simeon. Summer 1973. (*Steven Weed*)

Portrait of Patty's great-grandmother Phoebe Apperson Hearst, circa 1900. (*Bettmann Archive*)

Senator George Hearst, Patty's great-grandfather, 1888. (*California Historical Society*)

William Randolph Hearst keeping a watchful eye on Marion Davies, at the California State Guard Military Ball, 1942. (*UPI*)

The widow and five sons of the late William Randolph Hearst are pictured here following Mrs. Hearst's arrival in San Francisco to attend her husband's funeral service on August 17, 1951. Seated, *left to right:* John, Mrs. Hearst, and Randolph. Standing, *left to right:* George, David, and William Randolph Hearst, Jr. (*Wide World Photos*)

Mr. and Mrs. Randolph Hearst sitting on their luggage on a pier shortly after their arrival in New York City aboard the liner *Queen Mary* in June 1950. (*Wide World Photos*)

A snapshot taken by her father of Patty, aged three, in Beverly Hills.

One of the several pictures of Patty that Mr. Randolph Hearst brought out for newsme shortly after Patty was kidnapped. The pictu shows eight-year-old Patty at her first com munion. (*Wide World Photos*)

Patty as an eighth grade cheerleader at Sacred Heart School
in Menlo Park, California.
(*Courtesy Julie Gould*)

Patty and her sister Vicky,
1970.

On a Crystal Springs class tour to Japan, Patty is about to toss her class ring into the China Sea. Spring 1971.

Patty's class picture, Crystal Springs School for Girls. Spring 1971.

On a Menlo College "adventure-study" tour in Greece. Summer 1972.

Chatting between classes with friend and biology teacher Stu Olson. Spring 1972.

Patty and I at her family's Sugar Bowl condominium. Winter 1972/3. (*Mimi Swanton*)

At the Point Reyes seashore, north of San Francisco. Summer 1973. (*Steven Weed*)

At Duck Cove. Fall 1972. (*Steven Weed*)

At Duck Cove. Fall 1972. (*Steven Weed*)

In the garden of our Berkeley apartment. Summer 1973. (*Steven Weed*)

In Berkeley. Summer 1973. (*Patty Hearst*)

In Berkeley with Melissa our cat. Summer 1973. (*Mimi Swanton*)

Patty with Mimi Swanton and Melissa. In Berkeley. Summer 1973. (*Steven Weed*)

Patty standing on the porch of the "River House" at Wyntoon, where her grandfather William Randolph Hearst built his northern California mountain retreat, now owned by The Hearst Corporation. Summer 1973. (*Steven Weed*)

On the porch of the "River House," looking across the McCloud River to the old movie house where William Randolph Hearst would run films for his guests. Summer 1973. (*Patty Hearst*)

Patty and I at one of the old tennis courts at Wyntoon. Summer 1973.

The "Brown Bear House," where William Randolph Hearst would stay when visiting Wyntoon. Like the "Angel House" and the "Cinderella House," the "Brown Bear House," which partially leans out over the river, is decorated with fairy-tale murals. Summer 1973. (*Steven Weed*)

Looking across the lawn to the "River House," the only structure built at Wyntoon by Patty's great-grandmother Phoebe Apperson Hearst. Summer 1973. (*Steven Weed*)

In front of William Randolph Hearst's Egyptian statuary in the garden at San Simeon. Summer 1973. (*Steven Weed*)

Patty and I in front of the largest building at Wyntoon, nicknamed "The Bend." Converted from a modest hunting lodge into a castlelike structure, it houses the library and refectory. Summer 1973. (*Bob Purdy*)

An engagement picture taken in the garden of the Hearsts' home in Hillsborough, California. December 1973. (*John Gorman*)

Patty, her father, and sister Anne at Anne's debutante party at the Burlingame Country Club, Burlingame, California. Summer 1973. (*Wide World Photos*)

During our stay at a friend's cabin in Duck Cove on Tomales Bay, north of San Francisco. Fall 1972. (*Steven Weed*)

tell Chris about us, at which point Chris gave me a long lecture about not hurting Patty. Despite their suspicions, Patty never told her sisters. When Anne, who was also at Crystal that year, asked her whom she was seeing all the time Patty told her that it was an older guy named Harry. Unaware that I was the mysterious "Harry," Anne would stick her tongue out at me in the halls when I'd smile and ask, "How you doing, you skinny little thing?"

Patty's parents were not even aware of "Harry." Although they were unhappy about all the time Patty was spending away from home, sometimes complaining that "We never see you anymore," they were never able to pin her down. She was going to the library for a while, she would tell them, or visiting friends, usually Chris. Although Patty assured me that we had nothing to worry about, I sometimes insisted that we skip an evening together rather than risk upsetting her parents to the point where they would check up on her more carefully. Patty reluctantly agreed but pointed out that she was soon going to Japan with a small group of students, which would give her parents' suspicions time to cool, if indeed there were any.

Patty and I had only known each other for two months when she boarded the plane for Japan, but the trip was a turning point in our relationship: that is, it accelerated it. In the three weeks we were separated, I missed Patty very much and she missed me.

Not surprisingly, the girls' chaperon on the trip remembers that while Patty seemed to enjoy herself, it was in a very low-key way. She got along with the girls, but made no fast friends. If there was a single room where they were staying, Patty would always volunteer to take it, not out of any particular kindness, but because she preferred to be alone.

Kate, Patty's best friend on the trip, remembers Patty's impatience with the inevitable adolescent pranks—putting Vaseline on their chaperon's toilet seat, prunes in each other's pillows, and the like. "She acted as if she was older than everybody else, and in a way she was." And yet when the group went for a ride on a Chinese junk in Hong Kong, Patty shocked some of the girls with a stunt of her own. They were standing next to the guardrail, when Patty looked down at her Crystal Springs ring, which had the initials C.S. engraved on it. Patty mused, said, "C.S.: China Sea, Crystal Springs . . . chicken shit," held up the ring as Kate took a picture, then tossed it overboard. Most of the girls were flabbergasted. "That cost twenty-eight dollars," one of them said, looking at the spot where the ring had entered the water.

After Patty had been gone a week I sent her a letter giving the return address as "Capt. James T. Kirk, ret., U.S.S. Enterprise." In it I told her about my latest project:

> . . . I've been spending the bulk of my time designing and constructing a rather remarkable tree platform suitable for sun-bathing, star gazing, meditation, reading, and what-have-you. I think I can guarantee that it will be neighbor-proof, parent-proof, fuzz-proof, and maybe even Patty-proof. I'm hoping not. It's not much fun sitting at the top of an oak tree by your-self. . . . That's about all. Have a good time, but don't come home with the Rickshaw Rot or we're through. Sincerest Regards, Jim.

Kate remembers Patty looking at the letter at the hotel desk, then running upstairs. When she asked who it was from, Patty resisted the temptation to break the news and satisfied herself with a bit of barbed humor. "It's from an older guy named Ed," she told Kate. "He works at a school for retarded kids"—namely Crystal. For years Patty kept this "Star Trek" letter in her purse, fending off my occasional threats to destroy the evidence with, "You better not!" It was still in her purse, tattered and dog-eared, the night she was kidnapped. The woman assailant had thrown it on the floor with some other things when she was looking for Patty's driver's license and credit cards.

In spite of jet lag and general fatigue, the day Patty returned from Japan she hurried down to my house to present me with a white silk tie, a teapot, and a tape deck I had asked her to purchase for me. Mr. Hearst had met her at the airport and asked her about the large Sony carton she was lugging. Patty shrugged it off as a favor to some boy she knew in Hillsborough (in three short months I was Harry, Ed, Captain Kirk, and "some boy in Hillsborough"). "Well, you must really love the guy," he said, then used his influence to shortcut her through San Francisco customs. The rest of the Crystal group was infuriated and had to wait three hours, and Patty laughed to me about this later. She did not expect special privilege; in fact it sometimes irritated her. But not on this occasion. We hadn't seen each other in three very long weeks.

The spring was beautiful that year—deep blue skies, rain-soaked earth, rolling green hills, and, to the east, a lovely view of the San Francisco Bay . . . from my recently completed tree house. I was unabashedly proud of my latest achievement and insisted that Patty climb up to it with me. It was carefully lodged in the uppermost boughs of a huge oak, perhaps fifty feet off the ground, and creaked and swayed with the slightest breeze. Its only drawback was that most people considered it suicidal even to consider climbing up to the damn thing. "You're nuts, Weed," or "The hell with that, Weed," were the usual responses to my assurances of its solid design and construction. One look at it and Patty was in concert with the prevailing opinion. But with some gentle chiding on my part, she grabbed the first slat I had nailed into the trunk and began the ascent. I remember she was utterly terrified, locking each step in a death grip, shaking, refusing to look down, then summoning up her courage and taking another step upward. She breathed out an enormous sigh of relief when I helped her over the top.

We spent a lot of time in the tree that spring. Because it was always such an ordeal getting up to it we usually spent entire afternoons up there. I would make a couple of trips for books, wine and cheese, blankets, and a radio, and we would sunbathe in the nude, read, or just gaze off across the bay and listen to the radio. And when the nights were warm we would make the ascent and then just lie on our backs and look up at the stars. The tree house was a special place for us, a quiet little sanctuary removed from telephones and unexpected visitors, papers piling up, excuses to make, and questions to avoid.

But in contrast to our relaxed days in the tree, things at Crystal were as demanding as ever for me. Low man on the math department totem pole and without a classroom of my own, I continued to shuttle from class to class—five different rooms for five different classes—loaded down with books and ditto masters and would come home at the end of the day covered with chalk dust and carrying a stack of papers to be corrected that night. I had seventy students to worry about and little time to be bored with Crystal Springs. Not so, however, with Patty, as she herself described in that year's literary magazine:

> it's an all right day nothing
> special the sun's shining but
> overly warm it isn't children
> are playing outside laughing
> though no more than usual
> and the bird's singing pleasant
> it's true not as sweet as it has
> been other days I have a
> slight headache.

This is precisely what people at Crystal saw in Patty—a disparaging stance of detachment, boredom, and ennui. She was aloof and known for an offhanded negativity that even some of her teachers did not know how to handle. On one occasion I remember her history teacher stopping her in the hall and reminding her that her "A" average would fall to a "B" if she didn't turn in a late paper the next day. "Fine," Patty told her matter-of-factly, "I'll take the B." At this the teacher quivered a moment, unable to understand this attitude, then stormed off. But what this teacher saw in Patty was only facade, an affectation, or, more accurately, protective coloration. "Patty wore her coolness like body armor," a friend of hers said quite accurately. Beneath the armor was vulnerability, warmth, and excitement. For example, while Patty was considered "cool" and distant on her trip to Japan, when she returned that day with my tape deck she was really bubbling with enthusiasm. "It's just beautiful," she told me. "You'll love it. We have to go there someday."

In spite of her difficulty with some of her teachers Patty was doing quite well in most of her courses. Unchallenged by her junior English class, she transferred into advanced placement senior English and had no trouble competing with the older girls. But her geometry was still giving her problems. Even though I went over her homework with her almost every night she kept coming up with D's and F's on her exams. To salvage her grade I helped her with the project of constructing a geometric wood model of the five regular solids to make up for some of her poor test scores. But hte final examination was looming ominously on the horizon. Knowing that Patty's teacher—the aforementioned mumu garbed head of the math department—would put forth the least amount of effort in making up her tests, I obtained a copy of her previous year's final exam and spent three hours going over and over it with Patty the night before. But I had no idea just how little effort her teacher *would* put into her final exam. The next afternoon Patty came over after school and told me that she had gotten an 80 percent on the test, a B-minus in the class. It was the identical test.

"Perfect," I told her. "If you had gotten them all right it would have looked suspicious."

"I did try to get them all right," Patty said, laughing.

It was toward the end of that school year that a few people really began to suspect that Patty and I were involved with each other. Fortunately, most of these were friends of mine. One day Mimi cornered me in the parking lot and warned me that if the rumors about Patty and me were true I could get into a hell of a lot of trouble. I smiled, shrugged, and was generally noncommittal. Another time Diana Olson, a biology teacher and one of my closest friends, called my house and Patty answered.

"Who was that?" Diana asked suspiciously when I got on the line.

"My mother," I said with a straight face while Patty stifled a giggle next to me.

But soon enough it was summer and Crystal Springs faded into the background; Patty had discovered that she had enough credits to graduate a year early and had decided to attend Menlo

College, not two miles from my house. Yet the subterfuge continued. Patty took a course in biology at Aragon High School and I took a class at Stanford. Most of our weekends and evenings were spent raising a vegetable garden, lazing in the tree, going to the movies, picnicking at the beach or taking Patty's MG for a drive in the hills.

In late June of that year her parents went to Palm Beach for two weeks to visit Mr. Hearst's ailing mother, giving us a perfect chance to slip away on a trip of our own. No sooner had they left than we were packing the MG for a leisurely drive down the coast through Big Sur. As luck would have it, when we stopped for a Coke outside San Simeon, we ran into Patty's aunt and uncle, W.R., Jr., and his wife "Bootsie," who were summering at the castle. I quickly donned some sunglasses and ducked behind a postcard rack while they exchanged hearty How-are-you's and What-are-you-doing-here's.

"Shhh," Patty whispered with mock secrecy, "I'm on my way to visit a boy named George in Santa Barbara. My parents don't know a thing about it."

Her aunt and uncle smiled at each other like co-conspirators and promised not to tell her parents. Meanwhile "George" had wandered out to the MG, having found the selection of postcards wanting. We made our getaway.

After visiting one of Patty's favorite cousins, Willie's younger brother, Austie, who was holed up with his pet rat in a miserable motel in Santa Maria while "doing time" on a Hearst affiliated newspaper, we headed east into the Mojave Desert. I had this great theory that deserts cool off at night and suggested that we drive into Death Valley. Patty was not so sure about this but took my word for it. Six hours later at midnight she was crying on a picnic table in 105-degree heat at a godforsaken outpost called Furnace Creek. At one point she got up and started off into the darkness.

"Where are you going?" I asked.

She paused, then came back to the table. "I don't know, ' she said distantly. She was half-delirious.

After watching the sunrise at Zabriski Point we left the valley, the temperature soaring to 120 degrees, and headed for the Sierras. The misery of the night before was quickly forgotten in the crisp mountain air of Yosemite. We spent a couple of days hiking through Tuolumne Meadows, then headed home. It was our first trip together, and despite our misadventures at Furnace Creek, it was a good one.

When the summer ended, I went back to teaching at Crystal and Patty enrolled in nearby Menlo College, supposedly rooming with Nazi Rohani, a girl from a ruling class Iranian family. Nazi had a peculiar Middle Eastern disdain for most Americans, but liked Patty and respected her privacy. The arrangement worked out beautifully. Patty spent the entire school year living with me in my rented house, and Nazi had a room all to herself.

My house in Menlo Park sat on a half acre that was over-grown with brush and weeds, the remains of a fruit orchard and seven huge oak trees. The surrounding neighborhood had not decided which way it would go. There were lovely old homes sitting next to crackerbox houses, the rutted road in front lined with everything from Cadillacs to battered, abandoned cars. Our neighbors were also a real cross section of America—retired couples, hippies, blacks, Chicanos, lots of kids, and four identical poodles owned by our next-door neighbor, a swarthy ex-marine. There was also a group of Hells Angels living down the street, their choppers lined up proudly in front of their dilapidated, pink stucco house.

Since I didn't have the money to buy any good furniture, my house, which was soon to be "our" house, was crammed with odds and ends—old couches from aunts and uncles, a rug I had salvaged from my father's office, fraying wicker chairs, and a collection of mismatched utensils, pots and pans in the kitchen. On one living room wall I had hung a monstrous and equally ridiculous neoclassical manger scene—cows and sheep munching straw and tiny shepherds in the distance—that I had borrowed from an attic at Crystal. But it was not the painting that dominated the living room decor. It was an eighty-nine-cent dress shirt, a tongue-in-cheek gift from my mother. I had framed the shirt, still wrapped in cellophane, and hung it above the mantel. It kind of leaned off the wall and looked at you.

After Patty moved in, she was sometimes visited by her friends, usually while I was off teaching school. Although I was still uncertain as to the direction of our relationship, her friends were well aware that Patty had more in mind than just setting up a temporary household.

"Patty was trying very hard to be all the things she thought a mate should be," Kate remembers. "We would check out the newspapers to see which grocery stores had the best buys or talk about recipes while Patty was doing the dishes. Sometimes she'd ask me what our family had for dinner the night before and then say, 'How do you make that?' She didn't like the way Steve had 'decorated' the house, especially the shirt in the frame, and indicated that 'the shirt will go someday.' But she was biding her time until she was sure her thing with Steve was really solid, giving him no reason to break it off. One time we were talking about marriage and I asked her why she was so sure that Steve would marry her. She said she just had the feeling he would. 'He really does love me,' she said, said it very gently. 'And I love him.' Then she said she was coming into some money when she was twenty-one, implying that this would make her more attractive to him."

Chris Johnson remembers similar conversations about cooking, love, and sex. "She was so honest, so basic," Chris said. "Patty had the idea that if you were intelligent, good in bed and in the kitchen, everything would be great. We used to talk, sort of half joke, about what we called being a 'gentlewoman.' "

In the preface of a cookbook Chris hand-copied and gave to Patty she defined a "gentlewoman."

A gentlewoman is many different things to many different people. Some consider a gentlewoman that female who has resigned herself to the kitchen, dressed in yards of Cost-Plus bedspread, walking about as if her feet had been bound from birth. Some see her humming gently Judy Collins hymns, wafts of baking bread rising in the air as she goes about her daily household chores. They see her as that woman who is so elated at having her home clean by the time her man arrives, after a hard day's work, that she is driven to orgasm.

This is not necessary. One may be anything one wishes to be. Being gentle to me only means, in this sense, that one is efficient in domestic tasks. It also means that one takes pride in doing one's best to make cooking an art.

I have taken this collection of recipes from my gentle-woman-mother's magic potpourri of dining delights. I hope you enjoy them for many years and that you add some of your own recipes and thoughts about gentlewomanhood.

My friends were always stopping by and, despite Patty's age, they soon realized that she was by no means just a cute little teen-age girl and certainly not a spoiled heiress. Our evenings with our friends usually began with a good meal and fresh baked pie both carefully prepared by Patty. After a long relaxing dinner Stu Olson, Diana's husband, would invariably drag out his guitar and we would all accompany him in nasal folksongs, howling about good ole dawgs, dying ponies, and lonesome cowboys.

In all, our year in the Menlo house was a happy one. Patty was flourishing at Menlo College, earning A's in all her classes, taking up photography, and really enjoying school for the first time, while I survived well enough at Crystal. On weekends we might go to the San Francisco ballet, drawing disapproving looks as we lounged informally dressed in her mother's center box— which she rarely used—and enjoyed the performance as well as the drinks served between the acts. And then that winter, during Christmas vacation, I secretly rendezvoused with Patty at her parents' penthouse in Hawaii—which was also rarely used—and we spent some great days chugging around the island on a rented motorscooter. Patty was a rich girl and we unabashedly reveled in some of the advantages. That is, we had a hell of a lot of fun.

Naturally enough that year in Menlo Park was also a time in which Patty and I began learning to adjust ourselves to each other's sensitivities, expectations, and idiosyncrasies. As Patty began assuming the wifely, and sometimes the maternalistic role, I became, almost without realizing it—and certainly not admitting it—the husband and, as Patty used to tease, "a grumpy old man just like my father." Of course the teasing went both ways. One day I returned home from school to find her sitting crosslegged on the couch watching "Sesame Street" and filling in a coloring book with crayons. I pretended to be aghast and made a great show of grumbling and reproaching her paternally. And yet if I missed even so much as the opening theme music of "Star Trek," I was not fit to live with the rest of the evening, which Patty was always happy to point out. Even the difference in our ages was a source of amusement for us.

"Come on, Sweet Sixteen, put on your saddle shoes and your little Crystal dress for me," I'd sometimes tease her.

"You dirty old man," she'd scold back.

I remember Nate once looking at Patty and then telling me, "She's charming you, Steve," which was true enough. With the same single-mindedness that she demonstrated when we first met, Patty made the Menlo house a home, assuming the responsibilities of running the household as though I were incapable of looking after myself.

But all of this came on gradually. In fact it wasn't until months after she moved in that I realized a certain metamorphosis had taken place in my life-style. I remember one evening in particular. It was toward the end of the second semester, and I was sitting on the couch when I happened to look up at her. She was sitting across from me reading one of her school books, her skin deeply tanned and her blond hair hanging down over her maroon tank top to her waist. I remember thinking what beautiful shoulders she had, and beyond that, what a wonderful girl she was, and finally how lucky I was to have her. Sensing my look, Patty glanced up at me and smiled as if she was reading my thoughts. Shortly thereafter we began making plans to move to Berkeley together.

With a fine sense of timing, Patty decided to break the news to her mother when they went to a Menlo College awards assembly where Patty was to be honored as the top-ranked student of her class. The perfect setting was almost upset, however, when the Master of Ceremonies embarrassed Mrs. Hearst and some of the other parents with a few off-color jokes. Because of this Patty postponed the announcement until she and her mother were comfortably seated in a nice restaurant. Hoping for a quiet dinner with her daughter, Mrs. Hearst was dismayed by Patty's plans. "I thought you might tell me something like this," she said wearily. Patty told me about her father's reaction upon his return home the next day from New York. "What did we do wrong?" he asked, then warned her about getting a reputation as a "Sally Round-Heels." But after a moment he calmed down. "Well," he said, "let's meet this fellow. If the old man could sit up there on top of a hill [San Simeon] with the woman [Marion Davies] in full view of the world for thirty years, I guess we can handle this."

I for one, however, was not so sure how *I* was going to handle it. Between the time Patty made her announcement and the evening I was to meet Mr. and Mrs. Hearst, Vicky had received her report card from Crystal with a large F in algebra next to which was my name. I had sent home the usual progress reports noting Vicky's utter lack of progress and had even talked to Mr. Hearst about it on the phone earlier in the quarter. He was polite but had an attitude common to most Crystal parents. If his daughter was doing poorly, it was because her teacher wasn't "cracking down" on her. I explained that Vicky was extremely stubborn and simply refused to do any work whatsoever. At this he softened and mentioned his own poor grades in prep school. But Mrs. Hearst was not so understanding. It did not comfort me much when, the day before I was to be presented, Patty confided that "Mom's really pissed off at you for flunking Vicky."

I arrived at the Hearst home at promptly seven o'clock and was shown into the living room by Emmy. Mr. and Mrs. Hearst arose and greeted me, both of them as uneasy as I was. Introduced by Patty, who had hurried downstairs, I gave Mr. Hearst a properly firm handshake. Then, after a brief chat, we went into the dining room for dinner. The meal was excellent and the conversation warm and friendly, except for a visible tightening around Mrs. Hearst's mouth when Patty dismissed "coming out," the opportunity to be a debutante, as "stupid."

"It is not stupid, honey," she said sweetly. "It's a long and fine tradition."

The subject was fortunately dropped.

After dinner Mrs. Hearst and I walked through the gardens in the evening light and talked about the various varieties of roses, about which I knew nothing. Then Patty took my hand and led me on a tour of the twenty-room Mediterranean house. I hesitate to use the word *mansion* because it brings to mind pillared elegance, cavernous rooms, and formally attired servants standing at their stations, all of the careless opulence and ostentatiousness reminiscent of, say, Edith Wharton's portrayal of "the rich." In that sense the Hearst home was not a mansion, but rather a large, three-story house, the first floor consisting of two large living rooms and off these the library, music room, dining room, and kitchen. Upstairs were the family bedrooms and on the third floor, the servant quarters. When Patty and I had finished our tour we were in the music room, the walls of which were lined with, strangely enough, a fine antique gun collection. I was admiring these when Mr. Hearst entered.

"Are you interested in sports, Steve?" he asked.

I told him I had been on the track team in college and liked to play tennis. At this he looked somewhat amused and embarrassed at the same time.

"Oh," he said. "I meant duck hunting, sailing, that sort of thing." We both smiled weakly, then he offered me a drink. As minor as it was, that was our first misunderstanding.

On the whole, it was an enjoyable evening. Contrary to Patty's predictions, I found her parents pleasant, warm, and remarkably understanding in view of their daughter's plans to live with me in Berkeley. When it was time for me to leave, they walked me to the door and said good-bye. I thanked them for dinner, then Patty and I walked across the gravel horseshoe drive and up to my car.

"Well, what do you think?" she asked me. "Are you going to survive?"

"It wasn't so bad. I think your parents are pretty nice people."

I kissed her, then climbed into my VW and pulled out onto Santa Inez Avenue.

In a week Patty would be off for Europe. Sadly for us both, she had agreed to spend the last week before her departure at home with her parents.

4

PAST THE FBI AGENTS I could see that Santa Inez was lined with press cars, mobile units, and huge vans that were hooked up to the power lines, feeding off the city in exchange for the latest news, the on-the-spot reports from the Hearst mansion in Hillsborough.

When we pulled into the driveway, the newspeople surged around the car, though it was not the stampede that occurred at my exit from the hospital. Photographers held their cameras over their heads and fired away, interviewers crowded close and shouted questions at me as we made our way through them and up the front steps. Emmy opened the door and we entered the large foyer where Mrs. Hearst, wearing a black dress as though she were in mourning, her eyes swollen from crying, glanced, almost winced at the bloodstained shirt I was still wearing, then embraced me. Mr. Hearst shook my hand solemnly. Behind them I remember some other members of the family and a few close friends hanging back, nodding, and uttering a few words of greeting.

Mr. Hearst was starting to lead me into the living room when John Lester, a television reporter acting as the press liaison, asked me if I was going to make a statement.

"There's plenty of time for that later, Steve," Mr. Hearst said. "You don't have to go out there now if you don't feel up to it."

I didn't, but decided to get it over with. I told Lester I'd answer some questions, and he stepped outside and informed the crowd of newspeople who began readying their equipment. After collecting my thoughts for a moment, I moved to the front door with the Hearsts. Mrs. Hearst put on her dark glasses, then walked out into the television lights, Mr. Hearst and I behind her. We went down the broad stone steps to the gravel drive where some technicians were making adjustments on a ring of microphones. They moved back and crouched down below the TV cameras. Lester nodded to me and I stepped up to the microphones. The first question I was asked was about possible SLA demands.

"I just hope the Symbionese . . ." Lester readjusted the microphones and I began again. "I just hope the Symbionese Liberation Army makes demands that lead to a smooth transition," I said, adding that the Hearsts had only limited ability to meet political demands. "What I mean is, if they're talking about letting prisoners go, the Hearsts look at the situation as a family problem, but California and the FBI see it in a larger context. . . . And it's the state that has the final word on political demands."

A red-faced man in the back asked about my vow not to testify. "Isn't that withholding evidence?"

"I said that if Patty is released unharmed, neither she nor I will become further involved in any way. Under those circumstances we cannot be forced to testify."

While I was saying this a woman reporter had crept around to the steps behind me. "How old are you?" she suddenly shouted and I jolted a little. "Twenty-six," I told her. Another woman asked if my description of the kidnappers used to make the three composite drawings might not endanger Patty's life.

"I don't see how that would place her in jeopardy. Anyway, I've seen the drawings and they're not very good."

"How good a look did you get of the kidnappers?" a man half-shouted, standing on his tiptoes in the middle of the crowd.

"I saw one of the men face on, directly, right in the eyes," I said. "I had a very good look at his expression." Actually this was not quite true, but I was again hoping to give the SLA the impression that I had seen nearly as much as Patty.

"Do you think the kidnappers intended to kill you?"

"Looking back on it now, I don't believe they did. However, at the time I thought they intended to." In spite of the assassination of Marcus Foster, I dared not characterize the SLA precisely as assassins, for fear they might live up to it.

After that there were a few more questions about the attack, about my impressions of the SLA, and then the final question of the day: "Why have you come to the Hearst home?"

"For emotional and organizational reasons," I said.

With that the briefing was over, the klieg lights faded out, and the Hearsts and I went back inside.

In view of what was to happen in the following weeks, that last statement now strikes me as almost an entrance line. If Patty's kidnapping and my days in the hospital can be likened to a prologue, the press briefing that afternoon was the beginning of Act I of a strange absurdist drama filled with pathos and black comedy, an act in which, one by one, the characters begin to break down under the pressure, confusion, and despair. For much of this time the Hearsts, the rest of the family, and I were literally trapped inside the three-story home, while, outside, the press, like a Greek chorus, described and interpreted our every move to an audience of millions.

Emmy showed me upstairs to what would be my room for the next three weeks. She turned back the bed and fluffed the pillow for me, then her eyes began to well with tears. She handed me a pair of Mr. Hearst's pajamas, then went out the door, closing it quietly behind her.

To this day, that room is obsessively clear in my memory. The room was Catherine's, Patty's oldest sister. The shades were always drawn, because the windows looked down at the scramble of press people. I slept on the tiny sofa bed, my feet hanging over the edge. An old-fashioned console color TV filled the room, and on top of it was my toilet article kit and a box containing Patty's jewelry, which I had brought from our apartment.

The room was my place of escape—the place where I tried to sleep as much as I could—not only because I was still physically shaky, but because oblivion was more enticing than depression. But no matter how much I slept, I never felt rested. I would fall into a deep torpor for four or five hours and then awake to stare and think of too many things. Eventually, I'd fall back into unconsciousness, only to awake again, feeling drained and unrenewed.

During the evenings, my room was the TV news watching place for the Hearst sisters: Ann, in Patty's room, just across the hall; Vicky, in the room next to Ann's; and Gina and Jay, whose room adjoined mine. We'd sit on the deep-green carpet and stare at the tube, hoping and fearing to hear the latest news about Patty.

At around 11 o'clock the next morning I was awakened by Emmy's knock on the door. She brought in my freshly washed jeans and work shirt, the same clothes I was wearing the night of the kidnapping. I had forgotten to bring along a change of clothes when stopping briefly at our apartment with the FBI the day before. I dressed and went downstairs to find Gina and Jay about to leave for the airport. Packed among their things was an old Princeton nightshirt that I had given Patty, the "something personal" Mr. Hearst had asked me to pick up when he called me at the hospital. Gina and Jay were flying down to Los Angeles with it and some of Patty's other clothes to meet with Peter Hurkos. A rather prominent psychic, Hurkos had telephoned the house earlier claiming that he might be able to locate Patty if given something of hers to do whatever psychics do with such things. Neither

Gina nor Jay was particularly hopeful, or even serious, about the venture, but as would be the case with all of us, at that point they were willing to try anything.

After they left I wandered through the house trying to get a grasp on what was happening, what was being done. There was really no central gathering place, no one room where the family and friends huddled together to discuss plans, talk about the day's events, or simply seek some comfort. Rather, the house was like a small hotel bustling with the frantic comings and goings of up to twenty-five people, many of whom didn't even know each other's names—secretaries with stacks of letters and packages of every conceivable nature, servants carrying trays of food, FBI agents answering phones, friends and relatives dropping by to help out, buffet meals, served at irregular times to a constantly changing cast.

There was, however, a good deal of activity centered around the library where the FBI had set up shop. When I entered the room the first thing that caught my eye were their handguns lying on the mantel. The two .38s produced a weird still life, contrasting with the Renaissance Della Robba ceramic on the wall above them. The front blinds were drawn leaving the room in semidarkness, and a police band radio was set up on the carpeted floor, presumably to contact agents in the field. Three tape recorders sat on a coffee table next to a large stack of blank cassettes, and lined up on a card table in the corner were three specially installed telephones. The two agents in residence, a lanky westerner named Duane, who always wore a brown suit, a string tie, and a short sleeve shirt, and Steve, an extremely serious young man right off a Marine Corps poster, had been sleeping fully clothed under a couple of blankets on the couch since the day after the kidnapping and would continue to do so for weeks. On one occasion Duane inadvertently caused quite a stir when one of his fellow agents was spotted carrying a package into the house. The newspeople immediately surrounded him, and after fending off their questions about the mysterious contents of the package, the agent finally told them it was Duane's laundry.

Duane and Steve's primary job was to monitor incoming calls, and for the first few weeks there were hundreds of them. The entire house was jangling with ringing telephones—from the three in the library, the other three phones on the first floor, and Mr. and Mrs. Hearst's two unlisted phones upstairs. After the first communiqué, however, none of us really expected the SLA to make contact by phone, but there was always the chance that someone might call in a tip as to their whereabouts. When one of the phones would ring, Duane would push a cassette into the tape recorder, pick up an earpiece, then signal Jack or Phoebe Cooke, or whoever had phone duty that particular moment, and they would pick up the receiver.

"Hello?"

"Is this the Hearsts?"

"Yes, it is."

"Well, I just wanted to call 'cause my husband just walked out on me and I don't have anybody else to talk to. . . ."

At this Duane would stop the recorder and lean back, while Cooke, or whoever, would try to conclude the conversation as quickly as possible.

Patty's kidnapping produced an intense, almost personal feeling of loss in people all across the country. Every week there were hundreds of letters: whole congregations were praying for Patty; mothers whose daughters were named Patty grieved for the Hearsts. Donations, in the form of small checks, came in, and each check had to be returned to the donor. Indian tribes adopted Patty and consigned her to their protection. But those who made sympathy telephone calls, at a time when it was so important to keep the lines free, generally needed sympathy themselves. I remember Gina telling me about a long distance call from a Los Angeles woman who literally sobbed over the phone for fifteen minutes before Gina could ease her off the line.

There were also, of course, a few extortion attempts. One such call was traced to a couple who were later captured by the FBI after phoning the house nine times. But by and large most of the telephone calls could be placed into two categories—sympathy and crank. Mr. Hearst received one of the more outrageous of the latter.

"Listen," the caller said sharply, "I'm a radical from Santa

Barbara and I understand how these people operate. Now you can either listen to me or you can get your daughter's finger in the mail!"

Furious, Mr. Hearst slammed down the phone.

On another occasion, Charles Gould got a call from a man who told him of his plan to kidnap Angela Davis, Huey Newton, and a couple of other radical leaders. He would kill them one by one until Patty was released.

Jay got one of the more amusing crank calls. Duane gave him the nod.

"Hello?" said Jay.

"Hi," said a bright cheery voice. "Is this the Hearst house?"

"Yes."

"Well, this is Patty Hearst. I bet you all been wondering where I am. Well, I can't tell you exactly where, but I can give you some hints. . . ."

Duane frowned, waved Jay off the line, and stopped his recorder. "I know that girl," he said. "She's always calling the family of kidnap victims. A kidnap groupie from Texas."

So whereas everyone in the house was at first unnerved by the din of ringing phones, after they fielded hundreds of strange calls the tension lesened and telephone duty became just another task. There were still, however, some calls that had to be checked out. Willie got one of these. It was from a black man who claimed quite convincingly that he had a plan that could lead to Patty's release in the near future. "I've got some information," he said, "and in order for you to get this information you've got to meet me today." I remember Willie scribbling down the address, hanging up, and telling me about the call. "It's probably another nut," he said, but was not so sure that he could let it go at that. I told him that if he was going to meet with the guy, he'd better take a cop along just in case. Willie agreed, then went and got his raincoat.

Two hours later Willie returned, still nervous and a bit giddy from the meeting. He had driven through the rain to Oakland followed by two FBI agents. There he further discussed the strategy to be used with an Oakland cop, then headed for the rendezvous spot, a car wash/gas station called The Bubble Machine. He had his tank filled, his car was hooked up to the conveyor, and he was pulled into the whirring brushes, blasts of hot water, and steam. Peering through the soapy windshield, he gave all the attendants knowing looks, which were invariably misinterpreted. He emerged from The Bubble Machine with a clean car but no contacts. He hung around the car wash for another ten minutes, then shrugged to the cop and the FBI agents across the street and climbed back in his car. But just as he was about to drive away a black man pulled up in a frog-pond green Buick Electra, parked at the curb, and gave *him* a knowing look. Willie got back out of his car, his heart in his throat—there were fears that he too might be targeted for kidnapping—and walked across the rain-slick parking lot to the man's car. The Oakland cop also got out of his car and moved behind the Buick. The man motioned Willie to get in.

"Is it okay if I bring my friend, Rocko, with me?" Willie asked.

The man nodded. Willie and "Rocko" climbed into the car. "Well?" Willie said.

The man looked around nervously, then leaned close and said, "Do you play chess?"

Willie tightened. He did play chess, a lot of it. He nodded to the question.

"Do you know," the man went on, "that I've played exactly twenty-five games this week and every single one of them has turned out the same." He sat back in his seat.

"I don't quite see what you're driving at." Willie frowned.

"The plan," the man said. "The SLA makes a move, you make the same move. They make another move, you make the same move again."

That was it, the plan. Willie and Rocko exchanged glances.

"Look at all the winos and the trash around here," the man continued. "You pay to clean up this street and the SLA will relate to that."

Willie thanked him and got out of the car.

"You use my plan and I want an inventor's fee!" the man shouted after him.

Willie walked back to his car while the Oakland cop and

the two FBI agents checked out the man's identification. Later, the FBI informed Willie that the man was just another harmless nut, which hardly came as a surprise. But that's just about all the FBI ever told him or anyone else for that matter. Contrary to what one might expect, none of us, including Mr. Hearst, knew much more about the Bureau's investigation than the man on the street who read the morning papers. In the evenings FBI chief Charles Bates would drop by, but his arrival was always more of a casual visit than any kind of briefing. A trim, military-looking man, he would sink down into the long sofa in the living room while Mr. Hearst made some drinks at the bar in the music room. Then Mr. Hearst and anyone else who happened to be present— usually Willie, Jay, Gina, me, and sometimes Mrs. Hearst—would listen to him talk, gesturing expansively with his arms and leaning forward. Bates's ability to talk and say nothing was really something of an art, particularly where the press was concerned. For us there were random details: how many agents they had in the field, where they were concentrating their search, maybe a passing reference to a cabin in the mountains they were staking out, but never insights into the minds of the people who held Patty. During one of these sessions I asked him what the FBI would do if the SLA made a ransom demand. "We have our ways of handling drops," he said, but went no further. On another occasion I remember the subject of guns coming up. At this Bates set down his drink, unholstered his revolver, spun the cylinders around, then holstered it saying that he had had only two occasions to use it in all his years with the Bureau. True to form he did not go into them, and because of his expression, we did not inquire as to the results. Upon leaving, Mr. Bates would always assure us that the Bureau was working hard, that Patty's safety was their greatest concern, but that was about it.

Because of our utter frustration at knowing next to nothing and our need to try to do something, while the FBI was pursuing standard lines of investigation, we tried some highly unorthodox and invariably unsuccessful approaches ourselves. The first of these was Jay and Gina's flight down to L.A. to see Peter Hurkos, dubbed Swami #1. When they returned the following day they said his house was something out of a Bela Lugosi movie. Hurkos had evidently put on quite a floor show for them in his sorcerer's den, running his hands over Patty's nightshirt, then goofing around with a topographical map of California. But he came up with nothing. Before they left, however, Hurkos insisted they leave him one of Patty's blouses just in case he was struck by a sudden vibration.

But Hurkos's offer was not unique. During the first few weeks there were hundreds of such offers from psychics and seers from all over the country. While Mr. Hearst was skeptical, he was also of the opinion that it didn't hurt to try anything. "Hell, let them hang around awhile," I remember him saying about the latest offer. "Who knows, maybe they'll come up with something."

On this note, the Monday night after my arrival the two of us sidestepped the press corps in front by sneaking out a side gate to Santa Inez. An FBI car was waiting to drive us to the Airport Hilton where we were to meet Mrs. Helen Tully, from Nutley, New Jersey—Swami #2.

Mrs. Tully, we were told, had had some startling successes and had worked with police on a number of occasions. On one of these she located a ten-year-old boy who had been missing for days. After directing police to a certain location, she got out of the car, walked down a dirt road, then stopped and said the boy was there. He was—drowned in a drainage pipe that ran under the road. Or so we were told. I was told that my attendance at that night's session was imperative. I was still black-eyed and puffy, wearing the once bloodstained shirt from which it was felt that Mrs. Tully might be able to get vibrations. I was far more skeptical about the whole thing than Mr. Hearst—also having heard that upon her arrival, Mrs. Tully had asked two FBI agents to drag her out of our Berkeley apartment and throw her in the trunk of their car from which she would direct them to Patty (they refused)—but I tried my best to keep an open mind about her powers. It is an indication of how desperate I was that I agreed, not just out of politeness, to participate in something that normally would have struck me as totally ludicrous.

Mrs. Tully, her husband, her psychiatrist, and her hometown police chief did not look like the sort of people one would go to for spiritual guidance. The men were dressed in shiny slacks, pointy shoes, and Technicolor jackets; Mrs. Tully in what can only be described as a cute little pink outfit. But there was no doubt about their sincere concern for Patty. After the introductions, Mrs. Tully said, "Well, let's see what we can do," then lay down on the couch. Mr. Hearst gave her the same nightshirt; her psychiatrist sat next to her and placed his hand on her forehead. "Okay, you are going to sleep," he monotoned. "You are very sleepy. Very, very sleepy . . ."

That was all he had to say. To all appearances Mrs. Tully was in a deep hypnotic trance, her eyes closed and unblinking, her hands clutching Patty's nightshirt. Mr. Hearst sat down on the floor and leaned back against one of the chairs as the session began.

"You are at the apartment now," the psychiatrist was saying. "You are looking around. Do you see which way they went?"

"Yes. . . . Yes, I see them. They are driving north. They are in a great hurry!"

"Okay, do you see the car? . . . Can you see their car?"

Mrs. Tully saw the car, but she couldn't read the license plate. "It's too dark," she started saying.

Her psychiatrist was a man of fertile imagination. "Now you have on some infrared glasses," he said. "These glasses will allow you to see in the dark."

Mrs. Tully frowned, and then began listing off numbers and letters. While she was doing this her husband whispered to me that when she saw a number or a letter there was no way of telling if it was upside down or backwards. "I don't know how she does it," he whispered. "I just do not know how she does it." Meanwhile the two FBI agents were sitting at the table scribbling down the numbers and letters, which they latter phoned into the Department of Motor Vehicles, which produced nothing.

In all, the session must have lasted close to two hours. During this time Mrs. Tully named just about every geographical location imaginable. Patty was being held in a basement, then it was a winery, then a monastery. "I hear the sound of dripping water," she kept saying. If pieced together, her "feeling" for Patty's location would have been in a monastery, near an airport, by a large body of water, in a houseboat by the mountains in a valley somewhere. Throughout this Mr. Hearst was sitting on the floor. It had been a long, trying day for him and he was totally exhausted. After listening to Mrs. Tully ramble on for an hour or so, I looked over and saw that he had dozed off. Then he began to snore.

"I hear something," Mrs. Tully exclaimed. "Snoring. I hear someone snoring."

Everyone exchanged glances, but none of us knew quite what to do.

"There's evil here," she began saying. "I'm frightened. It's cold. . . . My feet are cold."

Actually her feet were sticking out from under a blanket her psychiatrist had placed over her. He pulled the blanket down over her feet. "I think she's just tuckered out," he told us, then placed his hand on her forehead again. "You can wake up now," he said quietly and she did. Then I woke up Mr. Hearst. Extremely disappointed by her performance, Mrs. Tully asked him if she could keep Patty's nightshirt to sleep with. Mr. Hearst said of course, thanked them, and we left.

The two of us stood in a cold drizzle and waited half an hour to be picked up by the FBI agents, who had left an hour earlier. It was nearly midnight when we got back to the house, having driven home in silence. Both of us were pretty gloomy, especially Mr. Hearst. He poured himself a Scotch and slumped down wearily on the sofa. I kept him company for a few minutes, then said good-night and went upstairs. Earlier that day, when asked by the press about the five days of silence from the kidnappers, Mr. Hearst had said, "If it's an attempt to make us feel badly, they are succeeding very well."

"Are you still certain that it is the SLA?" the reporter had then asked.

"I have to believe it's them. The only other possibility is that some absolutely crazy person has taken her off and killed her. . . . I don't want to believe that."

While we were all certain that Patty was indeed being held by the SLA, we did not rule out the possibility that they had already killed her. As he sat alone in the living room, I'm certain that this possibility was going through Mr. Hearst's mind that rainy night.

"They've got a message at KPFA!" Anne called excitedly through my door the next morning. Mr. Hearst had just called down the same news to the crowd of newspeople who hurried to their radios. Less than a half hour before, KPFA's Paul Fischer had been sorting through the morning's mail when he had come across a bulky envelope and torn it open. It contained a tape cassette and an eight-page leter emblazoned with a seven-headed cobra under which was written "S.L.A." Fischer played some of the tape and immediately called Mr. Hearst and told him that he had and that it sounded authentic. Mr. Hearst gave him the go-ahead to broadcast it at 10:00 A.M., then sent Willie off to get it as the station had refused to hand the tape over to the FBI.

I dressed and hurried downstairs to find the family and a few friends gathered silently in the library awaiting the broadcast. Duane tuned in the station. "We will now broadcast a tape-recorded communiqué allegedly sent to us this morning by the Symbionese Liberation Army," the news director was saying. Mrs. Hearst looked on the verge of breaking down but managed to maintain her composure and held tightly to Mr. Hearst's hand. There were a few moments of silence, then the voice of "General Field Marshal Cinque" filled the room:

"To those who would bear the hopes and future of our people, let the voice of their guns express the words of freedom."

Cinque announced that he had been ordered by the Symbionese War Council to convey the message that Patty was alive and safe, declared that the SLA's purpose was "to liberate the oppressed people of this nation," then launched into an incredible diatribe:

Randolph A. Hearst is the corporate chairman of the fascist

media empire of the ultraright Hearst Corporation, which is one of the largest propaganda institutions of this present military dictatorship of the militarily armed corporate state that we now live under in this nation. . . . Mrs. Randolph A. Hearst is a member of the University of California Board of Regents . . . one of California's largest foreign investors [that] supports through its investments the murder of thousands of black women and children of Mozambique, Angola, and Rhodesia, murder designed to destroy the spirit that all humanity longs for. . . .

Cinque stated that before any negotiations for Patty's release took place the Hearsts were to show a gesture of good faith "in the form of food for the needy and unemployed." In closing he added that he too was a father and held a "high moral value to life," but that he was quite willing "to carry out the execution of your daughter to save the life of starving men, women, and children of every race. . . . Let it be known," he said, "that even in death we will win, for the very ashes of this fascist nation will mark our very graves."

There was a pause in the tape and then, unmistakably, Patty's voice—"Mom, Dad, I'm okay. I had a few scrapes and stuff, but they washed them up and they're getting okay. . . ." She sounded weak and tired, her words coming out in almost a drowsy (some thought drugged) monotone. "I think you can tell that I'm not really terrified or anything," she said. "Try not to worry so much. I know it's hard. I heard that Mom is really upset and that everybody is at home, and I hope this puts you a little bit at ease. . . ." She was trying to be brave and make us feel better, but it had the effect of making all of us feel just that much more miserable at her plight and our helplessness. I just sat in the chair, staring at the radio, listening to Patty's voice and feeling a terrible mixture of utter relief and utter sorrow.

For whatever comfort and hope we gained from Patty's message, and whatever she was trying to say about her captors, her fear of a police assault, and her belief that her father could meet the SLA demands, was blotted out by Cinque's final statement:

"What happens to your daughter will be totally your responsibility . . . her life and the blood of that life will be on your hands only. . . . Death to the fascist insect that preys upon the life of the people."

The tape ended, but nobody moved or said anything. Then Mr. Hearst stood up, gestured feebly and said, "Well, the guy's got a Jamaican accent." Cinque's message was so overwhelming that was all he could say. I was sunk in depression as were the others in the room.

And finally the coup de grace: Fischer began reading the "good faith gesture" demanded: $70 worth of food for every person in the state who had a welfare card, social security card, pension card, almost any kind of a card. He went on to read a list of community groups designated by the SLA to coordinate the food distribution—Nairobi College, Glide Memorial Church, the Black Teachers Caucus, the United Farm Workers, the American Indian Movement, and others—but I hardly heard him. I was sickened by the realization that the demand amounted to hundreds of millions of dollars. Did the SLA really believe that Mr. Hearst could meet this demand, or had they cynically and deliberately put a price on Patty which they knew could never be met?

"We're never going to see her again," Mrs. Hearst said and then began to weep.

Of all of us, Mrs. Hearst was the most fragile emotionally. Under the strain of pressure and grief, Mrs. Hearst could become undone, and, in her agitation, say things that were morbid, nonsensical, or wrong. On one occasion, she announced to the press that over a million dollars had been donated to help pay Patty's ransom. Later, Mr. Hearst had to explain that she had become confused by talk of the possibility of raising that much if it were solicited—which it was not.

She sensed that her opinion was not respected, and more and more she began to relegate herself to tasks such as answering phone calls from well-wishers and replying to letters of sympathy. Thus, her sense of frustration increased, and she felt, perhaps more than any of the rest of us, that her ability to do something about Patty was slipping from her control.

But it was her reaction to that first tape that really revealed the depths of her disorientation and despair. Mr. Hearst tried to comfort her, to reassure her that they would get Patty back, then helped her up and led her from the room.

"Well, at least Patty sounds okay," Jack Cooke said after a moment. I couldn't say much of anything. I went up to my room, my stomach clenched like a fist. It was to be that way every time I heard a tape—a Pavlovian reaction. In fact, just hearing that a new tape had arrived would tie me up with hatred, fear, then nausea. After listening to them, I would usually lie down for an hour or, if it was sunny, sit in one of the deck chairs outside like an old man in a convalescent home, my thoughts, my emotions, everything turned inward.

A few minutes after the broadcast, Mr. and Mrs. Hearst went out on the front porch to address the press. It had begun to drizzle by then; the reporters and cameramen huddled under umbrellas and parkas as the Hearsts walked down to the ring of microphones. Mrs. Hearst held her husband's hand with both hands as he made a brief statement. "The important thing for us is that Patty's safe," he said. "Certainly we'll do everything within our power to comply with the demands." But aside from assuring the SLA that "nobody's going to go rushing up to some house and start shooting," there was little he could say. He and Mrs. Hearst went back inside and the newspeople hurried through the rain to their mobile units and vans.

With the arrival of this first taped communiqué, there was no longer any doubt in the minds of the press that Patty's abduction was not only a Big Story, but in light of the SLA's demands, it was also going to be a long one. They moved in accordingly. That same afternoon, despite the rain, four telephone crews were called in to set up a coaxial cable, while five miles away technicians from the three major networks were installing large microwave discs on the roof of an apartment building that would serve as a relay station to San Francisco for live coverage. And whereas the number of newspeople assigned to cover the Hearst home was already enormous when I had arrived the week before, after the first tape their ranks swelled. Santa Inez was clogged with press cars, huge mobile transmission units, and campers in which the reporters and technicians worked, slept, ate, and played gin rummy when there was nothing new to report. The ring of microphones and cameras at the base of the front steps became a permanent fixture, covered by plastic sheeting when rain threatened. Even the trees themselves became instruments of the press, special telephones having been attached to the trunks. A common crack among newsmen was, "You can reach me at my tree," or you couldn't because "my tree's unlisted."

But despite their numbers and the competition for news, the press corps, like millions of other people, were deeply touched by the Hearsts' plight and became uncharacteristically protective of them. They pooled their questions at press briefings, were careful to pick up their cigarette butts from the driveway, and checked out the credentials of strangers who appeared on the scene. On one occasion a rather suspicious-looking man was noticed hanging around in front of the house. He was followed by a couple of reporters who took down his license plate number and phoned it in to the police. A few blocks away the Hillsborough Police pulled the man over and found that there were a dozen warrants out for him on burglary charges. On another occasion a contingent of Italian newsmen, the paparazzi fresh from spying on Jackie Kennedy, showed up and tried to take the house by storm—climbing over the cyclone fence to get into the backyard, tramping through the flower beds, and sneaking up to the windows and French doors to take pictures. The local newspeople caught wind of this and removed them bodily, except for a few of the quiet ones who promised to behave themselves.

The press corps's genuine sympathy for the Hearsts' sorrow, along with their honest desire to see Patty safe, and the endless hours of day-in-day-out vigil combined to make their interest in the case almost obsessive—not unlike what happened to many correspondents in Vietnam. With their emotions uncharacteristically engaged by the human content of the story, and with the intense competition for a scoop, the psychological effect on many of the journalists was disruptive. By the end of the case, a dozen marriages were destroyed and careers had been made and broken.

As we looked out at the reporters from the second floor of the house, we might see a reporter and a cameraman running through the shrubbery, chasing Mooshy, the Hearsts' fat, gray cat, looking for some human interest for "The Six O'Clock Report," all the while being filmed by another news team, equally desperate for a story.

But on that Tuesday, the twelfth of February, the press was gorged with news. If there was ever a truly "symbiotic" relationship, it was between the media and the SLA, each one feeding off the other. The next day's newspapers, as well as television and radio reports, were filled with the latest communiqué, Patty's message, and financial analyses of the SLA's demand. According to experts it amounted to over $300 million.

The next afternoon Mr. and Mrs. Hearst made another statement to the press and again the camera zoomed in on Mrs. Hearst's hand tightly clasped to her husband's. "Patty, I hope you're listening," Mr. Hearst said. "We're really pleased to know you're okay. . . . I just wanted to let you know it's a little frightening because the original demand is one that is impossible to meet. However, in the next twenty-four to forty-eight hours I will be trying my best to come back with some kind of counteroffer that's acceptable."

Then Mrs. Hearst spoke: "We love you, Patty," she said tearfully. "We're all praying for you. They [the SLA] have good ideals. They're just going about it the wrong way. God bless you, honey."

The authorities' reaction to the SLA demand and, obliquely, to the Hearsts' announcement of a counteroffer was swift and to the point. "I've never seen anything good come out of compromising with a bunch of hoods," Charles Bates said. Attorney General William Saxbe went one step further: "You don't catch kidnappers or save the victim by doing what the kidnappers say. If authorities knew where Miss Hearst was being held, they'd go in and get her."

Saxbe's statement angered and upset everyone in the house.

"Mr. Saxbe is not the father of Patricia," Mr. Hearst said the next day. "And to make a statement from Washington that you're going to bust in and shoot the place up I believe is damn near irresponsible."

But if we were worried by Saxbe's statement, we were encouraged by the public outcry against the SLA. A leader of a large senior citizens' organization said, "We will go hungry before we accept food under threat of violence." The director of a halfway house for ex-cons said his men "would like to stuff the seventy dollars down the kidnappers' throats." But the denunciation of the SLA and their demands was not unanimous. Of the twelve groups named in the communiqué to coordinate the food program, six refused or did not respond: "Our only concern is for the safety of your daughter," said a telegram from Cesar Chavez of the United Farm Workers. "We have no relationship and do not support the SLA," said a handwritten note from Huey Newton of the Black Panther Party, but the other six groups formed a coalition and announced they would be willing—for varying reasons—to help organize the program. The Bay Area Left had been put in an uncomfortable position. There was little support *anywhere* for the SLA's brutal kidnapping, but at the same time, the plan to feed poor people *had* to be applauded. And there was the consideration that Patty might best be helped by helping monitor the program as the SLA asked. I did not know it at the time, but they had been privately asked by Mr. Hearst to do just that. Otherwise the SLA would have been backed into a corner and there was no telling what they might have done.

"The oppressive conditions of our society are a reality," said Cecil Williams, the flamboyant minister of Glide Church and the spokesman for the coalition. Williams became the self-appointed spokesman for a coalition, which sought to feed the poor *and* rescue Patty. "People I've talked to said they would take the food," said Popeye Jackson, head of the United Prisoners Union, in a radio interview.

Willie and I heard the interview while we were driving to Berkeley to make more permanent arrangements for the care of Patty's and my cats, our plants, and to pick up some more of my things. I was depressed by the whole prospect of a food program. "If we get into a program like that there's going to be trouble," I remember telling him. But I had no idea how true that was. I was thinking of the five weeks it would take to complete such a program before negotiations for Patty's release could begin. It seemed impossible that anyone in the house would be able to hold himself together for five weeks.

Our visit to the apartment that day did nothing to reduce my depression. Cold and stale inside, the bullet holes carefully marked with numbers, the doorways dusted for fingerprints, plants knocked over, the bloodstain on the floor, everything had been left exactly as the FBI and police had found it, except for our box of grass which they had taken out of our closet and placed neatly on my dresser.

Nate, Mimi, and Scott had come over to help console me. But it was soon clear that only attending to trivial details could do any good. Scott did the dishes; Mimi washed aluminum fingerprint dust off the walls with "409," while Nate, Willie, and I sat in the living room, sorting through a pile of old mail. I found that most of the mail fit into the same categories the Hearsts' mail had been sorted into: sympathy, crank, and extortion:

Dear Steve Weed: I hope this eventually reaches you. I have been writing to friends all evening and on an impulse have decided to write to you. I sort of wish I knew you personally so I could give you a hug. It's important that you know that you have friends you've never met, people who empathize with you. . . .

Feeling a bit better for that, I tore open another envelope that was lined with tin foil. The letter was five pages long, typed single space:

Dear Sir: If you wish that Patricia will be free please do the following. . . . Radiation is used on the people around the country to destroy them. It is a machine five feet high and two feet wide. I ask you to go on television and read my letter. Publicity is the only way to stop criminals from using radiation on people. . . . Maybe criminals paid Mr. Hearst a good sum of money so that is the reason he refused my offer. Don't cover-up the biggest crime and safety hazard to the public ever!

And then a letter typed in capitals on a scrap of paper:

DEAR STEVEN: WITHOUT FURTHER RHETORIC, LET ME STATE AS SECRETARY TO A SECRET GROUP THAT YOUR LOVELY FIANCE CAN, WITH SKILL, BE RETURNED TO YOU INSIDE A WEEK. . . . TO PERFORM THIS EFFORT WE REQUEST $800,000. REPLY AFFIRMATIVE BY INCLUDING IN THE CHRONICLE A BACKWARDS TELEPHONE NUMBER. YOU WILL BE GIVEN A CALL FROM "CHARLY" TELLING YOU THE EXACT LOCATION OF THE DROP. WE WAIT AND HAVE TRUST. PLEASE LET US DEAL AS MEN AND GENTLEMEN. WE ARE NOT ZODIAC OR ZEBRAS— cHaRLy.

After reading the morning mail Willie and I began packing some of the more valuable things, washing the dishes, and mopping the blood off the floor. Over the kitchen sink, on the windowsill, I picked up Patty's engagement ring. Upstairs I found her clothes still piled on her dresser and one of my philosophy books and some notes lying on our bed where I had left them when she called me down for dinner that night.

When Willie and I finished, I got into Patty's MG and headed for the *Examiner* garage where I was to leave the car. Driving down Benvenue, passing all the old houses, the students hurrying off to campus, left me feeling far worse than when I had arrived.

When I walked into the Hearst home, I was met in the foyer by Mr. Hearst. He said he had somebody he wanted me to meet. We went into the music room where he introduced me to a man named Jan Steers. I did not know what Mr. Steers was about, but was immediately impressed by his appearance. Thin and well-dressed, Steers's immaculately trimmed goatee and moustache, his erect posture, and thick Dutch accent gave me the impression of a man of razor-sharp intellect and penetrating insight. I sat down across from him and he fixed me with an unwavering stare. There was a moment of silence, then out of the blue he asked: "The girl with the red hair. Where have you seen her before?"

"Sorry," I said leaning closer.

He shook his head. "Alligator shoes. What does that mean to you? Where have you seen alligator shoes?"

I was starting to get this uncomfortable feeling in the pit of my stomach. "I don't follow you," I said.

"I'm trying to get you to beam out, Steve. You must try to beam out, because if Patty is beaming out you will meet and we will have something."

Jan Steers was Swami #3. He had called the house the previous night and had gotten hold of Jay. "I feel it! I'm coming up!" Jay tried to put him off, but to no avail. "I'm coming up! I'm coming up now, goddamn it!" The following morning he rang the doorbell, overnight bag in hand.

"Your friend who owes you a hundred dollars. Has he paid you back yet?" he asked. "What do you have under your bed?"

None of my friends owed me $100, I had a guitar case under my bed, and after going back to our apartment I just wasn't up to another Swami session. Steers asked me a few more questions, which I tried to answer as politely as possible, then excused myself and went up to my room to be alone for a while.

Jan Steers stayed at the house for the next two weeks. During this time he constructed an altar in the den to help him "beam out." It was a small table on which was a photograph of Patty, a flower vase, all sorts of maps, pencils, rulers, and a compass, all held down by one of her shoes. To Mrs. Hearst and her eldest daughter, Catherine, both devout Catholics, it bordered on sacrilege. But to me it was just another symbol of our futility and desperation.

The next afternoon, February 14, Mr. Hearst, Jay, Willie, and I drove to the San Francisco Hilton to confer with Cecil Williams, Paul Jacobs, and some representatives of the Black Panther Party. The meeting was designed to exchange views on the SLA and try to come up with some kind of approach with which to deal with them.

Because it was another gray, drizzling day, Mr. Hearst had given me one of his old black overcoats to wear. My fingertips barely peeked from the outsized sleeves. Walking into the Hilton I fell behind and found myself alone in the plushy carpeted hallway with a stuffy-looking matron who was giving me the once-over. In retrospect, I must have looked more than a little seedy—the back of my head shaved, my face still covered with yellow bruises, my eyes bloodshot, and my hands dug deeply in the pockets of the black overcoat. The woman looked me up and down, then sniffed. "That coat hides a multitude of sins, doesn't it, young man?" she said and harrumphed away.

When I entered the conference room, Mr. Hearst was talking with the two Black Panther Party representatives. Contrary to the popular, but outdated image—black berets, crisscrossing bandoliers, and rifles held at the ready—Elaine Brown and David Dubois were a striking couple. Extremely well attired, they were polite, articulate, and coolly professional, something of a contrast to the Reverend Cecil Williams in his brightly patterned dashiki, large pendant, and white bell bottoms, and Paul Jacobs, the totally bald Socialist and onetime editor of *Ramparts* magazine. The meeting, however, was not particularly productive except for the goodwill it produced.

It was generally agreed that the SLA was a newcomer on the radical scene, long on "collegiate, radical rhetoric," but short on any kind of a consistent political philosophy. But after two hours of discussion that's about as far as it went. No hard decisions were made and no policies were agreed upon, primarily because Mr. Hearst himself had not yet decided how to reply to the SLA demand.

We returned to Hillsborough at dusk, waded through the

army of newspeople, then began the standard evening routine—watching the news, *all* the news. Starting with the five o'clock report on channel 7, we would flip from station to station, two televisions going simultaneously, winding up at seven o'clock tuned into KQED, San Francisco's Public Television station. As a rule there was very little reported during these two hours that we did not already know. But on this particular night I stayed especially close to the TV, having heard Mr. Hearst mention something about a story on the identity of two SLA members that KQED was going to break. After the usual introduction, the camera went to Marilyn Baker, a rather hard-looking, blonde woman, who announced that she had learned the identity of "the mysterious Field Marshal Cinque" and the other black SLA member who'd taken part in the kidnapping. They were escaped convicts Donald David De-Freeze and Thero Wheeler.* Baker held up two photographs and the camera moved in on them. For the first time I got a good look at what I thought were the two men who had attacked us. It was a strange, discomforting moment, especially knowing that the SLA was probably watching the same newscast, being, as one reporter put it, "media freaks."

When Baker's report was over, I turned off the television, disturbed not only by the description of DeFreeze and Wheeler as small-time criminals-cum-revolutionaries, but by what effect the broadcast would have on the SLA, what they might do to Patty because of it. Mr. Hearst was extremely concerned about this as well. For over a week reporters like Ed Montgomery of the *Examiner* and Tim Findlay of the *Chronicle* had known the identities and backgrounds of Wheeler and DeFreeze, but were "sitting on the story" out of concern for Patty, in deference to Mr. Hearst, or at the insistence of their editors. (While many reporters agreed with this policy, others did not, especially Tim Findlay. His story

* Thero Wheeler was not involved in the kidnapping; he was captured in Texas a year later. As of this writing, the identity of the second man is still unknown. The FBI theory that the second kidnapper was Bill Harris in blackface seems possible, but unlikely, and published reports that the second kidnapper was Willie Wolfe are contrary to my firsthand experience of what the kidnapper looked like.

on the SLA, in which he described Cinque as having "a Manson-like power over his white middle class followers . . . like pilot fish to a shark," was not run until after Marilyn Baker had decided to break the story that night.)

Later that evening I went downstairs to find that Jay and Mr. Hearst had gone to talk with Paul Jacobs a half hour before. Not wanting to miss anything crucial, I got Willie, we jumped into the car and headed for Jacobs's large Victorian house in San Francisco. When we arrived we found the three of them loosened up with a few drinks and involved in a long, rambling discussion of socialism; or rather Jacobs was lecturing rather professionally, Mr. Hearst was interjecting impatiently, and Jay was dutifully taking down notes. While Mr. Hearst and Jacobs were talking, Jay showed me the back page of his steno pad on which he had jotted down Jacobs's suggestion, later described by Willie as "The Capitulation Theory." It called for a token amount of money to be donated to the food program—something like $500,000—coupled with other gestures of corporate repentance such as free newspaper space for a wide range of leftist writers, an examination of the *Examiner*'s hiring policies, and an offer to provide Remiro and Little with additional legal counsel. This last suggestion was especially timely. That same morning the two SLA "soldiers" had complained that prison officials at San Quentin were denying them visitor and exercise rights.

The meeting that night ended with Mr. Hearst thanking Jacobs for his time and his suggestions, which he would seriously consider. Unlike the earlier meeting with the Black Panthers which, if nothing else, produced remarkably good feelings between the Panthers and Mr. Hearst, the meeting this night produced nothing of the kind. To put it mildly, neither man had much respect for the other, thus the communication was nil. To put it bluntly, Jacobs considered Mr. Hearst "a strange bird," and Mr. Hearst considered Jacobs "a horse's ass." The two men shook hands and we left.

Saturday, February 16, produced the first relief, the first ray of light in two weeks of uninterrupted misery and confusion. Although Mr. Hearst had earlier announced that he would come back with a counteroffer within forty-eight hours after the first tape, the deadline had already passed and nothing had been put together. Dozens of people were still scurrying frantically around the house —secretaries, agents, reporters, family members, friends, and Jan Steers who was trying to get everyone to beam out. The meetings with the Panthers and Jacobs had produced nothing concrete. The pressure was building steadily, becoming unbearable, and then, on that Saturday, something finally broke.

At around 9:30 in the morning Cecil Williams called and said he had another SLA taped communiqué. He had found it in a bus station locker after receiving instructions from an anonymous telephone call at Glide Church. Mr. Hearst sent Jay off to get it, and when he returned we all gathered in the living room. But this time, after listening to the communiqué, I was able to sit down and begin a journal. I wrote almost as if I were writing to Patty, as well as venting my frustration and working out my thoughts. In a sense that first journal entry was the culmination of the entire week:

We received the third communiqué today, via Cecil Williams, and everyone is much encouraged (perhaps prematurely). The pressure seemed to reach a peak yesterday—after four days of confusion and ineffectual planning brought about by Cinque's verbose rantings and demands.

Yesterday evening Mrs. Hearst, who already had been showing signs of falling apart, lost control of herself, stood up and told us we were all fooling ourselves, that Patty was dead, that the schools had deprived all her daughters of their religion and Patty didn't even have that comfort; that men were no longer the Clark Gables they used to be, that in fact they had become homosexuals, and that she would personally track down and punish not only the SLA, but also the people from whence its ideas (she supposed) derived—Bruce Franklin of Venceremos, Cecil Williams, Angela Davis, etc.

Everyone in the room was stunned and embarrassed by her outburst, studying their fingernails, and Randy couldn't do much more than mutter, "That's not the point, Catherine." But we could all feel similar strains in ourselves, and if it hadn't been for the tape today it probably would not have been long before all of the principals suffered some sort of a breakdown themselves.

Overall, there were several encouraging elements in the tape. First, it was short and fairly much to the point. Second, Patty seemed healthy, undrugged and untraumatized. She gave the impression of having fallen in with a group of people who have *some* rationality that perhaps we can appeal to. Third, the SLA said in effect that any sincere effort would be accepted, leaving open the possibility of a reduced food program, or perhaps even some other "gesture of good faith." Fourth, it was clear from the tape that the SLA is beginning to feel the pressure both of the FBI investigation, and of the generally unfavorable public response to their first demands. They seem willing to consider a shorter timetable and more practical gestures on our part. It's not clear, however, if this tape was made before or after the news release Thursday and Friday claiming that Cinque and his sidekick have been identified (to his friends he is known as "Cin"). . . .

It was around noon when we had gathered in the living room to hear the tape. There were twelve of us—Mr. and Mrs. Hearst, the younger sisters, Jay, Gina, Willie, myself, Charles Gould, Emmy, Steers, and Dr. Frederick Hacker, an expert on terrorism who had been contacted by Gould.

A highly respected psychiatrist, Dr. Hacker (president of the Freud society who had recently helped in negotiation between the Austrian government and Arab terrorists) had flown up from his Beverly Hills clinic the evening before, showing up at about 10:30, just as Mrs. Hearst was finishing her stream of consciousness tirade about, as Hacker put it, "whether we were mice or men." A portly, distinguished, gray-haired man with a heavy Viennese accent, Hacker looked like a stock character, "the good doctor," in a '30s movie. He walked in with his briefcase, was introduced around, then sat down in the den and said in effect, "Okay, vat's dis about a kidnapping?" Willie and I exchanged looks, both of us thinking, "Oh Christ, not another one."

Dr. Hacker was not another one, but had been out of the country on business and was unwilling to make any off-the-cuff statements until he had completely familiarized himself with the case. Willie, Jay, Gina, and I stayed up late that night trying to fill him in as much as possible. At around midnight Gina made him a sandwich, discovering that he had not eaten since breakfast. The talk continued until 3:30, then Jay and Willie took him to the Airport Hilton, furnishing him with stacks of newspaper clippings. The following morning he arrived shortly before we gathered in the living room.

Duane pushed the cassette into the recorder and suddenly the room was filled with a high, squeaky voice, just intelligible enough to tell that it was Patty's voice. The tape, it turned out, had been made on a recorder with weak batteries. Duane and Steve, the other agent, fiddled with the machine, trying to slow it down, but were unsuccessful. Finally John Lester saved the day by digging up some weak batteries and putting them in the recorder. Duane pushed in the cassette again.

Dad, Mom. I'm making this tape to let you know I'm still okay and to explain a few things, I hope. . . . First, about the good faith gesture. There was some misunderstanding about that and . . . uh . . . you should just do what you can about that. I mean they understand that you want to meet their demands. So whatever you come up with is basically okay. . . . And do it fast as you can and everything will be okay. . . .

Once again: Because we were all so tremendously relieved just to hear her voice, because we did not know whether, and to what extent, she was speaking under duress, there were things she said, fears she expressed—primarily of an FBI assault—and an almost imperceptible shift in her attitude toward her captors that went unnoticed. All we really heard was her relatively strong voice and, in particular, one statement that reassured us all that she was still the same strong-minded Patty: "Mom should get out of her black dress. That doesn't help at all." I smiled at this, but Mrs. Hearst winced.

Patty closed by saying that we should all understand that the SLA had an interest in her return. "Take care of Steve," she said. "And hurry. . . . Bye." There was a pause, then the general field marshal added a final word:

People are awaiting your gesture. You may rest assured that we are quite able to assess the extent of your sincerity in this matter. . . . We are quite aware of the extent of your capabilities as we are also aware of the needs of the people. . . .

Despite Cinque's statement, everyone's spirits were buoyed by the conciliatory tone of the communiqué. Dinner that night reflected this. There was almost a giddy atmosphere to the gathering. Willie, Dr. Hacker, the family, and I were seated at the table when Jan Steers walked in. He looked around, then asked where Gina was. "You tell us, Jan," Willie said, referring to Jan's "powers." Everyone burst out laughing and Jan, quite pleased with himself, sat down and was quickly holding court, rambling on excitedly about alpha waves, the new sciences of the unknown, and the advantages of beaming out. The optimistic atmosphere was such that even Mrs. Hearst and Catherine seemed to enjoy the discussion.

After dinner we moved back to the living room and tried to get down to the business at hand, namely how much money to offer the SLA, for what purpose, how to word the offer, and what to demand in return. Aside from the dinner group, Charles Gould and two other executives from the *Examiner* were in attendance. Unfortunately the result of this was that there were too many people with too many opinions. The discussion became unwieldy, wandering off to unrelated subjects, breaking into separate talks, and then finally circling back to alpha waves and psychic phenomena. Sometime after midnight I excused myself, went up to my room, and sat down at my journal. While I was frustrated by the unproductive discussion, I was also encouraged by the latest tape. What I wrote that night had been building up inside of me since I arrived at the Hearsts'. It was less a criticism than an attempt to record my concerns and talk myself down:

Although today's tape was encouraging it contained one ominous note which seems to have gone right over Mr. Hearst's head—or at least he seems unwilling to discuss it with anyone. Cinque claimed again to be aware of the extent of the Hearsts' ability to act, his financial capabilities. But since we have already been asked for $300 million, and in light of the *Daily Cal*'s "of course the Hearst fortune is worth considerably more than that," and *Time* magazine's ". . . heir to one of the largest fortunes in America," I have been urging Mr. Hearst, and anyone else who will listen, like Charles Gould, to directly or indirectly get some information out that might show the SLA just what Mr. Hearst's ability to act really is, to ensure, as someone said to me today, that Randy doesn't become the victim of his father's image.

But Mr. Hearst does not seem to place too much importance on this point, partially because of a reluctance to spell out his financial situation, which admittedly is a somewhat humiliating thing to have to do, whether or not one has any money, and partially because he really doesn't seem to think it would do any good. "I can't go out there and cry poormouth," he says. "They're not going to believe me anyway." But my feeling is still that *some* means must be found to inject some financial reality into the situation before we can make an offer that we can stick to, and one that will have some chance of pleasing the SLA.

The lack of any plan for the last four days has been almost too much for me to take, and although a figure of $2 million was pretty much decided on tonight ($1/2$ million from the family, $1 1/2$ million from the Foundation), the way the "planning session" went tonight doesn't give me much cause for encouragement. Charles Gould, Tom Eastam, and someone else from the paper thought we should pretty much ignore the SLA's absurd demand and offer a sum like $100,000, a standard sort of kidnapping amount. Hacker thought we should, as much as possible, treat the SLA at face value, even to the point of incorporating their rhetoric in our replies, but that a figure like 1½ million seemed more sensible in view of the fact that this "good faith gesture" is only a preliminary demand. Hacker also thought we should demand a specific date for the beginning of "release negotiations" in return. I thought his ideas were fine, but was trying to push for something other than just a lump sum of money for food—perhaps just a token amount for food, coupled with some offers of the type Paul Jacobs suggested— free clinics, newspaper space, anything but an enormous food program.

More than anything else it seems necessary to practically plead with the SLA, show them a wide range of things we *can* do, and ask them not to make us try the impossible. But finally, after several people left tonight, Mr. Hearst decided that $2 million would be the figure. He feels he can't offer less and be able to convince the SLA that he's really made a sacrifice. He feels the only hope he has is to convince both the SLA and himself that he's acting in good faith. "I want to be able to take a lie detector test," he says. "I want to be able to dream that I'm not holding back."

I'm hopeful that it will work, but I am also fearful that the SLA, thinking in terms of hundreds of millions, will consider it to be a token, an attempt to get off cheaply. If that is their response, I hope Mr. Hearst is willing to defend his effort with some financial facts. We also hope that the movement leaders in the area will endorse the idea and put sufficient pressure on the SLA to make it work. Unfortunately, Mr. Hearst doesn't really seem to know if he is merely to ask that negotiations be started, or if he is to demand Patty's release. If our compromise is to be that negotiations start *after* her release, who will be left to negotiate with?

As sincere as he is, Mr. Hearst is truly an exasperating person to have to make plans with. Admittedly, he had a few drinks, is under enormous pressure, and is having advice thrown at him from all sides. Still, the degree to which he is unable to focus is quite incredible. He repeats himself, interrupts, argues trivial points, and every now and then will fall back upon such outbursts as, "If they kill her, they're dead!" To further confuse matters, he is very sincere about wanting to help the disadvantaged and from time to time the discussion tonight would stray to the issue of whether the extorted newspaper space might help or hinder the Left (who gives a shit at this point?).

In short, it is almost impossible either to influence him with suggestions, or to get him to prepare anything before stepping in front of the cameras, feeling best about playing his press conferences by ear. His disorganized (from my view) approach is at once his strength and weakness—his strength because he has managed to convey his sincerity, but his weakness because he just seems to be stalling; he certainly must be confusing the SLA about our intentions.

Yet despite all of this, it is still quite possible that Mr. Hearst's day to day approach will prove to be the most successful—I don't know, and at this point I have no choice but to do it his way. At present it seems an 80/20 chance that Patty will be returned in the next few weeks.

The next morning Willie and I drove Dr. Hacker to the airport. While awaiting his flight we sat in the cocktail lounge talking about the case and especially the SLA. "Sure is kooky," Hacker said at one point and Willie and I burst out in nervous laughter. Then, after discussing similar cases, Dr. Hacker made two very important observations, which stuck in my mind but which I didn't think were applicable to Patty: that prisoners, particularly kidnapping victims, often develop sympathies with their captors and that like prisoners of war, kidnapping victims return to people who have come to resent them, making readjustment difficult for both sides.

After seeing Dr. Hacker off, I took Willie to Hillsborough, then headed for Berkeley to spend the night with the Swantons and stay out of Mr. and Mrs. Hearst's hair. We had had a couple of run-ins the week before. One of these came about when I questioned the publication of some of Patty's baby pictures, saying that a play for sympathy might anger the SLA and decrease our credibility. At this Mr. Hearst had snapped, "I know something about this business and you don't. Some little old lady somewhere might just see these pictures and call in a tip to the police." There was another flare-up over dinner one night. That day's *Washington Post* had run a story claiming that Patty had been kicked out of Santa Catalina for smoking pot, which was untrue. The Hearsts were furious and bitterly attacked one of Patty's girl friends whom they suspected of feeding the lie to the press. Not having the good sense to stay out of it, I interjected a few words in defense of the girl, suggesting that if she were the source, she might have thought she was helping Patty by making her look better in the SLA's eyes. Mrs. Hearst blew up. "We don't need friends like that," she said, "and we don't need people defending her in this house!" With that she got up and left the table. A few days later I decided it would be wise to absent myself for a while.

The next day, while I was in Berkeley packing some more of our things and carting our houseplants around, Mr. Hearst was spending a very long, trying day consulting with his financial advisors, IRS officials, and the state attorney general. The following afternoon he met with the coalition leaders who had offered to monitor the food program. Held in a suite in the Hilton Hotel, the meeting got off to an acrimonious, almost portentous start. In attendance were Cecil Williams and a few of his assistants from Glide Church, Yvonne Golden and a few of her assistants from the Black Teachers Caucus, Popeye Jackson and his secretary from the United Prisoners Union, and much to all of their displeasure, Russell Means, Dennis Banks, and John McLean of the American Indian Movement along with at least thirty Indian bodyguards who stood solemnly against the walls, one half bodyguarding the other half. Despite the similarity of their plight, Indians and blacks are hardly known for the spirit of brotherhood between them. When Mr. Hearst arrived the sharp-tongued Yvonne Golden, recently acquitted of inciting a riot at a school board meeting when the American Nazi Party tried to attend, marched up to him. "We could have brought fifty of our brothers too!" she shouted angrily. "We will not hold a meeting like this!" Then Popeye Jackson got into it. "Where's my fuckin' bodyguards!? *They* got bodyguards!" he yelled as Cecil Williams danced around trying to get the brothers and sisters "to dialogue, relate."

After cooling Golden, Mr. Hearst conferred with Banks and Means, finally persuading them to leave their contingent of bodyguards outside. Meanwhile scores of newspeople, tangled in their equipment, pushed and shoved in the narrow hallway, their klieg lights driving the temperature up into the nineties. At one point a cart of sandwiches was rolled up to the door but two "warriors" insisted on testing it for poison before allowing it inside. The reporters got some good shots.

Finally, after a grueling four-hour meeting in which he was harangued, shouted at, and upbraided, Mr. Hearst emerged from the suite looking tired and rumpled. The newspeople crowded close as he sat at a card table covered with microphones and read a carefully prepared statement. A two-million-dollar "gesture of good faith" to the SLA would be delivered to a tax-exempt charitable organization "for the benefit of the poor and needy." He also announced that William Coblentz, a prominent San Francisco attorney, would act as an ombudsman at the Little and Remiro court proceedings to see that they received due process. Asked by a reporter if he thought his offer would satisfy the SLA, he responded wearily: "That's all there is in the kitty."

When I returned to Hillsborough on Tuesday, spirits around the house had brightened considerably. After days of floundering around with this proposal and that, just the idea of finally settling on an offer was cause enough for optimism. Even Mr. Hearst was hopeful. He had just introduced on the front steps two Washington State officials who had offered to organize the food program—Peggy Maze and A. Ludlow Kramer—and it seemed the coalition would accept them as directors.

The next day provided further cause for optimism. It was February 20, Patty's birthday, and Charles Bates, in a moment of carelessness he would soon regret, told reporters he had a "seat of the pants feeling" that she would be released. He was not alone in his feeling. Outside the Hearst home a reporter hung up a hand-painted sign that read, "Welcome Home Patty," while inside the house Jan Steers was bubbling around proclaiming that she had in fact already been released. He abandoned his altar and stationed himself expectantly by the telephone, ready to receive her call. There was even some talk of buying a birthday cake and some presents for Patty's return.

Dinner that night was nervously, self-consciously cheerful, as if optimistic feelings might somehow affect the situation favorably. Willie was in top form, breaking everyone up with his imitations of Dr. Hacker—"So vat's dis about a kidnapping?"—Cecil Williams—"Dialogue, brothers and sisters, relate!"—Popeye Jackson—"Hey, where's my bodyguards?"—and even Cinque himself—"Speaking poisonally for mahselve I would like to take this opportunity to say . . . please pass the salt."

At approximately 8:30 that same evening Cecil Williams's phone rang again. The message was a short one: There was another letter and a taped communiqué in a phone booth on Pine Street.

I was in my room scratching down some thoughts when Gina entered in tears. "They've just got another tape calling Dad's offer 'crumbs to the people.' They're demanding another four million in twenty-four hours." Unable to say any more, Gina left. I sat there a moment, then picked up my pen.

I am writing this now not for the record, but just to steady my nerves. If I think about the stupidity and the callousness of these people for even a few seconds I am filled with visions of putting a bullet in Cinque's head. . . . I am out of ideas and cannot even continue writing now.

I turned off the lights and lay down and tried not to think.

5

ALTHOUGH WE MUST HAVE LISTENED to the tape later that same night, I cannot remember when it arrived, who delivered it, or even in what room we listened to it. It hit me that hard. As crushing as the first tape was, it did not have this kind of impact. The communiqué of February 12 seemed detached from reality, the tape recorder issuing a disembodied voice which matter-of-factly announced Patty's arrest, stated the crimes of her parents, and then made demands that were so grandiose, so absurd that they seemed to beg for a counteroffer, or at least some grounding in reality. This tape begged for nothing. Fired with hatred and rage, it spat at us and all our efforts, laid waste to any hopes we had. It assaulted us directly. *Cinque* assaulted us directly. He said he knew us and now we knew him. His hood had been removed, his picture plastered across the front page of every newspaper in the country, and now, listening to this tape, we were face to face with him, Donald David DeFreeze, an escaped convict, a paranoiac, a self-proclaimed general field marshal with an automatic rifle. That is how communiqué #6 hit us, directly, face-to-face, the worst of it so far.

"Greetings to the people," the communiqué began. "General Field Marshal Cinque speaking." In a controlled voice he announced that the "SLA War Council and the Court of the People" had directed him to clarify "the request of the people." This amounted to a total, across-the-board denunciation of Mr. Hearst's counteroffer.

> The Hearst empire has attempted to mislead the people and deceive them by claiming to put forth a good faith gesture of two million dollars. This amount is not at all a good faith gesture, but rather an act of throwing a few crumbs to the people, forcing them to fight over it amongst themselves. . . .

To prove this he began reading a long list of Hearst holdings, many of them nonexistent. He stated that even if Mr. Hearst were to give everything he had to the people—in the SLA's judgment, "hundreds and hundreds of millions"—with personal friends like Howard Hughes and the Shah of Iran, he would suffer no losses. Whatever hope we had that the SLA had some grasp of reality, at least some notion of the system they were attacking, vaporized with that statement. And this was only the beginning.

Next came the new demand. If Mr. Hearst wanted to protect another one of "his possessions, his daughter Patricia," he would come up with another $4 million within twenty-four hours; and if this demand was rejected, all further communication with Patty would cease. Moreover, if there were any attempts to rescue Patty or injure Remiro and Little, "the subject is to be executed immediately."

On the heels of that, Cinque moved to the next section of the communiqué, his voice now betraying his self-righteous rage. He accused those organizations that had voiced criticisms of the SLA of accepting "reform and revisionism," and "sliding up next to the enemy's power." And then finally the diatribe: Cinque began reading what was apparently his own writing, his bitter response to his unmasking by the press.

You do, indeed, know me. You have always known me. I'm that nigger you have hunted and feared night and day. I'm that nigger you have killed hundreds of my people in the vain hope of finding. I'm that nigger that is no longer just hunted, robbed, and murdered. I'm the nigger that hunts you now. Yes, you know me. You know us all. You know me, I'm the wetback. You know me, I'm the gook, the broad, the servant, the spik. Yes, you know me. You know us all and we know you—the oppressor, murderer, and robber. And you have hunted and robbed and exploited us all. Now we are the hunters that will give you no rest. And we will not compromise the freedom of our children. . . . Death to the fascist insect, that preys upon the life of the people.

A pause. Then, as though she were reading from a slip of paper, Patty's voice: "Today is the nineteenth and yesterday the Shah of Iran had two people executed at dawn." That's all she said, all she was allowed to say, but the warning was clear. Mr. Hearst's "personal friend" had executed two people. The SLA was quite willing to execute one.

I made a short entry in my journal later that night:

I have just listened to the lengthy tape and it has succeeded in making me physically ill with depression and hatred. The speaker no longer sounds political to me, but simply bitter, ignorant and nearly insane. The chances of getting Patty back now seem about 25%. For the first time something has clicked inside me, the idea that they actually may intentionally kill her. The entire family is pretty much shattered.

The family was indeed shattered, but unlike the times before none of us was able to pick up the pieces afterward. The arrival of communiqué #6 marked the sixteenth day since Patty had been taken. During that time the Hearsts, the various relatives, and I had, despite our differences, presented a fairly united front. The mutual fears, the shared grief, but most of all the hope that any day Patty might be escorted by the FBI through the crowd of newsmen and up to the door had produced a common bond among us. The February 20 tape utterly destroyed that hope. She was not going to be released any day now; there was no end in sight. In destroying our hopes of a foreseeable resolution, the tape also began to undermine the sense of unity those hopes had fostered. It was in this new atmosphere of waiting and futility that my standing with the Hearsts began to crumble.

"It's like feeding a goddamned alligator," Mr. Hearst said bitterly the following night. He got up and poured himself another Scotch. "The more you feed them, the hungrier they get." He was referring to the additional four-million-dollar demand.

Mr. Hearst, Charles Bates, Willie, Jay, and I were sitting in the living room, all of us feeling desperate, backed into a corner, except, perhaps, for Mr. Bates, who repeatedly assured Mr. Hearst that the SLA would eventually be captured. He could guarantee that. True to form, however, he did not say much else.

"They can't kill the girl," Mr. Hearst went on. "They'll alienate the entire Left." He sat down wearily on the couch. "How in God's name do we get Patty out of the box?"

Bates said the Bureau was working around the clock, following every possible lead to do just that. Although he did not give Mr. Hearst any specific advice about how to respond to the SLA's demand for an additional $4 million, it was clear that he was sticking to his original comment that "he'd never seen any good come out of compromising with a bunch of hoods." "I can assure you that Patty's safety is our first concern," he said, repeating the FBI's constant refrain. Since the Bureau had not the vaguest idea of where she was being held, this comment was hardly a comforting one. After a few minutes Bates finished his drink, got up and said good-night. Mr. Hearst showed him to the door while Willie, Jay, and I sat in gloomy silence. When Mr. Hearst returned, we sat up with him late into the night.

The remainder of the evening bore little resemblance to the wandering strategy sessions of the Saturday night before. Now there were few options to be discussed and, while it was clear to everyone that another $4 million had to be offered the SLA, it was becoming equally clear that we were dealing with people whose demands were insatiable. Therefore, the additional money would be made available only upon Patty's release. But aside from that there was little else Jay and I could do or say except keep Mr. Hearst company. Everything was on his shoulders, not ours. He had spent another exhausting day phoning his fellow members of the Board of Trustees, meeting with a constant stream of coalition leaders, and consulting with Peggy Maze and Ludlow Kramer about the food program that was already in full swing in the Hearst Building in San Francisco. Throughout all of this, and despite the enormous pressure he was under, Mr. Hearst had been remarkably controlled. Only later that night, sitting with us in the living room, was he able to vent his anger and frustration.

"If they so much as lay a hand on the girl, the next million will be on their heads," he said. "There won't be a radical in this country who'll have a thing to do with them except to turn them in. The FBI will call out the troops and it'll be like Cowboys and Indians." He went on to talk about how the SLA was actually counterrevolutionary, how they were "screwing up" every legitimate effort in the country to really help the poor and needy. "There's already been one hell of a backlash to this thing," he said. "People pick up the *Examiner,* read all that crap we've been forced to print, and throw it down in disgust. You can't tell me that doesn't affect their attitudes about minorities." He slumped back. "They can't be allowed to push foundations around like this."

And yet Mr. Hearst knew that was precisely what the SLA was doing—using him as an instrument to exact a "gesture of repentance" from the Corporation and Foundation. He was chairman of the board and perhaps the most influential of the thirteen trustees; what he wanted done usually got done. But increasingly Mr. Hearst began to find himself caught in a bind between the SLA and "his" business empire. More than most people realized, and more than it seemed possible to explain, the other twelve trustees began to feel that things had already gone far enough. Resistance began to develop not so much over the loss of a few million dollars—a loss that would probably have been made up by the end of the year—but over the precedents that were being set as a result of our capitulation. The other four Hearst family trustees—Randy's brothers and nephews—were justifiably concerned that such large sums of money might encourage other kidnappers to go after their own children. Influential nonfamily trustees, some of them old, conservative executives who had been around since the days of W.R., Sr., began to explain to Mr. Hearst that, as much as they sympathized with him, in their judgment the more the SLA was given the less likely that Patty would be released. A rationalization, perhaps, but one that had some grounding in reality and was not easily dislodged. In view of this, when Mr. Hearst and Charles Gould stepped out on the porch the following morning, they carried an offer that for many reasons was not likely to be improved upon—whatever Mr. Hearst and the SLA had to say about it.

"The size of the latest SLA demand is far beyond my financial capabilities," Mr. Hearst said solemnly, his face downcast as he read the statement. "Therefore, the matter is now out of my hands." Ignoring questions from reporters, he turned and went back inside as Mr. Gould stepped up to the microphones and introduced himself as a representative of the Corporation. "The Hearst Corporation is prepared to contribute to People In Need a total of four million dollars for a food distribution to the poor and needy," he said, "provided Patricia is released unharmed." He stated that $2 million would be contributed immediately upon Patty's release and $2 million in January 1975, then added, "Neither the Hearst Corporation, nor the Hearst Foundations, are controlled by members of the Hearst family. No other funds will be contributed by the Corporation or the Foundations under any circumstances." There was no more to be said, no questions, no answers. He too turned to the door and the television lights faded out.

Twenty-five miles to the north, on the fifth floor of the Hearst Building, the People In Need operation was mobilizing for its first food giveaway. The distribution sites had been announced in the newspapers, on television, and radio. A. Ludlow Kramer was confident of success. "We have spent only fifteen thousand dollars on the purchase of food," he announced. He believed that a million dollars' worth of free food had been donated. When asked if the donations could make up the additional $4 million demanded, he was equally confident. "We will be far in excess of that amount if the current rate of gifts is maintained." He was certain the program would bring Patty home.

A reporter asked whether some needy people might refuse to pick up free food "under these circumstances."

Peggy Maze responded: "People's attitudes are our biggest problem. Maybe when the press coverage dies down people will feel free to go in and out of the food banks."

The food bank in East Oakland was scheduled to open at 11:00 A.M. By 10:00 A.M. a crowd of five thousand people jammed the streets. By 10:30 the crowd became unruly, and then the rioting broke out. One of the PIN delivery trucks was surrounded and broken into. Cartons of crackers, milk, and frozen turkey legs were thrown into the crowd, injuring some of the bsytanders. Fistfights erupted. Reporters and cameramen were beaten, their equipment smashed on the sidewalk. A passing motorist was hit by a rock, lost control of his car, and crashed into a building. Another motorist was hit and was blinded in one eye. A fire bomb was lobbed into a hardware store, but burned itself out before much damage was done. The angry crowd began throwing rocks and bottles, windows were smashed, stores looted, then the Oakland police moved into the area in force.

In the aftermath twenty-one people were being treated for injuries at nearby hospitals. Although Oakland was the worst of it, chaos prevailed at most of the other food banks as well. PIN had expected to feed twenty thousand that day but only nine thousand actually received food, and those who did complained that there was little of it and that it was of poor quality.

The evening news highlighted the disaster. Gina, Jay, and I sat in depressed silence watching six young blacks pick up a bicycle rack and heave it through the front window of a market, then loot the liquor section. The scene cut to three cops dragging a man into a police van. "Thirty-five people have been arrested," the newscaster said. "There is still some rioting going on at this hour in Oakland." Then a close-up of an old black woman. "I'm only here because I'm poor and not for any other reason," she said. "But I didn't think it was going to be like this. The Hearsts got their millions and we ain't got nothin'." The camera swung to a sign carried by two young men—"More Cinque," it read. Then a shot of three people on stretchers being wheeled into Highland Hospital. Then to Kramer: "It's obviously a problem of logistics. With so little time to set up the program," he said, "we tried the impossible and it nearly worked." He announced that the food banks would be closed for three days of reorganization.

There was little said after the newscast. Gina and Jay went to their room and I put on the same black overcoat, intending to take a long walk. As Mr. Hearst and I had done a week earlier, I went out the back door, across the wet lawn where I was greeted by Mike, the Hearsts' large Labrador. Starved for attention, he jumped up and barked happily. I patted and shushed him, then went out the side gate onto the darkened street.

The night was clear and cold. A slight wind rustled in the pines along Santa Inez as I walked head down, my hands deep in the pockets of the overcoat. It had been an awful day. An hour before, Marilyn Baker had given some more information on Donald DeFreeze, his career as a petty crook, arrests for beating up prostitutes, and an arrest involving stolen guns in which DeFreeze had led the police to a friend's house in order to save his own neck. The bitterly self-righteous voice of the "general field marshal" was never very far from me during these weeks . . .

the voice of a criminal. What a travesty to think that his politics were anything more than a facade, an excuse or occasion for De-Freeze's warped personality to express itself. And Nancy Ling Perry. In the letter she had sent to the media a month before, there had been one line that had particularly stayed with me: ". . . because I have learned that what one really believes in is what will come to pass." It was hard to comprehend the sort of fanatical mysticism we had fallen victim to. There was little chance we would be able to please such people. Could they execute her in cold blood? Foster had been shot in the dark, his assailants fleeing, not having to deal with the bleeding corpse they'd created. Or would they wrap her up in a blanket and then shoot her? I had nightmares about Cinque firing at Patty, still tied up. I had dreams, waking and sleeping, fragments of dreams: a closet, a dank, concrete utility porch, a windowless basement, a cot perhaps.

My thoughts were interrupted by a car pulling up behind me. I turned and was blinded by a flashlight. "Are you a resident of this neighborhood, sir?" a voice asked.

It was the Hillsborough police. I told them I was staying with the Hearsts. At this they both got out of the squad car, keeping the flashlight on me.

"Your name?"

"Steve Weed." I started to dig out my wallet, but they sloughed it off, now recognizing me.

"We're just checking everybody out, Mr. Weed," one of them said. "Can we give you a lift anywhere?"

I told them I was just taking a walk.

"Oh . . . well, I guess you can use one." There was an awkward pause. "We're sorry about everything, Mr. Weed. Sure hope she's returned soon."

I nodded. There was not much I could say.

"Don't get lost." They climbed into their car and pulled away. I started walking again but had only gone a couple of hundred yards when another squad car pulled up. We went through the same routine almost to the word. "No, I'm just taking a walk. Thanks." When a third squad car pulled me over a few minutes later, it was obvious that "just taking a walk" was impossible. The Hillsborough police had been cruising the neighborhood in force since the kidnapping.

"You're heading into San Mateo Park," one of the officers said. "Streets get pretty tangled up out here. We'd better give you a lift."

I climbed into the back seat and asked them if they could let me off at the side gate. They did. I made my way into the backyard, was again intercepted by Mike, then went inside. Mr. Hearst was standing in the living room, apparently startled by the dog's barking. "Where have you been?" He frowned. I told him out for a walk. "Well, don't just wander off like that without telling anybody." As walks go, it had not been a successful one.

The next day I read the papers and listened to the newscasts, but that's about all I did. I was still depressed about the rioting the day before, as was the rest of the family, except Mr. Hearst. He was angry and frustrated. I made the mistake of venturing into the living room that evening to find him talking to Willie. He'd had several drinks; there was a chip on his shoulder; I quickly became the target of his frustrations.

"You know it's *your* SDS that started this whole goddamned thing," he said sharply. "You intellectuals content yourselves with raking the system over the coals. You build up overnight expectations in idiots like DeFreeze and they go out and start shooting for the revolution. DeFreeze," he muttered. "DeFreeze couldn't lead a goddamned picnic to the beach on a hot day!"

I glanced at Willie, who was obviously wishing to be elsewhere. "I hate to say it," Mr. Hearst went on, "but you just rub me the wrong way. You spook around the house, you upset Catherine, and you damn near go to pieces when anybody points a camera at you. You know you might try to be a little more helpful around here. Help Emmy in the kitchen once in a while."

"Look, I'm sorry but there doesn't seem . . ."

"That's right," he cut me off. "You're so goddamned liberal, you tell me what this is all about!"

Although I was upset by Mr. Hearst's outburst, I was aware

of the terrible pressure he was under and tried not to take his attack personally. Still, the number of irritations between the Hearsts and me had been steadily increasing, especially in the last few days: the arguments over the swamis, Patty's baby pictures, and my ill-considered defense of her friend who supposedly leaked the "marijuana story" to the *Washington Post*. Even the fringe that Patty had sewn around the cuffs of my Levi's was a source of irritation to Mr. Hearst. "Why the hell would anyone want to wear something like that?" he asked Willie.

Taken by themselves these irritations did not amount to much, but as a whole they were indicative of a larger feeling of resentment. As I wrote in my journal that same evening:

> I also have the unmistakable feeling that on a certain intangible level the Hearsts blame me for the situation, or more accurately, that I am the closest thing in the house worthy of blame. Of course they cannot say it, nor do they even *think* it really. Rather, it's a question of my being somehow tainted with life in Berkeley and the kidnapping itself.

If Mr. and Mrs. Hearst held me accountable for Patty's kidnapping on a subconscious level, the FBI went one step further. A few days earlier, on Tuesday, February 19, I was summoned to the FBI office in Berkeley for a three-hour "interview."

Located on the tenth floor of one of Berkeley's few downtown, high-rise office buildings, the FBI offices are effectively isolated from the rest of the building's occupants by a large wooden door with a peephole in it. I rang the buzzer outside, an eye appeared in the peephole, then the door opened and I was shown into the small waiting room by one of the secretaries. I took a seat, was glancing through a pamphlet entitled "Ever Consider a Career with the Bureau?," when Don Jones, the tall, cleancut Berkeley FBI chief, entered the room and greeted me with a handshake. I followed him into his office, a medium-sized room with a view of the bay, a desk covered with photographs of Jones's wife and kids, and large portraits of J. Edgar Hoover and Billy

Graham on the wall. Two other agents and a secretary came in behind us, pulled up their chairs, and took out their note pads. The interview began.

Friendly at first, their questions soon began to narrow in scope and focus on what they obviously considered the unsavory aspects of Patty's and my background.

"How much money did Patty get from her parents?" one of them asked.

"Three hundred dollars a month, but she also had eight thousand dollars in a bank account."

"That's all?"

"Her father gave her a thousand to buy furniture for our apartment when we first moved in."

"Then any time you wanted money her parents would give you a thousand or so?"

"Not really. Patty didn't like to ask them for money."

"Well, she pretty much supported you."

"No, my income from my teaching assistantship was higher than hers. We shared expenses."

"You met Patty at Crystal Springs Girls School, is that right?"

I nodded.

"How many other girls did you have 'friendships' with?"

"Like Patty? None."

"Did you and Patty ever smoke marijuana?"

"Of course we did. Look, let's stop playing games. You found that box of . . ."

"What about harder drugs?"

"We never had anything to do with harder drugs, except LSD on a few occasions."

"Have you ever sold any marijuana?"

"I sold some at Princeton during my senior year."

I was starting to get the depressing feeling that my interviewers—who alternated their questions so that my head was constantly turning back and forth—were more interested in trying to trip me up than in getting my help.

"What about your radical friends at Princeton? Do you ever see them anymore?"

"Some of them, yes."

"Who?"

I listed them off.

"What are your politics?"

"I'm pretty much apolitical."

"Who knew about you and Patty? You must have mentioned her background to someone."

"I didn't go out of my way to mention . . ."

"Can you trust all your friends? We have reason to believe that there is some word-of-mouth connection between you and the SLA."

"No, you're really wasting your time on that angle. We have a small group of friends that . . ."

"Princeton friends?"

"A few of them, yes. Princeton friends."

"To your knowledge have they ever been connected with a terrorist-type organization?"

It went like that for three hours, the agents going over and over the same questions about finances, dope, my "radical" connections, and particularly our Berkeley friends, the secretary taking down everything in shorthand. Although I was irritated by their moralizing attitude, which they made no attempt to disguise, and frustrated by their unshakable belief that there was a "missing link" between Patty and me and the SLA, I tried to answer all their questions as forthrightly as possible. I didn't care about their opinion of me, or even if I had unwittingly put myself in some sort of legal jeopardy. My only concern was to convince them that I was holding nothing back so that they would stop wasting their energies on me. Unfortunately, my honesty produced the opposite result. By the end of the interview, it was obvious that from their point of view it was "suspicions confirmed." I was a drug-taking closet radical, who had been exploiting Patty for three years. I was free to go.

That I began to find myself at odds with the FBI came as no surprise. The combination of my "unsavory" background and their narrow, almost peephole view of the world could produce nothing other than mutual distrust and suspicion. But by the same token, while the deteriorating state of affairs between the Hearsts and me was a result of the differences in our personalities, as well as the pressurized situation in which we found ourselves, it was also due to their particular view of the world. Like the FBI, the Hearsts are as much of an organization as a family.

From the day I entered the Hearst home after Patty's kidnapping, I found myself in the midst of a conflict in which I had no real role and, because of this, no power to resolve. To the SLA I was simply an embarrassment, the boyfriend who had been left beaten and bereaved—not good PR for the Revolution. To the Hearsts I had always been a source of some discomfort, but was now a considerable aggravation. Dressed in my Levi's and work shirt I looked, as one of the Hearsts' friends put it, "more like one of them, than one of us." And to the media, who were not only responsible for defining the scenario, but the characters as well, I was really not much more than a sidelight, a diversion of sorts. They were quick to see that it was the Hearsts and the Hearst "empire" that had been forced to stage center by the SLA and commanded to perform, not me. In that sense Patty's kidnapping was something that had happened, for want of a better word, to "Hearstdom" as much as it had happened to Patty herself. What happened to me was incidental. *I* was incidental. Because of this I found myself living in the same surroundings, trying to operate under some of the same constraints that I had so often heard Patty complain about. For me it was just one more problem in an already impossible situation. For Patty it was far more. It was something that she had lived and breathed all her life—until the night of February 4, 1974.

When Patty and I first met I paid little attention to her plan to change her name. I was aware, of course, that her family was highly unusual, that she was bound to have had unique problems of adjustment, but I assumed that her preoccupation with "being a Hearst" was primarily an adolescent one. In fact it was, but with a twist: it was an adolescent reaction to something undeniably real, something I sensed almost subconsciously on my first visit to her parents' home. I remember looking over their collection of antiques and historical memorabilia—some from the Hearst Castle at San Simeon—and thinking that old W.R. must have been an impossibly difficult act to follow. But it was only in the years following that first visit that I gradually became aware of just how true this was, how all of the Hearst heirs, including Patty, had had to make their various accommodations to W.R.'s legacy and, more importantly, to his legend. The Hearsts were people who lived in the wake of something. I remember one day in particular when this came home to me.

It was in the late fall of 1973 and Patty and I were flying down to San Simeon in a rented plane with her parents. We broke through the clouds at five thousand feet and banked around the Disneylandlike castle a couple of times. Waving from one of the terraces below us were Patty's uncle and aunt, Bill and Bootsie. We circled low, then landed on the private airstrip, where a car was waiting for us.

Of W.R.'s five sons, Bill's accommodation to his father's legacy is the most easily understood: he embraces it fully, plays it to the hilt. In this sense, Bill is the perfect Junior, not only in name and appearance, but in his life-style as well, from hobnobbing with heads of state, movie stars, and society people, to his weekly column and its peculiar brand of Hearst Americanism, all the way down to his personalized "W.R. Jr." license plates.

One would have to say that Bill's third wife, Bootsie, is perfect for him. A former society gossip columnist, Bootsie Hearst is a woman of irrepressible energy and larger-than-life, almost theatrical proportions. Up early every morning and exercising for two hours to cassette-tape music with a piece of clear plastic adhesive tape between her eyes to keep from getting "squint lines," she counts Zsa Zsa Gabor among her friends, calls everyone "Dahling," and is an absolutely fearless horseback rider (she was once thrown and fractured her hip, but was back in the saddle before her cast was removed).

Bill and Bootsie are quite a pair and it was always pleasantly unreal to visit them at San Simeon—driving up the long winding road to the gleaming white castle, poking through the huge warehouses crammed with the remains of W.R.'s possessions, most of which hadn't seen the light of day since they were crated some forty years before, going for wild horseback rides with Bootsie through the surrounding countryside, playing tag in the Neptune pool under the eye of Grecian statues, blowing the dust off a bottle of 1824 Burgundy in the castle's wine cellar, and on this particular occasion having a picnic on the lawn behind the large Victorian ranch house, the oldest dwelling at San Simeon and a spot that had once been the very heart of Hearstdom.

In 1865 George Hearst and his young bride Phoebe had built the ranch house on 48,000 acres, purchased after George had struck it rich in the Homestake Mines. They had each planted an acorn—now two enormous oak trees—to symbolize their marriage, and every year they made the journey by carriage from San Francisco with their only child, William. In the spring, when the weather was good and the countryside green, the family would often mount extravagant expeditions, complete with tents and an entourage of servants, up to the hills above the ranch house for a day of picnicking. As the story goes, little W.R. dreamed of building a castle on "Picnic Hill" someday. Fifty years later he did just that, as well as expanding the ranch to nearly a half-million acres. After his death in 1951, however, the Hearst holdings at San Simeon were gradually reduced to their present size of 80,000 acres, the hilltop castle and grounds being given to the State Parks Service in 1957.

Sitting on the lawn, the castle shimmering in the distance, our picnic group that day reflected the life-style, attitudes, and interplay between the third- and fourth-generation Hearsts. There were no more tents or servants now, but Styrofoam coolers and aluminum tables and chairs set up on the wide lawn. Ever the bustling organizer, Bootsie took charge of things, seeing to it that everyone was seated in order of seniority. "Oh, no, Dahling," she said to me when I started to sit down, "that's Catherine's seat. Your place is over here"—at the end of the table.

After the picnic ended, Bootsie insisted on taking the group on a tour of the ranch house which was being renovated by the Corporation under her direction. A beautiful two-story building with twelve-foot ceilings, tall windows, and wood-paneled rooms, the ranch house had fallen into disrepair in the years following W.R.'s death. At one point during the tour, Patty and I found ourselves alone with Bootsie. Patty said something about how well the renovation was progressing.

"Oh, yes." Bootsie smiled. "We're going to fix it up for the use of V.I.P.s," meaning the friends who so often came to visit her and W.R., Jr., at San Simeon—not the "junior" members of the family.

"Oh," Patty said, "you mean like me?"

"Yes, Dahling," Bootsie said icily.

On the flight back Patty took this up with her father. "I don't see why we can't use the ranch house sometimes too."

"You're goddamned right," Mr. Hearst said. "If the grandchildren don't have the right to something like that, nobody does. Bill gets up there on that hill and he thinks the Old Man's talking to him."

Of all the sons, Randy is probably the best put together, the least affected by both his position and his heritage. The oldest son, George Hearst, was severely affected by his unusual upbringing. An obese man, he went through seven wives and died in 1972 leaving daughter Phoebe and son George, Jr. (who runs the *Los Angeles Herald-Examiner*), both part of the archconservative wing of the family. The middle son, John Hearst, a bit of a playboy, died in 1958, his children representing the prodigal wing of the family —one daughter running off with an entire mariachi band, another marrying a dogcatcher who was later found trying to "catch" deer at San Simeon. David Hearst, Randy's twin brother, is the nominal director of the Hearst Corporation, but, as Patty used to tell me, "has a thing about his father," stays out of both family and Corporation affairs almost entirely, and refuses to go to San Simeon. This leaves W.R., Jr., firmly and happily ensconced at the castle, and Randy, a down-to-earth man who appears to be the only exception in a group of rather odd characters. And yet his statement to

Patty about the rights of the "grandchildren"—not *his* children, but his father's grandchildren—is an indication that like his brothers he too operates with the Old Man's gaze upon him.

It was this second-generation attitude of subtle obeisance to the memory of "The Chief" that was at the heart of Patty's disaffection with being a Hearst and came to be part of her character. As one of the grandchildren she was made acutely aware of what it meant to be an heir, which in some ways was more oppressive than the actual demands made of her. Viewed in this light, then, I don't think Patty's plan to change her name was really an expression of disgust for Hearstdom per se, but for "heirdom" and all the expectations and assumptions that went with it. But whatever the case, while most of the other family members accepted their role as heirs and lived within its boundaries, Patty did not. She resisted it, especially when it came to her parents.

"The rich are very different from you and me," F. Scott Fitzgerald once told Hemingway. "Yes," Hemingway responded, "they have more money." In Patty's eyes, particularly when I first met her, this was all her parents had, except for the self-consciousness of being Hearsts. To her mind they had opted for a rather mundane existence. They lived sheltered, uneventful lives, had no genuine interest in art or culture, and no appetite for social gatherings. They were first and foremost Hearsts, and this drove Patty crazy. She had little patience with their concern about maintaining old Hearst privileges and traditions and preserving the old Hearst hierarchy. Her irritation with these things comes out clearly in that same tape-recorded letter she made at age seventeen for her sister Anne. In it she describes how the caretaker of Wyntoon, Bob Purdy, threw some friends of a nonfamily Corporation Trustee off the ranch:

> We went up there (Wyntoon) three weeks ago and this really nice guy, Mike Peterson, and four friends—long hair, but really nice . . . anyway, Bob Purdy was giving this guy, Mike, all this trouble and about three weeks ago he told Mike's friends that they had to be off the ranch in thirty minutes or he'd throw them all in jail because Bob's a sheriff also, aside from being the caretaker of that place. . . .

This is all well and good except that you have to under-stand that Mike Peterson's father is not only editor of *Good Housekeeping* magazine, but he's also a Trustee of the Hearst Corporation, which is what Dad is also. Now since Wyntoon is Corporation-owned, that means that Mike and his friends can come up there anytime they want to. They have every right to be there and Bob Purdy had *no* right to tell them to get off the ranch.

Anyway, I told this to Dad and of course he got really mad at the idea that, you know, that it was Corporation-owned. He was saying things like: "Well you know the other men [trus-tees] are polite enough not to go up there." Like this should be reserved *only* for Hearsts. As a matter of fact, it's not *like* he was saying that, he *was* saying that. He said, "Well, your grandfather built it and we're the only ones that belong up there." . . . The Hierarchy . . .

It is important, here, to take the Hearstdom/Heirdom distinc-tion one step further: while Patty was disgusted with the idea that growing up as a Hearst was to grow up with a place in the "hier-archy," she was at the same time proud of the achievements of her forebears. Ironically, she was unable to go a single day without being reminded of both. On the Berkeley campus alone there were the George Hearst Mining and Engineering Building, the Phoebe Apperson Hearst Gymnasium, and the William Randolph Hearst Greek Theater, monuments to her family's illustrious history. But there were also the reminders of the way things were now—Hearst business announcements that would appear in our mailbox, state-ments to sign, monthly allowance checks that came not from home, but from a Corporation bookkeeper in Los Angeles, as well as all the warnings and concerns she heard so often. "They'll take you because of your name," her father used to tell her, referring to potential kidnappers. The worry was real to Randy, having grown up with two bodyguards during the Lindbergh era. But not to Patty. She would scoff at these concerns, claiming that her parents were just overprotective and paranoid. "Because I'm a Hearst I have to have two million dollars' worth of car insurance," she said wearily one day. But these irritations were relatively minor compared to the very real pressures Patty felt to have a career and a life within the Hearst business sphere.

Of all the Hearst girls, it was Patty who pretty much bore the brunt of her parents', and especially her father's, expectations. Catherine had been seriously ill as a child, was frail as an adult, and had gone into religious work. Gina had not distinguished herself as a student and until recently had shown little interest in a career of any kind. Anne was something of a problem child at that time, and Vicky was simply too young to consider. So it was Patty who naturally seemed, by her character, strength, and intellect —and in the absence of a Hearst son—to be the one to carry on the family tradition. Aside from these qualities, she also had the most generous helping of old W.R.'s fiber, spirit, independence, and combativeness, which only served to further convince her father that she would bear the family standard. Patty was trapped in a sense. The more resistance, the more "spunk" she showed, the more Mr. Hearst's expectations and hopes for her rose. But to Patty the Corporation was the very incarnation of the second-generation attitude and the hierarchical accommodations she so wished to avoid. I remember her considerable irritation at being greeted by her cousin George, Jr., with: "Say hello to your Uncle George" —a none too subtle reminder that he was some twenty years her senior and thus occupied a higher place in the Hierarchy. "He knows damn well that I'm his cousin," she said to me as George was walking off.

All of this then, the reminders, the expectations, and the inbred seniority system, was enough to convince Patty at an early age that she wanted no part of the Hearst organization and its perquisites—she wanted desperately to make it on her own. When she was sixteen she decided that she wanted to be a veterinarian. A few years later she took biology courses at Menlo College and, encouraged by her good grades, told her parents of her plans. They were not enthusiastic. Nothing could be further from *their* plans. Adamantly refusing her mother's offer to help in getting into U.C., Patty began a biological sciences program at Berkeley, but at the end of two mediocre quarters, began to realize that her talents lay in the humanities, not in science and math. Her parents were relieved. Patty was back into English and art history, something "useful," something that could be applied to Hearst newspaper or magazine work.

And yet had Patty been of a different temperament, had she been less stubborn and more philosophical, she might have been able to slough off her parents' attitudes. But she could not. Her hackles would go up at the slightest provocation. It was not in her nature to try to mollify anyone, least of all her parents. In view of this it is open to question whether Patty was totally justified in her discontent, and whether by that discontent she aggravated the problem. But what is undeniable is that Patty felt suffocated by her family and the Corporation, the borders of which literally stretched all over the world and well into both the past and the future.

So despite my vague, unfocused awareness of this, it was not until those first few weeks in Hillsborough, when I too found myself caught in the wheels of that rather odd machine, and discovered firsthand that there was indeed suffocation, that I realized I had not given Patty's complaints a fair hearing. Because I was an outsider from the Hearsts' world, and what they considered *their* problem, my first attempts to take part had been squelched. There were many times when Mr. Hearst would ignore my suggestions or simply blow up, times when Mrs. Hearst would look right through me, that I felt like shouting that I had only one Patty and they had five daughters. But I didn't.

The Hearsts were not ultimately to blame for my frustration, of course, nor my feelings of helplessness. I knew that. It was the SLA with their impossible demands and their terrible cruelty. It was the irrational situation, the steadily mounting pressure, and my own confusion and indecision about what the next course of action should be. All I could do was bear it, hoping that Mr. Hearst's approach would prove successful. But then came the bitter February 20 communiqué, the PIN riots, and it had become painfully clear that his approach was failing at the seams. Worse, he didn't seem to realize it. It was then and only then that I began to realize the time had come for me to take a stand of my own. When the next tape arrived I did just that and in so doing prepared the way for my exit from the family's good graces, such as they were.

A few days after the Oakland riots, around February 27, Mr. Hearst began "normalizing the house," as he put it. Jan Steers, Swami #3, was the first to go, his departure hastened by an outburst from Jay, which was indicative of the mood around the house at that time.

"Can't you see that you're bothering everyone?" Jay shouted in response to one of Steers's exhortations. "Why can't you just leave us alone?"

Although Steers was hurt, he said nothing, but quietly packed his bags and left later that afternoon. Shortly thereafter the various secretaries took their work to the Examiner Building, the eldest daughter Catherine flew back to Los Angeles, the Cookes stopped coming by every day, and I began staying with relatives and friends, returning to Hillsborough only when necessary. "Hearsts in Seclusion," read the newspapers. Day after day passed with no word from the kidnappers.

On March 3, almost two weeks after the February 20 tape, Mr. and Mrs. Hearst made a plea that Patty be allowed to send them a message, "a note or something to let us know that you're okay," Mr. Hearst said. Mrs. Hearst told her to keep her courage up and pray. "You've never harmed anybody," she said tearfully, "and I know that pretty soon God will touch their [the SLA's] hearts and they'll send you home again."

On March 6, in a letter smuggled to KPFA Remiro and Little stated that if granted a nationally televised news conference they would present a list of proposals that could lead to Patty's release. Alameda Sheriff Frank Madigan took the request under consideration. Still no word from the SLA. By March 8 the third and fourth PIN giveaways had been completed with considerably more success. Still no word.

On the evening of March 9 I was at the Swantons'. We were just finishing dinner when the phone rang. It was one of Patty's old classmates from Crystal calling to tell us that KSAN had just received another tape and was broadcasting it over the radio. Mimi and I sat silently on the couch, braced for the worst, as Scott tuned in the station.

For the most part the tape was unintelligible. Washing in and out of the static came the bitter voice of a woman who identified herself as Gelina, a general in the SLA. For fifteen long minutes she assailed the PIN program, the Hearsts, and the FBI. Although we could not make out much of what she said, her angry, self-righteous tone and her affected ghettoese were enough to tell us that the SLA's position had hardened, if that were possible. "The true meaning of the Hearst empire's sincerity [is] deception and lies," she said. "PIN also tried to sham the people by trying to distribute hog feed. . . . The plans of the police state agency are to see to it that Patricia Hearst is killed and then to use her death to further rally middle America." After demanding to know why the SLA should honor the Hearsts' request to hear from Patty and stating that until Remiro and Little were granted their news conference there would be no further message from Patty, there was a pause, and then Patty's voice.

Although we could only make out bits and pieces of it, there was definitely an angry, accusatory tone to her voice—"Mom, Dad . . . all you want is to hear from me sometimes. . . . I don't know who influenced you not to comply with the good faith gesture. . . . I'm starting to think that no one is concerned about me anymore. . . . I no longer fear the SLA. Only the FBI and certain people in the government stand to gain anything by my death."

What followed was another woman's voice: "Comrade sisters, resistance fighters . . . we women know the truth . . . turn our rage towards the enemy in a direct line down the sights of our guns. Until we meet again may we have a strong back like that of the gravedigger. . . ." And finally Cinque: "I call upon the people to join the Federation . . . answering this call to arms with the sound of your guns and your commitment to save the children."

Scott turned off the radio, then poured me a glass of wine. After the Swantons went to bed, I picked up my journal.

I strongly feel I have to do something now—talk or write through the media and try to influence the SLA even slightly. I feel I will have no credibility with the SLA unless I actively disassociate myself from the Hearsts and the FBI. There are too many elementary things that the SLA does not seem to understand about our efforts and intentions. Perhaps they may listen to me a little, though I have no delusions that I can change their whole outlook.

What followed were four pages of notes, sixteen points that I felt had to be made, and then a postscript to myself: "Perhaps the SLA will be amused by all of this. It remains to be seen if these things that seem so important to me now will later look as feeble as some of the things I thought so important three weeks ago."

After writing I covered myself with a sleeping bag, put in my usual hours of staring at the ceiling, then finally fell asleep.

When I arrived in Hillsborough the next day, the rest of the family had already heard an improved duplicate tape that the SLA had sent to KPFA. I listened to it alone in the library.

Our first impressions were correct. Gelina denounced as cowards and opportunists the various members of the Left who had decried the SLA's tactics and described the "enemy state" as forcing the poor to buy back the goods they themselves had produced with blood. "To this our bullets scream loudly," she almost spat. "The enemy's bloodthirsty greed will be destroyed by the growing spirit of the people and their thirst for freedom." Then she got down to particulars. The Hearsts had avoided making any sizable contribution to PIN, then had sabotaged it by misplacing the food and delaying the delivery trucks. They had shown no regret for their crimes against the people and their well-known lies didn't "make no bag of cabbages into meat." As for the FBI's claims that Patty's safety was foremost in their minds,

The FBI, with the sick permission of [Patty's] parents, willingly and without regret, [will] sacrifice the life of Patricia Hearst in order to attempt to kill the members of the Symbionese Liberation Army.

While Gelina's hateful message could obviously be taken at face value, such was not the case with Patty's eleven-minute statement. There were parts when she was clearly upset, even angry: "You said it was out of your hands; what you should have said was that you wash your hands of it." But then her voice would change to a pleading tone. "It's hard to believe that my sisters and cousins aren't saying anything. Steven, what do you have to say? Willie, I know you really care about me. Make Dad let you talk. Please listen to me because I'm speaking honestly and from the heart."

I just did not know how much of her statement to believe. If all the nonpolitical sentences were taken out and strung together it was definitely Patty. The rest, however—her fear of the FBI, her attacks on the media for portraying her as a "helpless, innocent girl," and her anger at her parents—could have been written by Gelina, or Cinque for that matter. But in spite of its ambiguities, Patty's message confirmed my feelings of the night before: I had to do something.

After listening to the tape I spent much of the day talking to Ludlow Kramer and Peggy Maze of the PIN program, who had come down to Hillsborough, and then joined the Hearsts for dinner, hoping for an auspicious moment in which to catch Mr. Hearst's ear. It was a common saying around the *Examiner* that "the last person to talk to Randy gets his way," as was the observation that "If he's in a good mood you get everything. If he's in a bad mood you get nothing," except, perhaps, a tirade. I had certainly gotten my share of tirades during my stay with the Hearsts and thought it likely that I was in for another one this night. I was about to broach a subject that had become a very sore spot between Mr. Hearst and myself.

For the past three weeks I had been suggesting, then encouraging, and finally bugging Mr. Hearst to clarify his financial position, his "ability to act," which Cinque claimed to understand so well.

At first, I considered it important that we convince the SLA that our two-million-dollar offer was not demeaning: a mere morsel from the banquet table of the Hearst empire. When the angry communiqué of February 20 arrived itemizing Hearst assets, it was clear that the SLA *did* consider the Hearst offer to be offensive. What's more, so much of the SLA information was grossly exaggerated or simply wrong that it cried out for rebuttal. I remember cornering Randy in his bedroom one morning and asking him if he owned any stock in Safeway Stores. He said he didn't know, but was courteous and concerned enough to call his stockbroker, George Mercader, who told Randy that he owned no Safeway. His response to me, "Well, what did you expect?" contained the seeds of bad feeling that would grow between us on the matter of financial disclosure to the SLA. Randy inferred that he was being called to justify himself in front of people who had no right to cast his integrity in doubt and that to ask him to do so was to sympathize with the enemy. Of course, my motives were different: they were to show the SLA's data to be preposterous. Randy would not back down, however, and none of the claims of the February 20 tape were ever countered.

The SLA made good use of Randy's silence: "It is no coincidence that Mr. Hearst has remained silent about his vast interests in Safeway Stores, Inc." The SLA appeared to be furious that the "Hearst empire" had not dignified its claims with a response. "The enemy cannot afford . . . to reveal to the people the total extent of the sum of the wealth that it has robbed from the people."

Finally, in frustration, and left with little else to do, I began looking into the Hearst Corporation myself, if only to better understand Mr. Hearst's position and his reluctance to make that position clear. I read everything on the Hearst empire I could get my hands on, from W. A. Swanberg's *Citizen Hearst* for historical background, to every newspaper and magazine article written on the Hearst conglomerate, a Byzantine arrangement of foundations, trusts, subsidiaries, and interlocking directorships. But it was slow going. Between 1951, the year of W.R.'s death, and the present, there was only a handful of articles on the subject and these were incomplete, oversimplified, and reflected the Hearst empire's long-standing preoccupation with keeping its business affairs under wraps. And then, in the midst of my research, this overriding concern with absolute privacy was brought home to me firsthand, when I asked Helen Mehawk, Mr. Hearst's secretary, if she could get me a copy of W.R.'s will, the founding document, the blueprint of the Hearst Corporation. Assured by her that there would be no problem, I returned the following day to find Mrs. Mehawk looking somewhat chagrined. "You'd better talk with Mr. Hearst," she said, nodding toward his office door. I went in and found him shuffling through a stack of papers. But before I could explain why I wanted to see the will, he shook his head. "You don't have any business looking at that," he said. "Now I'd just as soon you drop the whole thing." He went back to shuffling papers. End of conversation.*

Randy's discouraging my investigation I did not think particularly suspicious. I knew the $2 million figure he had publicly given as his net worth to be essentially accurate; I knew that his ability to push things past the other twelve trustees was already being strained to the limit. Indeed, a week after the March 9 tape Randy came home from a board meeting in New York fuming. Several of the other trustees had begun to have second thoughts about offering an additional $4 million for the return of a girl who was starting to sound ungrateful. They had suggested that a stipulation be added that Patty come home "clearheaded" before the money be released.

In Randy's irritable responses to my urgings, I sensed an element of self-deception—a need to feel that the only real issue was money, that the situation was analogous to a union negotia-

---

* It was about this same time that the 128-page Hearst will—the largest ever filed in California—was, along with seven volumes of probate proceedings, being sequestered by special court order, at the request of the Hearst attorneys and the state attorney general.

tion. For it was Randy who was tortured by the tension of deciding how much to offer in order to get his daughter safely returned. I had no doubt that, if the proper occasion had arisen, Randy would gladly have traded all of his personal wealth to get Patty back. His financial resources were limited—and at least that offered him some solid ground. But to have me hanging at his elbow, pointing out a whole realm of potential SLA humiliating demands that could affect his family, his corporation, and his country was bound to evoke from him another annoyed reaction.

But I was *equally* desperate at how clear the source of the SLA's rage had become, and so there I was that Sunday night, at the dinner table, waiting for the opportunity to try one last time. Although I was prepared for the worst sort of criticism, this night was different, something totally unexpected: not only did Mr. Hearst listen to my suggestions, he agreed with them.

When the meal ended Mr. Hearst and I were sitting alone at the dinner table, the first bottle at our elbows. He asked if I cared for a "splash." I did. We talked a bit, then another splash, then another. Two hours and two bottles later Mr. Hearst and I found ourselves talking like old cronies. We were both a bit drunk by then, and in that common state the differences between us had temporarily disappeared.

These differences, I might add, had been evident from the first day we met. Mr. Hearst, like his father before him, had an instinctive distrust of academics, of "intellectuals" as he called them. He considered me a part of this class and himself a solid American businessman, a pragmatist who didn't mind unwinding with a drink or two after work. There was more than a little truth to these stereotypes. While we were equally miserable over Patty's situation, we expressed it in different ways. After listening to the latest tape, I would sit silently, trying to put every contingency together in my mind before speaking, which meant that I didn't speak much. Mr. Hearst, on the other hand, would often say the first thing that came into his head or fly into rages, sometimes at me. Later, however, he would often regret his outbursts and ask Willie, "Why doesn't he just haul off and belt me when I give him all that crap?" But the upshot of our one-sided confrontations was that he considered me at best bloodless, at worst gutless, and I thought him scattered and irrational.

On this particular night, however, we were both feeling our wine.

" 'Nother splash, Steve?" he asked. We were halfway through our third bottle. "I want you to understand that I have a great deal of respect for PhD's," I remember him saying. "It's just that sometimes I'm hard put to say just what the hell it is they do outside of libraries."

I laughed, then apologized for upsetting Mrs. Hearst and admitted that perhaps I *had* been acting strangely the last few weeks.

"No, I apologize," he said. 'I had no right to fly off the handle like that."

When the conversation circled back to that morning's bitter communiqué, I saw my chance. "Isn't it about time we said a few things to defend the effort we're making?" I asked him, mentioning some of the SLA's latest attacks on "Hearst trickery," the "measley two-million-dollar offer," and the "Hearst Empire's deceit and silence concerning its interests." Bracing myself for an annoyed reaction, I was surprised to hear him agreeing with me: "Maybe you're right, maybe we should say something." A few encouraging minutes of this and the talk went to the PIN program. We rambled on about the riots, the continuing problems that were plaguing the program, then my and others' suggestion that we get it over as soon as possible, using all the remaining money to buy high quality beef and handing it out in one massive distribution. Mr. Hearst nodded. "Looks like that's the way we gotta go, all right," he said and then invited me to accompany him to the next Coalition meeting. I quickly accepted. I did not accept his offer of "another splash," however. I stood up slowly, said good-night, and tottered into the kitchen.

I was listing badly and aiming for the stairs when Gina and Anne happened in. The next thing I knew they had me under both arms and were helping me up the stairs. "Poor old Steve." They laughed, and I laughed too. "Come on, just one more step." In both sisters there were certain looks and speech habits that were

Patty's. I remember thinking of that, then thinking of her, and all the ache and sorrow sunk back into me. "Never drink with my father," Gina scolded me. They eased me down on the bed, took off my shoes, and covered me with a blanket. "Good night, Steve," Anne said quietly and closed the door.

The next morning, showing no signs of the night before, Mr. Hearst stepped out on the porch to answer questions from the press. Visibly angered by one reporter's suggestion that "some people" believed that Patty was a willing participant in her own kidnapping, he responded in characteristic style: "Anyone who listened to her on that first tape and believes she was part of this has got to be a dum-dum. Patty's just a normal kid who has read something besides *Peter Rabbit*."

Answering a question about the PIN program, Mr. Hearst said he had made the mistake of thinking that an ongoing program would be more desirable than one that would be over quickly. He would now attempt to follow the SLA's original instructions to the letter. But from my point of view, the most important statement he made that morning addressed itself to the SLA's exaggerated assessment of his power. "I am only one of thirteen members on the board," he said, "and the Hearst family makes up only five out of the thirteen members. Go read the will of my father filed in 1951 and it can be understood how the Corporation operates."

"Aren't you the chairman of the board?" a reporter asked.

"I am the chairman, but the chairman can't go in and tell the rest of the board what to do. I cannot force them to do anything. I have some influence, but I cannot go up and say, 'This is what you will do.' "

Gina, Jay, and I listened to the press conference on the radio in the front hall. After a few more questions and answers, the big front door opened and Mr. Hearst stepped back inside. I told him that I thought his statement was a good one, though I feared it had come too late, then left the house to meet with newswoman Marilyn Baker to discuss the possibility of my doing a taped interview for KQED. Baker had called earlier and had spoken with

Mr. Hearst, who reluctantly agreed that maybe I too should make a statement, as Patty had asked.

It was around seven o'clock that evening when I returned to the house to find Mr. Hearst and Duane, the FBI agent, talking in the living room. They were discussing the possibility of offering the SLA safe passage out of the country *if* Patty was released, a suggestion that had come out of a meeting Mr. Hearst had had with a convicted murderer called "Death Row Jeff." An hour before, Mr. Hearst had returned from Vacaville prison, this the first in a series of secret meetings with Jeff, who claimed to be the founder of the SLA. He had in fact been visited in 1973 by several SLA members and had exchanged cryptic letters with Willie Wolfe and Russell Little up until the week of Marcus Foster's assassination. Despite this, however, Mr. Hearst had his doubts about Jeff's credibility. "Hell, I don't know if the guy's got any clout or not," I remember him saying. Still, he was definitely interested in Jeff's idea of offering the SLA a plane out of the country. Duane, on the other hand, was at best lukewarm.

"The Bureau cannot make a public statement insuring these people safe passage," he said. "In this case the SLA would just have to settle for a gentleman's agreement."

There was something so patently absurd about this that I couldn't help butt in. "A gentleman's agreement between the SLA and the FBI?" I asked incredulously. "Do you seriously think . . . ?

"And if they refuse," Duane continued, "we'll just have to go in and take her out by force."

"Go in and take her out? Maybe I'm missing something, but . . ."

"You are *not* part of this conversation, Steve," Duane said. "I am talking with Mr. Hearst." I glared at him but realized there was nothing to be gained by getting in a fight with an FBI agent in the Hearsts' living room. Mr. Hearst said nothing. Shaking with anger, I got up and left the room. It was obvious that the FBI's concern for Patty's safety was giving way to their concern about their already tarnished image in the case.

At two o'clock the following afternoon I walked down what was becoming a well-beaten path across the back lawn and through the side gate. Waiting for me in her car, the collar of her trench coat turned up, her jaw firmly set, was Marilyn Baker. "Just be careful what you say to that woman," Mr. Hearst had warned me as I was leaving. I should have heeded his advice.

The interview was held in a comfortable home in San Mateo, a suburban community just south of Hillsborough. The video tape machine was set up in the living room. Marilyn and I took our seats by the fireplace, and the cameraman cued us. The questioning began.

She asked me about Patty's apparent fear of an FBI break-in. Could the Bureau be trusted *not* to break in?

"To a point. I do not believe the FBI wants Patty to die, but I think the SLA would be wrong to trust them entirely."

What about the sessions between the FBI and Mr. Hearst? Are they productive?

"Unfortunately, they're almost comical. Mr. Bates comes in and sits down. He's poured a drink, then Mr. and Mrs. Hearst and whoever just sit down and chat. The comical part about it is how adept Mr. Bates is at not telling us anything." So much for the FBI.

What about Mr. Hearst? Did I agree with his handling of the matter?

"Actually we disagreed somewhat over the importance of divulging his finances. He did not seem to understand how people, very intelligent people, could fail to understand his financial status. One of the problems, though, is that Mr. Hearst is getting too much advice—from friends, relatives, the authorities, even the cook."

And Mrs. Hearst. How did I view her voting record on the Board of Regents?

"Neither Patty nor I would have appointed her. And we certainly would never have voted, in almost all cases, the way she voted."

So much for Mrs. Hearst. Now it was my turn.

"Would you be willing to act as a substitute hostage?" Baker asked.

The question caught me by surprise. When Russell Little's father had offered to take Patty's place, I thought the offer, while well intentioned, was pretty foolish; that is, it would be laughed at by the SLA. But in answering Baker's question I looked worse than foolish.

"It uh . . . it depends on the circumstances," I said. "I wouldn't rule it out."

"What do you have to say to Patty?"

"I . . . I want to tell her to try to hold on as she has been. I want to see her. . . ."

"Thank you for talking with us," Ms. Baker said coolly. The camera clicked off.

Even before I saw the edited version of the interview at the KQED studios, I had the sinking feeling that I had blown it. Because the Hearsts' credibility with the SLA had hit rock bottom, it had been my plan to actively disassociate myself from them and from the FBI. It had not been my plan to be gratuitously insulting, however, and yet that is exactly what I was, even managing to offend Emmy, the cook, with a careless remark. Under the TV lights I was less conscious of Baker's presence than the collective eye of the SLA. I knew they were watching, and in my nervousness I could think of no other way to ingratiate myself with the SLA than to belittle the Hearsts and FBI. What's worse I was certain that my ploy had been obvious, that the SLA and everyone else would see through it. No one saw through it. The following was typical of the avalanche of disapproving mail my interview prompted:

To see you on TV made me sick. Why in the Cockeye world don't you get a man's haircut and stop complaining about the Hearsts? As for the FBI I see nothing at all comical about Mr. Bates. He's doing everything in his power to bring your finance [sic] back while you sit around on TV. Cut off the g-d moustache or trim it.

Aside from Willie and Gina, Mr. Hearst was the only one who understood what I had tried to do—partially, perhaps because I had forewarned him. Upon my arrival at Hillsborough that night he opened the door. "Go say hello to Catherine," he half joked. "I thought you did all right. But when they ask you if you want to say anything to Patty, tell her you love her." It wasn't an order so much as puzzlement that I hadn't, that I had missed what in retrospect was the most important reason I should have agreed to the interview.

Catherine was indeed furious. The next morning I got up early to accompany Mr. Hearst to the Coalition meeting and found her and Phoebe Cooke in the kitchen talking about the "despicable things" I had said in the interview. Although I was standing only five feet away they continued, referring to me in the third person. "He's despicable," Phoebe said. "His smoking marijuana, selling it at Princeton." Apparently the FBI had discussed my interview with the Hearsts. At that point Mr. Hearst entered, his mood considerably changed from the night before. He ushered them out of the room, then returned. "There's really no point to your coming to the Coalition meeting," he said, then left. I was still standing there when Emmy passed through. "You didn't say anything nice to Patty." She frowned.

That was it. Everyone, from the master of the house to the family cook, had pretty much had it with me. I went to get my things.

As I was leaving, overnight bag in hand, Duane stepped out of the library. "Remember you have a sodium pentothal test on Saturday in Berkeley," he said.

I told him I'd be at the PIN warehouse.

"We've got a man flying up from L.A. for this thing. We'll call you Friday to double-check."

I resisted an impulse to tell Duane what the Bureau could do with its sodium pentothal test and went out the door.

6

It was march thirteenth when I backed my car out the horse-shoe drive, past the wrought-iron gates in front of the Hillsborough house, and headed down tree-lined Santa Inez. Eight days later, bumping over railroad tracks, passing grimy factories, lunch stands, and the lines of truck-trailers in San Francisco's industrial area, I pulled up in front of the China Basin warehouse. I was about to become involved in the PIN food program and was slated to work the midnight to seven shift.

If the Hillsborough home was the command post in the early stages of the operation, the facilities in the China Basin warehouse were the front lines, and I was like some green recruit. In my four days and nights with the PIN program, I was to see and learn about tragicomedy on a grand scale. I was only one of a cast of thousands, an incredible coming together of the dedicated and the selfless, the strange and bizarre, and the outright insane. There were pimps and city officials, housewives and ex-cons, along with society matrons, Mission Street winos, private detectives, body-guards, and even a contingent of burly Samoans. There was every sort of person imaginable working, sleeping, laughing, shouting, and cursing inside that cavernous, dimly lit building. The atmosphere was charged with energy and emotion, conflict and co-operation. And outside, all over the Bay Area, were the tens of thousands of people who would wait in long lines for their bag of groceries from the China Basin warehouse. On one hand, PIN was an enormous happening, a dance of the lunatics; on the other, it was a tragedy, a tale of wasted effort, disappointment, and dashed hopes.

The program had been struggling along for four chaotic weeks before I appeared on the scene, and, while I could have involved myself in that struggle, I did not. From the outset, from the day of its announcement, I feared that such a huge, hastily organized operation was destined to fail, perhaps to collapse altogether. The outbreak of rioting in Oakland during the first food giveaway realized my fears. Apart from my generally weakened physical and emotional condition, I was so specifically depressed by the hopelessness of the situation that I simply was not up to dissecting PIN's corpse, nor to involving myself in its resurrection. The mechanics of the program—answering telephones, stacking crates of onions, loading trucks—all the physical activity seemed to have so little to do with my belief that Patty was locked and blindfolded in a room somewhere. Her fate seemed to depend entirely on some cruel or insane whim of the SLA or the blind luck of the FBI.

But then the bitter March 9 tape: "I don't know who influenced you not to comply with the good faith gesture," Patty had said. "So far it sounds like you and your advisers have managed to turn it into a real disaster." With this it was suddenly clear that PIN and all the mechanics involved in revamping it had everything to do with Patty. Despite her captors' original four-hundred-million-dollar demand and their denunciation of PIN, it still appeared that they were looking to a successful food program as the only way out for them and for Patty.

A few days later, Jay telephoned me in San Francisco and asked me to round up as many people as I could to work in the warehouse. He explained that the entire operation had been reorganized, primarily by Mr. Hearst who, despite legal restrictions and against the advice of some of his advisors, had stepped in and taken charge. Experts had been called in, security guards had been hired, and friends and family members were massing for one final, improved food giveaway. I told Jay that I could come up with at least ten dependable volunteers, then hung up and started dialing. After calling everyone I could think of (fellow philosophy students, friends, and friends of friends), the next night, March 21, I climbed into my car and headed for the China Basin warehouse.

I parked next to a row of rusting boxcars, jogged across the rain-slick parking lot, and ducked in the door to find the entranceway jammed with volunteers. Aside from those I had called, it was wall to wall with an amazing cross section of people. A Hillsborough housewife, dressed in jeans and a Stanford sweatshirt, was chatting cheerfully with her two teen-age daughters, while behind her three women in tight satin dresses and spike heels were laughing with a grizzled old black man in a Goodwill overcoat. A couple of boys in high school lettermen's sweaters stood silently in the corner, beside them an elderly Chicano woman sitting sound asleep on the Naugahyde couch, her shoes in her lap. All of them had come to work in the warehouse, packaging goods, bagging vegetables for the last People In Need giveaway.

After greeting my friends, I made my way to the door leading to the suite of offices and looked inside. It was a scene of barely controlled pandemonium—jangling phones, people rushing around the desks, checking and double-checking their instructions—and above it all a large poster of Patty that had been thumbtacked to the wall. "She is what this is all about," read the handwritten caption below it.

"People, make sure you have all signed in with the guard here," I heard somebody say and turned to see a warehouseman in a knit cap standing on his tiptoes to be heard above the crowd.

A few minutes later, around midnight, the work shift changed. "Give them room," the warehouseman called out as a hundred tired volunteers began filing out of the warehouse, some carrying large boxes of food. Then those of us who had been waiting moved one by one past the security guard, giving our names before moving into the warehouse proper. Because it was dark outside and the concrete interior of the warehouse was lighted only in the work areas, the place had a subterranean atmosphere that made the group instinctively huddle together as the warehouseman led us past stacks of pallets, crates of produce, and cases of meat. Suddenly a horn blared out and a few people jumped out of the way of a forklift that came wheeling around the corner, driven by one of the shaven-headed members of the Delancey Street organization, a halfway house for ex-cons.

"If I can have your attention, people," the warehouseman shouted above the whine of the retreating forklift. He told us that we would be divided into three main groups: the vegetable brigade, the meat-packers, and the assembly line workers. Three volunteers who had been working since 7:00 A.M. then led the groups to their respective areas and began instructing them on the procedures. I found myself with the meat-packers. Our instructor, a tired but patient middle-aged man, a butcher who had taken a week off work to help PIN, lined us up along the assembly line and showed us how to break down the 100-pound cases of frozen meat. "Watch your fingers," he warned, holding up a mashed thumbnail, then demonstrated which and how many pieces of meat were to be put in plastic bags, and how many bags were to go into each box. A man sidled up to me. "Ain't you Patty's fiancé?" he asked quietly. When I told him I was, he nodded. "I think this is gonna work out for her," he said, patting me on the back.

"And if you have to use the bathroom," the butcher was saying, "it's way over there, the first door past the garbage pile." Everyone turned to look past the garbage pile, a huge avalanche of empty crates, rotten produce, and trash. "Any questions?" There were no questions. "Then let's do it."

With that the work began. Forklifts and hand dolleys were used to haul the crates of vegetables and cases of meat from one side of the loading dock to the work areas where they were broken down, packaged, then moved to the final assembly line to be boxed.

At the end of the line two women sealed the boxes with a tape machine, then pasted an SLA sticker on the sides. From there the boxes were loaded onto empty trailer-trucks, which all night backed in and pulled out with their cargo. Three security men patrolled the dock, smoking cigarettes, waving the trucks in, then watching them move out into the darkness.

Except for two ten-minute breaks and a half hour off for "lunch," the work went on without interruption until seven the next morning. There was at once a sense of urgency, esprit de corps, and friendly rivalry among the three main groups. Throughout the night there were calls for "Oranges! We need oranges over here!" "Ham! We're running out of ham!" "Hey, where's the goddamn onions?" Every so often someone from the vegetable brigade would sneak into the meat-packing camp and tell us we were dogging it.

"We're doing two bags of veggies for every one of your meat bags," one infiltrator said, grinning and shaking his head.

"We're hung up on ham, man," came the answer from a huge Samoan on the line next to me. He had an SLA sticker pasted to his forehead. "The forklift crew's holdin' up our ham," he explained, "and our main ham man here just bashed his thumb righteous." I had. A couple hours later I bashed it again.

By 3:00 A.M. the warehouse had grown cold and damp. People were working in their jackets, some of the women wrapping their feet in plastic bags to keep warm. By then fatigue was setting in and a few people were running around shouting giddily. Still the work continued at an amazing pace amidst the roar of forklifts and trucks firing up, the shouted instructions, the laughter and the groans as another pallet of food was wheeled up to the assembly line. By the time the midnight shift was over, four hours later, everyone was tired and dirty. As we filed out of the door and into the entranceway, the same warehouseman handed out chits that were good for one box of food. Many of the volunteers did not take them; those who did deserved them.

"What's it like in there?" I heard a young man ask from the crowd waiting for the morning shift.

"Don't let the forklift crew short ya on ham," the Samoan

said, sounding very much like the seasoned veteran.

Outside, I thanked my friends for helping out, then drove to Ed Stow's apartment. An old friend of mine from Princeton, Ed had been gone for a few days and had left me his key. I let myself in, collapsed on the couch, then made an entry in my journal before trying to get some sleep.

> I've just returned from the warehouse, am beat to hell but feel-
> ing good for the first time in nearly two months. Overall I'm
> quite optimistic that Patty will be released. At this point it
> seems only a matter of time and that thought, if not good, is
> better than any others I've had so far.

My optimism that morning, based on the good feelings and the sense of accomplishment that had pervaded the warehouse, was short-lived. In the narrow perspective of that night, I actually believed that the PIN program had recovered from most of its problems. But I was dead wrong. In reality PIN's fate had been sealed four weeks earlier by the rioting in Oakland. "Black people have lost more dignity today than they've gained in ten years," said a black leader in the wake of the riots. This loss of dignity was highlighted by the press who had trained their cameras on con-venient racial stereotypes—the young punks pushing through the food lines, the drunks trying to sell their food for wine money, and the flashy dudes loading up their Cadillacs with PIN boxes. All of this could produce nothing but rage in the SLA. They claimed "their" program had been sabotaged, resulting in the arrest, injury, and degradation of the people. "The people can never expect the enemy to feed them," Gelina said on the March 9 tape. "I call upon the people to shed no more blood of the innocent, but rather to bring death to the makers of fear," said Cinque. This was the last time the PIN program was even to be mentioned by the SLA. They buried it.

My first inkling of the internal strife and confusion in the operation came four days after the Oakland riots, when I talked briefly in the Hearsts' living room with Ludlow Kramer and Peggy Maze, the leaders of the PIN program. The week had obviously taken its toll on both of them, especially Kramer. He already looked defeated—tired, haggard, his hand shaking when he sipped from a glass of water on the coffee table between us. And yet just six days before they were brimming with confidence. As Washington State's secretary of state, Kramer was variously described as "a human dynamo who does everything from climbing mountains to building houses with his bare hands." Maze's praises were more subdued. She was the head of "Neighbors In Need" (NIN), a highly successful program to help feed Washington's poor and needy. Both of them had been in Olympia, the state capital, and after discussing the Hearst food program, Maze had her assistant, Pat Colton, call Charles Gould and offer their help. The offer was gratefully accepted, and a few days later Kramer and Maze flew to San Francisco. After consulting with Mr. Hearst, they held their first press conference in front of the Hillsborough house. Kramer did most of the talking. He spoke forcefully, punctuating his speech by pounding an invisible podium with his fist. "We are the technicians," he said. "The coalition is in effect the executive board. Our job is to start hard and fast. We don't have time for standards. We want to feed people."

The following day, Wednesday, February 20, temporary headquarters for the PIN program were set up in the Hearst Building in San Francisco. Thirty volunteers were flooded with incoming calls from food suppliers, truck drivers, housewives, and students, all offering help. The place was a madhouse. "People ask when we are going to get organized," Peggy Maze said to a reporter. "Well, we *are* organized. This is it. We're used to operating under crisis conditions."

Maze was right about the crisis conditions, but wrong about there being any kind of organization whatsoever. Answering two phones at once, the volunteers furiously scribbled down names, addresses and offers, but no one seemed to know how to coordinate the donations. "Twenty thousand people will be fed by Friday," Kramer announced confidently, adding that a million dollars' worth of food had already been donated to the program. Much to his chagrin, this figure was almost immediately revised downward to $150,000. (The actual figure was considerably less.) It was soon discovered that Kramer's other claims about the amount of warehouse space available, the number of volunteers signed up, the trucks and other equipment supposedly donated had to be similarly revised, downward. In short, neither Kramer, Maze, nor anyone else had any real idea of what they had, where it was going, when it could be expected to arrive, and who would be there to distribute it. PIN was twenty-four hours away from its first food giveaway and confusion reigned supreme.

Upon this scene came one Charlie Walker, a black trucker and a real wheeler-dealer (whose company has since been the subject of a grand jury probe). Walker had some friends to introduce to the increasingly desperate Kramer, the Black Muslims of Shabazz Enterprises, who had the trucks, manpower, distribution sites, and even some of the food. Kramer and Maze went for it, unaware that the Muslims were no better prepared for the giveaway than they were. The outcome was inevitable—Oakland exploded.

"We tried the impossible and it nearly worked," Kramer said the following morning. He was badly shaken by the fiasco and, although he tried to bounce back and maintain his "action-man" image, never regained his balance; he never had time.

That same afternoon Charlie Walker and his two Muslim friends paid Kramer another visit. They were extremely well dressed, extremely polite, and impossible to put off. Unnerved by their presence, Kramer kept them waiting outside his door for two hours, hoping they would just go away. They did not go away. They had come to inquire about PIN's insurance, claiming they had lost food and sustained damages to their warehouse to the tune of $99,000. Kramer blanched. He explained that there must have been some misunderstanding. PIN had no insurance. There was no misunderstanding, Walker said firmly. Peggy Maze had assured them that the program did have insurance, and the community would not be very pleased to hear that Kramer and Maze had lied.

It was two days later that I was sitting across the coffee table from Kramer and Maze in Hillsborough. Kramer mentioned the $99,000.

"What are you going to do?" I asked.

"We've already paid them," he said. "We were threatened. They were going to disrupt future distributions if we didn't."

That's about all Kramer would tell me that afternoon. A few minutes later Mr. Hearst called him and Maze into the den, leaving me confused and further disheartened.

In the week following the first disastrous giveaway, there was an attempt to reorganize the program from the ground up. Meanwhile another group entered the picture, the Western Addition Project Area Committee (WAPAC), presided over by a very big, very tough black man named Arnold Townsend. Like many other community groups, WAPAC was federally funded, having been established in the mid-sixties by the Economic Opportunities Council to organize San Francisco's Western Addition for community action. Unlike most of these groups, however, from the outset, from the first SLA communiqué demanding a food program, WAPAC had publicly announced that they would accept food from the Hearst program. The SLA had immediately responded on the February 20 tape by requesting that WAPAC head the previously named coalition with full veto power. A few days later WAPAC accepted. Holding a press conference in a vacant lot, Townsend said that his organization was interested only in feeding the people. "We don't talk about the kidnapping or the SLA," he said. But behind him, spray-painted on the side of a building was, "SLA Power!" and "SLA Feeds People!" Later, an abandoned SLA hideout was discovered in the Western Addition.

Rumor had it that the SLA was angered by the Reverend Cecil Williams's statements that he would act as a mediator between them and the Hearst family. They knew of his private meetings with Mr. Hearst and, through an intermediary, ordered him out of the program. Whether or not this rumor had any foundation in fact, it was obvious to anyone who heard the February 20 communiqué that the SLA was indeed unhappy with

Williams. In it, Cinque specifically demanded that the coalition was *not* to act as mediator, which was clearly a slap in the face of the Reverend Cecil and his well-publicized pronouncements. So whatever the case, WAPAC's entrance on the scene marked Williams's exit. The limelight was now on Arnold Townsend.

In line with the reorganization plans, on Sunday, February 24, Kramer and Maze met with the coalition to nail down the details of the next distribution. It did not go well. The coalition's first order of business was to force Kramer to publicly accept responsibility for the first disastrous giveaway. Kramer tried to sidestep this by persuading the coalition to take responsibility for choosing, operating, and providing security for the next distribution sites. The coalition refused, and a minor shouting match ensued. Finally John McLean of the American Indian Movement (AIM) intervened between Kramer and his fellow coalition members. He reiterated the duties that had been agreed upon at the Hilton Hotel meeting: Mr. Hearst was to provide the money; PIN, under the directorship of Kramer and Maze, was to purchase and distribute the food; and the coalition was to observe and report. Period. Then Townsend spoke up, or rather laid down the law. The coalition rejected absolutely Kramer and Maze's "supplementary approach," namely supplementing people's diet with seven dollars' worth of food per month for a year, as opposed to the SLA's demand that seventy dollars' worth of food be handed out over a one-month period. The coalition, Townsend said, didn't give a damn about Kramer and Maze's "detailed comparison" between their program and the SLA's. They were doing it the SLA's way. Another period. At this Kramer and Maze sputtered a protest, turned and marched out of the room, drove to the airport, and flew all the way back to Washington. Thus ended PIN's first reorganization meeting.

Kramer and Maze were still in Washington, steadying their nerves no doubt, when, during the second week of the operation, the PIN headquarters were being moved from the Hearst Building to the China Basin warehouse. In the absence of Kramer and Maze, PIN's executive secretary was left to manage things. Her name, Sara Jane Moore. Having involved herself in the program because "God sent me," Sara was shrill, abrasive, and totally unpredictable. It is a telling fact that she was also, given the confusion she found in the new facility, one of the most competent people to walk into the huge warehouse.

Donated by the city, the administrative offices in the China Basin warehouse had recently been repainted, new equipment installed, and expensive graphics hung on the walls to entice prospective rentees. But when Sara Jane arrived, she found the place in a state of total disarray. The walls were smeared and dirty, the graphics stolen, and there was garbage everywhere. In short, the offices had become a crash pad for anyone who walked in off the street. The smell of marijuana filled the air; people were lying on the floor in sleeping bags; and winos were slumped in the alcove. When Sara tried to move them out and lock the offices, she was confronted by a long-haired kid of sixteen. "Hey, that's elitism, lady," he told her. Finally she got the warehouse guards to usher the crashers out the door.

But this did not end it. The next morning she returned to find all of the volunteers, among them Mike, the twenty-two-year-old warehouse foreman, huddled around a secretary who was coming down off a drug trip. The secretary, it turned out, had been in a mental hospital and was currently an outpatient.

"It's been like this all night," Mike told Sara. "She started coming down last night."

"We've got to get her out of here," Sara snapped. "Deliveries are scheduled; food has to be packed. We can't let the whole program come to a grinding halt while we wet-nurse Nancy."

"People like Nancy is what this program is about," Mike said.

"No, it's not. We're here to get Patty Hearst out."

Sara took Nancy into the next room.

"I don't want to hurt the program," Nancy said. "If I'm hurting the program, I want to go."

"Nancy, you are hurting the program."

"I don't want to go," Nancy began to sob.

Now Mike entered the room.

"Get out there and get those people to work," Sara told him.

"I can't leave Nancy. Nancy needs me."

"If I'm a detriment to the program, I'll leave," Nancy continued to sob.

Sara finally called an ambulance, but Nancy refused to leave in it. A volunteer took her home.

Two days later Mike burst into the office shouting hysterically, then began to cry. Sara called Kramer in Washington and was told to get rid of him.

"But who's going to run the warehouse? We've got forty people out there and none of them know what they're doing."

"Just do the best you can," Kramer said and hung up.

The day after Sara Jane had arrived, a private detective walked into the warehouse and introduced himself to her. His name, amazingly, was Jack Webb. Hired as a "letter bomb expert" after the amount of hate mail addressed to PIN became disconcerting, Webb was unaware that he was soon to become the program's new head of security. And if his Levi's, cowboy boots, and work shirt did not fit the private eye image, his background most certainly did. A tall, rangy Irishman in his forties, Webb was a twenty-year veteran of the San Francisco Police force who had been shot, stabbed and, on one occasion, tear-gassed by his own department. If you wanted to know what was coming down in the Fillmore, the Tenderloin, any part of the city you asked Jack Webb. He knew every hustler, shakedown artist, and stoolie on the street and they knew him. What's more they liked him.

Jack Webb was not a man easily unnerved, but what he encountered in the parking lot at the China Basin warehouse gave him pause. In the empty stall next to his car, a six-foot-eight mental case, calling himself Pablo Neruda St. John, was chanting, shaking his jewelry and the garlic cloves that decorated his poncho, and doing a war dance around a campfire on the asphalt. The scene inside the warehouse was not much more encouraging. Webb entered to find three Pinkerton guards watching the rear door, while a fourth loaded his car with cases of frozen meat. The night before another "Pink" had turned in his pistol and scurried off because he feared for his safety. His fears were not groundless. Moving through the crowd of volunteers, Webb spotted at least a dozen he knew both personally and from mugshots. Many of them had, as Webb told me, "heard the candy store was open," and were moving as much food as they could carry out the door. A forklift driver pulled up behind him and jumped down smiling.

"Hiya, Jack. Want me to send a couple cases of chicken out to your place?"

If Webb's problems multiplied in the following weeks, one distraction disappeared. Pablo Neruda St. John was arrested a few days later for dancing with a dog.

By the time Kramer and Maze returned on Wednesday, February 27, the operation at China Basin had been tightened up considerably. Ten distribution sites were announced in the papers, and Thursday morning, under gray, drizzling skies, the trucks began pulling away from the warehouse. For the most part they reached their destinations on time and delivered the bags of groceries. Unfortunately, some of the sites ran out of food before they were scheduled to close and many people had to return home empty-handed and disappointed. The next morning Kramer announced to the press that PIN had proved to the SLA that "Damn it, the system works!"

Kramer was ignoring serious problems in the system. At Grove Street and the Sacred Heart Church, two sites in the Fillmore under the direction of WAPAC, groups of street people threatened to empty the food banks before the giveaway began. The call went out for help and within minutes Arnold Townsend and some of his men were moving the people back and restoring order. "They worked their asses off," one volunteer said. "Risked their lives too. I mean there were guns in that crowd."

There were problems at Norman Johnson's West Oakland food bank as well. One of Webb's men filed the following report:

A woman, her two sons, and their friend worked in one of the food distribution centers in Oakland. She telephoned us to report that she would not be returning to work at the center because the person in charge, a black man, was treating the helpers most rudely. She reported that he had a gun, and that he waved the gun around. She felt the situation was just too dangerous . . . and didn't feel she should take any chances.

A few hours later Webb received an anonymous telephone call corroborating the report. The man with the gun was suspected to be Curtis Baker. Baker had a police record three pages long, was known in the ghetto as "Black Jesus," and could often be seen walking down the street with two very large Doberman pinschers. Webb drove to the West Oakland site to nose around, then filed a report to Kramer.

I was told by several people around Market and 21st Streets that it was common knowledge in the area that Curtis Baker was selling large amounts of food, and that he has always been considered the "big gangster" in the area. The people could not understand why we would allow someone of his background to run one of our centers. One very nice lady, who was counting out pennies for the egg man while I was talking to her, related how her daughter has been volunteering at the 14th Street center and has been told that there is no meat for the people. This lady pointed out Curtis Baker's house, and the other house down the street where the meat and other items are being sold.

Webb inquired at the Baker house and was told that Baker was Norman Johnson's chief of security, for two thousand dollars a day and, apparently, all the money he could make selling PIN food. "How do you know he ain't gonna give the money he makes to the poor people?" Webb was asked. The door was closed in his face.

Later Webb was contacted by the Oakland police, who had also been to Baker's house and seen the stolen food there. They wanted authorization to make arrests so badly they could taste it. Webb called Maze; Maze spoke with the coalition; and the coalition, with the backing of Mr. Hearst, said that no complaints were

to be filed. It might antagonize the SLA. "The sergeant was notified of this decision," Webb wrote in his report, "and he did not
receive it very well." Especially since he had just been requested
to release another man for selling PIN food.

This was to be the policy throughout the program—no police
interference, which resulted in all sorts of characters coming up
with their particular angle to get a piece of the action. Jimmy
Beasley, for example.

A few weeks after the first giveaway, when the newspapers
broke the story of the Black Muslims' successful $99,000 claim
against PIN, Beasley came running. For over an hour he harangued
the coalition, claiming that the ubiquitous Charlie Walker, who
had since taken to hanging around the warehouse incognito, had
somehow authorized him to buy and distribute food. Beasley said
he bought $9,600 worth of food and that all of it had been ripped
off during the riots. But, when questioned, Walker said he had
given him no such authorization. Beasley was furious. He said he'd
been double-crossed and he wanted his money.

The coalition listened rather passively to his story, then
Arnold Townsend said that PIN's finances were controlled by
Kramer and Maze. At this Beasley and his bodyguard edged into
Kramer's office back to back, like Siamese twins. Peggy Maze, John
McLean, and Lipset Security man Jack Paladino looked on as
Beasley tore into Kramer. "You better pay me my money or else,
Kramer," he shouted at one point. Kramer was intimidated. Mc-
Lean and Webb tensed, but Paladino seemed relatively unper-
turbed.

"Come on, man, it's time for you to go," he said flatly and
opened the door. Beasley straightened up slowly, knowing his
bluff had failed and moved quietly out the door with his bodyguard. The next morning he sent Kramer a letter apologizing for
losing his temper, but this was not the end of it. A few days later
he turned his sights on Sara Jane Moore, presenting her with a
list of the food supposedly stolen from his truck. She scanned the
list, then called Mr. Edward Milani, owner of the Sunset Produce
Company, who told her that it would have taken at least three

trucks to haul the amount of food on Beasley's list. "Yeah, that's right," Beasley said. "Three trucks."

"Where are your bills of lading, warehouse receipts, and invoices for the food?" Sara asked.

Beasley said he didn't have the paperwork because it was "hot food."

"Well, if you stole the food, go back and steal the paperwork."

"You paid the Muslims!" Beasley started shouting.

At this point Webb entered. "C'mon, Jimmy, let's go out in the hall for a cigarette."

"They're trying to cheat me!" Beasley shouted.

"Now, Jimmy, we've known each other a long time," Webb said quietly. "What would you do if somebody came in with a cock-and-bull story like this?"

"You saw it on TV, how they ripped me off."

"Okay, where'd you get the money to buy the stuff in the first place?" Webb asked. "You must have the canceled checks or the receipts."

"You know I don't have that stuff, Jack. It was my dope money."

Webb showed him to the door. A diehard to the bitter end, Beasley later wrote up and distributed what he called a "Citizens Communiqué."

On the first day of the free food giveaway, I supplied oranges, bananas, bread and fish at a cost of $9,600. The cost to the PIN program was $15,000. As you can see, my profit margin was very small. When you take into consideration that three (3) truck drivers received $250 a piece, which comes to a total of $750, you can see my profit margin was very small . . . I submitted my bill of $15,000 to the Hearst Foundation two times . . . I had another meeting with Mr. Krammer [sic] and Ms. Mays [sic] today. When they came into the PIN building, I was told they would be with me in a few minutes and was told to sit down by a gentleman who follows Mr. Krammer everywhere he goes with a trained dog very angrily . . . I think its time we, the poor people, come together and not let food or money separate us . . . Money separated us first, now it is food. I am calling upon all concerned people to stop this regression upon our livelyhoods . . . I, James Beasley, am going to speak out about the injustice done to poor people . . . God gave Noah the rainbow sign, no more water, fire next time. Wake up people we're burning. Peace if we can have it.

By that time what somebody had was forty thousand dollars' worth of meat and poultry, which had been taken from a PIN truck stopped in Hunter's Point by armed hijackers. According to the driver's story they had forced him out of the truck and had driven away in it. A few hours later he "found" the truck and drove it back to the warehouse. Again the police were asked not to press the matter because it might anger the SLA. A SFPD investigator asked Sara Jane how he was to make out his report on the hijacking. "Start it with, 'Once upon a time there was a truck,' " Sara suggested.

While many of PIN's problems came from the outside, from the likes of Jimmy Beasley, Curtis Baker, and the Black Muslims, problems within the organization were just as debilitating. In fact, there was a good deal of rivalry, hostility, and bitterness within the coalition itself. In the February 20 tape, Cinque had demanded that the program, including the coalition, "be run in the true spirit of a revolutionary cooperative with no bureaucratic overseers," and then had invited any and all community groups who wanted to participate to join in that cooperative. While cooperation was hard to come by in the coalition, revolutionary spirit was not. Many coalition meetings included up to thirty-five individuals representing groups as disparate as Haight/Ashbury's 409 House and Oakland's Citizen's Neighborhood Assistance Program Computerized. All had to be given a full hearing which, more often than not, was carried out at full volume. During one meeting the representative from Hunters Point boasted that their operation had gone smoothly because they had the foresight to hand out numbered tickets to the recipients in the line. Townsend's lieutenant, a fiery fellow known as DW who was considered both streetwise *and* tough, took offense at this. "Fillmore niggas and Hunters Point niggas are different!" he shouted. "You got your Model Cities and your H.U.D. in Hunters Point. Orderly niggas. . . . Shit, you can't hand out no numbers to Fillmore niggas. You get shot!"

Tempers and time were short, the pressure great. Although the coalition was hardly the White Knight of the program, it is fair to say that their position was an increasingly difficult one. They soon found themselves saddled with duties they had not anticipated, problems that seemed insoluble, the very real possibility of riots exploding in their own neighborhoods and the whole operation blowing up in their faces. Mixed in with this was their genuine desire to feed the poor, their fear of police reprisals, their fear of the SLA, and the realization that their original roles as monitors had expanded to the point where they were practically responsible for running the whole show. In view of this, then, and despite Arnold Townsend's sound leadership, it is not surprising that the coalition was a touchy, acrimonious lot.

If he had tried, Kramer could not have succeeded in provoking the wrath of the coalition more than he did. He referred to them as "the SLA's representatives," he violated their agreement not to hold press conferences when they were not in attendance, and when a professional nutritionist came down to examine PIN food, he enraged the coalition by announcing that "she's from our world, not yours." Kramer also very nearly got his face flattened one night.

After the Muslims had gotten their $99,000 out of PIN, they continued to hang around trying to do more business. One day a leader of the Black Muslim businessmen talked his way into Kramer's office. "Hello," he said politely, but firmly. "We hear you need eggs. We sell eggs. How many do you want?"

Again Kramer was unnerved. He said PIN needed fifty thousand dozen.

"Fine, our price is eighty-two cents a dozen."

Anxious to get the Muslim out of his office, Kramer agreed

and directed him to Sara Jane who would draw up the purchase order.

As it turned out some of the eggs didn't even have to be transported by the Muslims. They were stored in a nearby cold storage locker, and the Muslims had the option to buy them, which they did, at forty-two cents a dozen. In his moment of panic, Kramer not only failed to negotiate the price, he didn't even inquire about the quality of the eggs. When they arrived, many of them were pullet eggs. Kramer was furious. He turned to Arnold Townsend and shouted, "Look at the eggs *your* Muslim friends delivered!" Townsend was enraged, barely able to restrain himself.

Adding to the animosity between Kramer and the coalition was the fact that Kramer seemed unable to get the delivery trucks to the food banks on time, forcing the coalition members to hold back the impatient crowds, sometimes for hours.

"Tell me this, Mr. Kramer," McLean said in a controlled voice at one of the meetings. "Why is it that the secretary of one of these fifty states of ours is unable to get twenty trucks to ten distribution sites on time?" Kramer said he was doing the best he could. "To fuck it up," Popeye Jackson said to McLean later. "When it comes down to time an' money, a white man don't fuck it up unless it's on purpose." This was in line with the suspicion among some of the coalition members that Kramer was a government-paid saboteur. "If an Indian is told he's gonna get a million dollars at twelve o'clock," Popeye went on, "he gets there at twelve thirty. If a black man's told the same thing, he gets there at twelve fifteen. But if you tell a white man he's gonna get a million dollars at twelve o'clock, he's there at *eleven*—Right now! Now you tell me who this man is workin' for?"

After the first distribution, Kramer and Maze ordered most of PIN's food from Washington suppliers instead of local people; because they wanted to deal with their own kind, it was said. Even fish was ordered from Boothe Fisheries in Washington, despite the many suppliers in San Francisco. Only one local fish salesman did business with PIN—John Alioto, cousin of Mayor Alioto. A PIN secretary told McLean that the mayor's office had called to say they would appreciate any courtesy that would be shown to Mr. Alioto. On another occasion Kramer was overheard talking to an executive of Fisher Products in Washington about food *and* a donation of 70,000 bumper stickers for Kramer's forthcoming congressional campaign—"We Love Lud" the stickers proclaimed. Because of this, McLean approached Jack Paladino, whom he had known since their days together at the Lipset Detective Agency.

"Is Kramer in it for the money, the kickbacks?" he asked Paladino. "I don't care how, or who's involved, but I've just got to know if he is."

Paladino promised to check Kramer out with his contacts in Washington. A couple of days later he got back to McLean. "I can't find any dirt under the carpet, John," he said. "The guy may be inept but I can't find anything dishonest."

In fairness to Kramer, he was trying to do an impossible job under impossible circumstances, but in fact he *was* inept. He was also scared. The Muslims, Charlie Walker, and Jimmy Beasley, not to mention the loud voices on the coalition, had him intimidated to the point that he feared for his life, or so he said. At fifty dollars an hour he hired another bodyguard named Phil Ellsworth. A former piano mover, Ellsworth stood six foot seven and was always accompanied by a vicious German shepherd he claimed to have trained with a cattle prod. But the dog was more for appearances than protection, and the only time it moved into action was when it took a bite out of Jack Webb's hand.

It goes without saying that Kramer was not much of a leader. Faith in him and, through him, in the entire program was non-existent. Fearing that PIN might go bankrupt at any moment, food suppliers would send special couriers to China Basin to pick up their checks on the day of delivery and take them directly to the bank. Some vendors, following Kramer's lead, would not even poke their heads in the warehouse without protection.

From an outsider's point of view Peggy Maze's position in all of this was somewhat difficult to understand. Originally *she* was the one slated to direct the program, having three years of experience with the NIN program, and Kramer was to operate primarily as her front man. It didn't work out that way. As a white, middle-class, church-oriented charity organizer whose sole purpose, it appeared, was to expand her NIN operation, Maze was hardly popular with the coalition members. At the outset many of them refused to work with her, referring to her as "The Bitch." Stymied by the coalition, Maze's influence in the program was further diminished by Kramer himself. Although he had no official position in PIN, from the first press conference in Hillsborough Kramer gave the impression that he was running the show and, much to Peggy Maze's irritation, let people think that she was *his* assistant. But it was not long before Kramer became victim of his own pretension. A few weeks into the program and he wanted out, but to his and everybody else's disappointment nobody else would even consider the job. Kramer was stuck and Mr. Hearst was stuck with him. Under these conditions the PIN program limped into its third week.

On Wednesday, the thirteenth, four days after the March 9 communiqué, and for the first time in three weeks, Mr. Hearst again met with Kramer, Maze, and the coalition at the Airport Hilton—this, incidentally, the meeting from which I had been disinvited. True to form, the meeting got off to a shaky start when West Oakland's Norman Johnson stood up menacingly, put his foot on his chair and tossed his bill on the conference table— $15,000 for damages to his West Oakland food bank and the $2,000 per day for his security guard, Curtis Baker. Although the coalition had previously agreed that none of them would present their bills until all members had examined them, no one said anything as Johnson shouted at Kramer about his supposed losses. But when he turned his sights on Mr. Hearst a coalition member spoke up, firmly reminding him that they had already agreed on the procedure. "Yeah, that's the way it is, Johnson," Townsend said coolly. "We'll deal with it later." Johnson hesitated, demanded that Mr. Hearst "keep that dog Webb" off his back, then sat down.

Once that was settled, the meeting got under way, talk turning to how, when, and what could be done to meet the SLA's latest demand. But within minutes tempers flared again. DW stood up angrily and called Kramer and Maze liars, accusing them of sabotaging the program. Kramer shouted back at him, then slumped in his chair as Peggy Maze stood up and announced that they had come up with a plan to meet the SLA demands.

The plan, which was agreed upon, called for seventy dollars' worth of food each for one hundred thousand people. It would all be given out in one final distribution. Each box would have a sticker with the seven-headed cobra on it and a similar poster would be placed over the door of every food bank. The food for the operation would be ordered in huge quantities, and the China Basin warehouse set up like a General Motors assembly line— empty boxes at one end, full ones at the other. When all was said and done, according to their foggy figuring, the approximately $700,000 remaining in the PIN account would be used up. Kramer promised that the trucks could be rolling in less than a week. Townsend warned him not to make promises he couldn't keep, but Kramer remained firm. The trucks would roll next Thursday.

As the meeting was breaking up, Kramer announced that he and Ms. Maze would be in Washington for the next few days and that Jack Webb would oversee the operation while they were gone. Since everyone was preoccupied with the details of the enormous giveaway, no one saw the incredible error, no one thought to multiply.

An hour later Jack Webb and John Lester, the press liaison man, were having a buffet lunch with Mr. Hearst in Hillsborough. As Mr. Webb recalls it, midway through the meal something dawned on him. "I'm no mathematician," he told Mr. Hearst, "but it seems to me that seventy dollars times one hundred thousand is seven million dollars." Mr. Hearst was taken aback for a moment, then shrugged it off as the wholesale/retail differences added on to the value of the food PIN already had in the warehouse. Something like that. No one else at the table seemed particularly excited about the question, and the conversation moved to other things. Still, Webb was unsettled. That afternoon, driving Kramer and Maze to the airport, he raised the question again, but now Kramer was preoccupied with other things. "Just do the best you can," Kramer told him, climbing out of the car.

Webb did the best he could. The following morning, Thursday, he tried to rent the second and third floors of the warehouse to house the expanded operation and the hundred trucks needed to carry the goods. The second floor was not for rent and even fifty trucks would be nearly impossible to get. Webb started getting nervous.

Meanwhile, Sara Jane and a half-dozen other people were on the phone ordering legs of lamb, chickens, peanut butter, everything in hundred-thousand quantities. Still feeling uneasy about the operation, Webb went back into the warehouse and talked with Paul Andrews, the head warehouseman, who was uneasier still. With the space available and the limited numbers of volunteers, there was no way they were going to move one hundred thousand boxes out of China Basin. "It's out of hand, Jack," Andrews said. "Something's really out of whack." After being reassured by Kramer and even Randy Hearst himself, it was the warehouseman's statement that set Webb in motion. He went into the office and called Kramer.

"It's impossible, Lud. We can't do anywhere near a hundred thousand boxes."

"How many can you do?"

"Hell, I don't know."

"Just do the best you can." Kramer hung up.

At this point John McLean walked into the office and Webb filled him in. McLean then called Mr. Hearst, thus beginning what were to be four very good days for the telephone company.

On Friday, after mulling over McLean's call, and making some inquiries of his own, Mr. Hearst realized that they had made a seven-million-dollar mistake and called Sara, telling her to cancel all the orders immediately. Sara began doing so and then called Maze in Washington and explained the situation. Maze told her that she and Kramer would be down the next day to straighten things out. What they did upon arrival, however, was turn Sara around and get her ordering again.

It was not until the following Monday that Mr. Hearst called

Sara just to make certain that she had canceled the orders, then blew sky-high when she said she hadn't. "Cancel the goddamn orders!" he told her. She said she would tell Maze of his decision and, after hanging up, did so.

"He doesn't have any right to tell me what to do!" Maze said angrily (which was legally quite true).

"Yes he does, Peg," Sara countered. "It's his money and his daughter."

"It's *my* money and I'll do what I want with it!"

Sara then called Mr. Hearst back and informed him of Maze's attitude. Mr. Hearst roared that he was coming down to the warehouse "to throw that bitch out personally!"

When Mr. Hearst arrived at the warehouse he had regained his composure. He talked to Maze, then phoned Kramer, who had shuttled back to Washington. Kramer finally appeared to understand the problem and agreed that the orders had to be canceled. Mr. Hearst then climbed back in his car and headed for Hillsborough.

In the meantime Webb called Kramer just to double-check on everything. "No," Kramer shouted into the receiver. "I'm not going to cancel those orders! Just do the best you can!" At this Webb called Mr. Hearst again. "Randy," he said, trying to keep his voice level, "there's a man up in Washington who doesn't seem to understand." Another explosion, then Mr. Hearst called Kramer and let him have it. Finally it was settled. Sara Jane began canceling the orders, with Maze and the others now helping. In one case her call came just in time to stop a special night shift the Langendorf Bakery had organized to meet the enormous bread order. She was not in time to cancel an order for 54,000 cardboard boxes at a cost of roughly $20,000.

Jack Webb was a weary man when he left the China Basin warehouse that evening. It had been a long day, but it was not yet over. As he walked out to his car, two large trailers sitting at the far end of the parking lot aroused his curiosity, and he went over to check them out. When he unbolted the door on the first trailer he was overwhelmed by the warm stench of rotting collard greens, a ton of them. When he unbolted the second, he was literally knocked down by a tremendous whoosh of chemical fumes. Three hundred cases of bananas, that had long since turned to black goo, had been fermenting inside the locked trailer for over a week. Fearing an explosion, Webb had Sara Jane call the fire department, which roared up to the scene and hosed down the inside of the trailer.

After they left, Webb went inside, called the truck rental agency, and arranged to have the two trailers hauled to the city dump to be cleaned. He then climbed in his brown Toronado with the "Mr. Webb" license plates and headed home. Despite his exhaustion, Webb got an idea that made him smile. Maybe he'd send Townsend and the coalition some "I Love Lud" bumper stickers.

It was the following day that Jay got hold of me in San Francisco, asking me to round up some volunteers and explaining that Mr. Hearst and a second echelon of volunteers, which included Webb, Sara Jane, Willie, Paul Andrews the warehouseman, John Piziali of Co-op Markets, and several others, were now directing preparations for the last distribution. Although Mr. Hearst was still, theoretically, barred from "interfering" in his own PIN program—a financial contributor to a nonprofit, tax-exempt organization is by law prohibited from trying to influence how his money will be spent—it had by now become abundantly clear that *something* had to be done. Expenses were rapidly climbing over the two-million-dollar mark, more money was needed to stave off a total financial collapse, and distrust in the organization was such that Mr. Hearst had to send out his personal guarantees that all future bills would be paid in full. Because of this, and against the advice of some of his counselors, Mr. Hearst stepped in and took charge. Indeed, when I arrived at the warehouse the next night and looked inside the administrative offices, there was little to indicate that Kramer and Maze had any say in what was now going on. The power struggle among Kramer, Maze, and Mr. Hearst had left the Washington people on the outside. Kramer was still there, however, looking over shoulders, moving around to check on things, and giving the impression that he was still in charge. But in reality he was finished. His rumpled suit, strained voice, and sour expression marked him as a beaten man. I remember asking him how things were going, before I moved into the warehouse with the rest of the volunteers. "I haven't slept in three days," was the reply, "and I've been bleeding internally." Although he was a sad, almost pathetic figure, many were of the opinion that A. Ludlow Kramer had finally gotten his due.

The following night I drove back to the warehouse. Fifteen hours later, and another midnight shift behind me, I returned to Ed's apartment. He was getting ready to go to his law office when I walked in and he made me a cup of coffee. I drank it and promptly threw up.

"Don't tell me that's from the PIN food," Ed said. I shook my head and lay down on the couch.

"I think it's the flu."

At noon I went back to the warehouse to find, much to everyone's surprise, that most of the packaging had been completed. After calling off my platoon of volunteers, it was back to Ed's couch. At midnight I returned to China Basin, and Jay, who naturally tends to take charge of things, sent me off to deliver last-minute instructions to some of the distribution sites. In my memory of that night, the four food banks I visited come back as a montage of the People In Need program and how it looked to many of those on the receiving end.

The Vallejo center, in the North Bay, was run by a group of young blacks who were kicking around, playing cards, drinking coffee, but quite conscientious about feeding their communities. They were upset by the prospect of having to turn away the hungry when the food ran out, as it inevitably would. In spite of this they were well disposed toward me, offering me coffee and expressing their sympathy and hope that Patty would soon be released. There was, however, a very large woman with a fishwife's tongue who was absolutely certain that I was not Steven Weed, but a police spy.

"You ain't no Steve Weed," she said loudly. "I seen him on the TV and you ain't him. He's skinnier. . . . Don't say nothin' to him," she warned the others, who were laughing as they showed me out.

At the first center in Richmond, I was greeted by a small, soft-spoken black man, the Reverend Mr. Harris. He gave me a tour of the food bank, an old Baptist church, proudly pointing out how well it was organized. "No riots here," he said. "We're going to feed people with dignity." When we went outside, he looked up at the poster of the seven-headed cobra over the door and frowned. "Savin' that poor girl means more to me than anything," he said quietly. When we shook hands good-bye he asked my name.

"Steve," I told him. Then he recognized me.

"May God bless you, Mr. Weed." He waved to me as I pulled away from the curb.

The second Richmond distribution site was housed in a run-down community center in a forlorn industrial area. The silhouette of the enormous Standard Oil refinery loomed above it, while across from it ran a murky estuary. When I arrived, a large group of toughs were hanging around outside, many of them drunk, swaggering around and threatening to break in and "liberate that food!" Over Ethel Dotson's dead body. A thirtyish black woman representing the Welfare Rights Organization, Dotson was rattled by the goings-on outside and compensated with a very loud voice. After moving as inconspicuously as possible through the crowd and knocking on the door, I entered to find her sitting on one of the counters shouting at everyone. "You tell those muthafuckers to git outta here or I'll shut the whole place down!" Two young men tried to slip by her with boxes of food, but were stopped in their tracks. "That goes for you too!" Dotson fired at them from her perch. "Put that food down an' git!" The two tried to shout back an angry explanation but were cut short by "Bul-l . . . *shit!* Git outta here!" They got out. "An' who are . . . oh, the Weed kid," she said.

John McLean, Jack Webb, and Sara Jane entered the room from a small kitchen. They had heard there was trouble in Richmond, that Dotson was at the end of her rope, and had come out to help—Sara with the inventory, Webb and McLean with security. It was not until I saw that they were somewhat nervous that I realized the situation was a precarious one. McLean told me not to go anywhere near the Oakland site, where people were cruising around with shotguns, and to be careful at my next stop, Marin City. Being overprotective, he called the Marin site after I left and told Nesbitt Cruxfield, the leader there, that I was coming and to look out for me. "Don't worry," Cruxfield said. "I'll shoot 'em with my twelve gauge."

McLean's precaution turned out to be unnecessary. The Marin site, located in a modern church, was quiet and peaceful. When I entered the building I almost stumbled over one of the twenty volunteers curled up in sleeping bags on the linoleum floor. Cruxfield stuck his head in the darkened room and nodded me over. He and another sleepy but curious volunteer went into a side room and talked with me until daylight.

I learned a lot from Nesbitt Cruxfield that night. An extremely articulate young man, he was also extremely bitter about, and suspicious of, the rich. Like a lot of other people he assumed that a man in Mr. Hearst's position was almost omnipotent and refused to believe that he had even tried to put forth a good faith gesture. I told him he didn't understand the incredibly difficult position Mr. Hearst was in. "What do you mean difficult?" he demanded. "The SLA asked for four hundred million dollars, and he gave them two million. With the money and connections he's got, he could have hired the best people around to help him put this thing together. And you're telling me he couldn't come up with something better than this?" As far as Cruxfield was concerned, Mr. Hearst and his ruling-class advisors had sabotaged the program to disgrace the SLA and the black community.

"Look at those people," he said, nodding outside toward the men and women who were already beginning to form a dark, silent line in the fog. "Nobody paid a goddamn bit of attention to them—

shit, they didn't even know Sausalito *had* a ghetto—until this happened. Then they went out and blew the program to make damn sure it didn't happen again."

There was no getting through to Cruxfield that night, especially since much of what he said was true. All I could do was listen rather apologetically and nod my head. But by the time it started getting light outside, the edge had gone from his bitterness—at least that part directed at me. "Come on," he said, "the truck's here."

It was drizzling when we started unloading the enormous truck-trailer. The volunteers worked hard and fast, with the same spirit I had witnessed at the warehouse, and I was hard pressed to keep up with them. When the job was done Cruxfield watched the truck pull out, then shrugged. "I hope this gets her out for you," he said, then turned and walked back into the church.

At five o'clock that evening I pulled myself off Ed's couch and turned on the news. After thirty-four hectic days and nights the PIN program was over. Thousands of people all over the Bay Area had braved the wind and rain to line up at the distribution sites to receive their box of food, or as many of the sixty-pound cartons as they could carry. In San Francisco one man rolled two boxes away in a wheelchair. In Vallejo a woman balanced one carton on her head, while her two small sons struggled with another one between them. There had been no violence, no major problems. In all 35,000 cartons, each containing forty-five dollars' worth of food had been handed out. "It is agreed," said the newscaster, "that the operation went smoother and was more efficiently coordinated than its predecessors."

The China Basin warehouse, once the scene of frenetic activity, was now quiet and empty. Janitors and trash collectors began cleaning up the huge building, while maintenance men took apart the assembly lines. All that was left of the estimated two-and-a-half-million dollars' worth of food were a few pallets of peanut butter, a few stacks of Zoom, and some miscellaneous crates of meat in the cold storage warehouse. The administration offices were empty; the phones silent. Before leaving, John McLean had taken Patty's picture off the wall. She was indeed what it had all been about.

It is safe to say that throughout the thirty-four-day life of PIN, Patty's image was often in the minds of the people who had worked so hard to overcome the utter confusion of those first three weeks and make the last distribution a success. They had done just that, and now there was nothing to do but wait and hope for some word that their efforts had not been in vain, that the SLA was prepared to release Patty. But somewhere in a dingy Fillmore flat a group of people had already decided on a course of action that would stun every volunteer who had filed past the picture of the girl it * was all about.

* The legacy of PIN lives on and it is not, for the most part, a happy one: six lawsuits have been filed against the organization; a number of producers and suppliers are demanding reimbursement for their "donations"; A. Ludlow Kramer, who stated that seventeen threats against his life were made during the program, flew back to Washington and promptly lost his bid for a Congressional seat; and then there is Sara Jane Moore, who, for four weeks, had been at center stage during the program, then found herself cast adrift again when it was over. Desperate for attention, she knocked around from one political group to another, and then publicly announced that during PIN she had been a paid FBI informant. But nobody seemed to care. Finally, on September 22, 1975, she attempted to assassinate President Ford as he was coming out of San Francisco's St. Francis Hotel. A few weeks before, she had called Jack Webb asking that he lend her a pistol and take her shooting, "like you did Steve," she said. Webb begged off and now thinks back on it. "Can you imagine what my reputation would be if I had [taken her to the rifle range] and she'd nailed Ford between the eyes?"

7

MY FIVE DAYS WITH THE PIN PROGRAM had the effect of temporarily pulling me out of myself. If nothing else, the physical activity, the hours of repetitious work on the assembly lines steadied me. But with the completion of the program, I was back to nothing but the wait. Although PIN officially ended on Monday, March 25, I did not expect an SLA response to the last giveaway until the next weekend, when the coalition would hold a press conference and issue its final report. That gave me five days to put together everything I knew about the SLA: their personalities, their past behavior, and what I guessed to be their view of their options. I tried to be as rational, as logical in this as possible. But for all my efforts to remain objective, just below the surface I was desperately trying to prepare myself, to brace myself for the SLA's next move, simply because I didn't think I could handle another unexpected blow.

For seven weeks, since the night Patty was taken, it had been one shock after another. And then all those days in between when I would wake up, stupefied at first, but then it would all roll back into me, sicken me with the realization that it was still going on. I could never shake it nor achieve any distance from it except when writing in my journal. I lived and breathed it every day. And it was not like experiencing a tragedy, the death or injury of someone you loved, or enduring some terrible fait accompli. Rather, it was still *happening,* it was still going on. But now, with the PIN program completed, it appeared that the end was in sight. And although I tried to temper my uneasy optimism with reason, with reminders of all the disappointments we had suffered in the past seven weeks, now more than ever there really was cause for hope.

On March 26, the day after the last giveaway, Mr. Hearst flew back to New York to meet with the Board of Trustees and make final arrangements for the additional $4 million the SLA had demanded in the February twentieth communiqué. The money was to be put in escrow under the control of three Left-leaning trustees: Willie Brown, a black assemblyman, Vincent Hallinan, an old-Left radical lawyer, and Ernesto Galarza, a Chicano leader; apparently to convince the SLA that the money would indeed be released to a cause or program of the SLA's choice—once they freed Patty. That same night I went before the cameras at KQED to emphasize these terms and to assure the SLA that even without the escrow arrangement the Corporation could not renege on its public promise of the $4 million. I also asked them to hold off on any decisions they might be considering until they heard from their captured comrades, Remiro and Little, because I had been told by Remiro's attorney, William Gagan, that the two SLA soldiers were sending an open letter to the media. Two days later, on Thursday, March 28, their letter was read over radio station KPFA. It was further cause for optimism. In a portion of the letter Remiro and Little addressed themselves directly to Patty:

Patty, we feel that we have already done the most concrete thing we can do to assist in your safe release by exposing the true intentions of the FBI, etcetera, to the public. We feel confident that when you are released you will continue to be strong and speak your mind! We realize, as do you, that the SLA has consistently referred to our safety and well-being, but that in reality, you will not be harmed for anything that might happen to us. You're in no better position than us as far as the reactionary forces' intentions—they want to make an example out of your death as well as ours.

Actually, you're in a better position only as long as the SLA can protect and keep you well hidden until you can be released and returned safely to your fiancé. Who knows—you might even look back on this as a worthwhile experience where people were fed and you and the public were exposed to the cruelty and inhumanity of the corporate powers who rule this country. . . . We look forward to receiving a visit from you, Patty, after you are released.

Later that week, when Mr. Hearst had returned from New York, I was staying down the peninsula in Saratoga with Diana and Stu Olson, trying to gauge the effect of these hopeful signs, while at the same time trying to guard against setting myself up for another bitter disappointment. As I wrote in my journal on Friday, the twenty-ninth.

I am allowing myself to be cautiously hopeful for the first time. If the SLA doesn't see that now is the time for a graceful exit I will have nothing left but to conclude that as a group they are either incomprehensibly stupid or simply suicidal and insane.

Those words, suicidal and insane, registered the dark side of my thoughts. Was the SLA even capable of seeing and acting upon anything but their own delusions? Or were they too far gone, too immersed in messianic self-righteousness and hatred to make a rational decision? From what I knew of two key members of the group, Donald DeFreeze and Nancy Ling Perry, I felt reason to fear the worst.

Donald David DeFreeze—the general field marshal—whose

communiqués spat out rage and bitterness from some unknown world of paranoia. Donald DeFreeze, the man with the bizarre arrest record: twelve arrests in ten years, half of these for possession of firearms and homemade bombs—an alcoholic it was implied. I had learned from a journalist how DeFreeze's fascination for firearms began at age fourteen, when he bought his first handgun with which he intended to murder his father who, he claimed, used to beat him with a hammer and had broken his arm three times. Then came a string of foster homes and reform schools, then city jails and state prisons. At some point during the kidnapping, Dr. Hacker who, coincidentally, had been appointed in 1968 to examine DeFreeze while DeFreeze was in jail, showed me a probation officer's report on the man. In the report the officer recommended probation, but with mandatory psychotherapy, admitting that "It is recognized that releasing the defendant on probation with his past history of being involved with weapons and his often mentioned 'mental confusion' does represent something of a hazard. . . ." But more frightening than any reporter's analysis, or the observations of his probation officer, was DeFreeze's own description of his life in a letter he wrote to Supreme Court Judge William Ritzi in 1970:

I am going to talk to you truthfully and like I am talking to God. I will tell you things that no one has ever before know.

To Start a story of a mans life you can start at the end, but at the start, this start will begin at the age of Sixteen.

At that age, I had Just gotten out of a boys school in New York after doing 2½ years for braking into a Parking Meter and for stealing a car, I remember the Judge said that he was sending me to Jail for boys because he said it was the best place for me. I was sixteen at the time and didn't have a home, life in the little prison as we called it, was nothing but fear and hate, day in and day out, the hate was madening, the only safe place was your cell . . . I had only two frights, if you can call them frights, I never did win. It was funny but the frights were over the fact that I would not be part of any of the gangs, black or white. I wanted to be friends with everyone, this the other inmates would not allow, they would try to make me fright, but I always got around them somehow, they even tried to make a homosexual out of me, I got around this to. After 2½ years I found myself hated by many of the boys there.

When I got out of jail, people just could not believe I had ever been to Jail. I worked hard, I didn't drink or any pills nor did I curse . . . But I was still lonely. I didn't love anyone or did any one love. I had a few girl friends but as soon as there mother found out I had been to Jail, that was the end.

Then one day I met my wife Glory, she was nice and lovely, I fell in love with her I think . . . We had just met one month before we were married. My wife had three kids already when I met her.

We were married and things were lovely . . . Then seven months later I came home sooner than I do most of the time from work and she and a old boy friend had just had relations. I was very mad and very hurt . . . Then one day I found out that none of my kids had the same father and that she had never been married.

I thought that if we had kids or a baby we would be closer, but as soon as the baby was born it was the same thing I had began to drink very deeply, but I was trying to put up with her and hope that she would change.

But as the years went by she never did and she told me that she had been to see her boy friend and that she wanted a divorce because I was not taking care of her and the kids good enough, I was never so mad in my life . . . I could have killed her, but I didn't. I through her out of the house and I got a saw and hammer and completely destroyed everything I ever bought her and I mean everything!

For months later she begged me to take her back and she said she had made a mistake and that she really loved me. I was weak again . . . I took her back . . . But I couldn't face anyone any more. I started drinking more and more and staying at my job late . . . I started playing with guns and firer works

and dogs and cars. Just anything to get away from life . . .
I finely got into trouble with the Police for shooting off a rifle
in my basement and for a bomb I had made out of about 30
firer works from forth of July.

I told my wife I would forget all that she had did to me . . .
But I was wrong again. I started playing with guns, drinking,
pills but this time more than I had ever before did. I was
arrested again and again for guns or bombs. I don't really
understand what I was doing. She wanted nice things and I
was working and buying and selling guns and the next thing I
knew I had become a thief . . .

You sent me to Chino and I lied to them and didn't tell them
all the truth. They think I am nuts . . . But you should not
have never sent me back to her. The day after I got home she
told me she had had Six relations with some man she meant
on the street when I was in Chino . . .

Sir Don't send me to prison again, I am not a crook or a thief
nor am I crazy. I hope you will believe me . . . Sir, even if
you don't ever call me back or want to see me again Thank
you for all you have done and all I can say is God Bless you,
                                Yours Truly, Donald DeFreeze.

DeFreeze was sent back to prison again, the judge deciding
that DeFreeze was too unbalanced to remain on the outside.

And then there was Nancy Ling Perry, "Fahizah," another
disintegrated personality, another casualty of the Berkeley youth
ghetto. Intense, searching and desperately lonely, Nancy had
drifted from one cheap apartment to another, before marrying
Gilbert Perry, a black musician, and getting heavily into drugs.
Though she was devoted to Gilbert, "a barnacle on his shell," the
marriage didn't last. Shattered by this, Nancy began dating other
people only to return to her apartment one night to find that
Gilbert had painted bright scarlet "A's" over all the doors. When
she and Gilbert separated for the last time, Nancy was plunged
into guilt and self-hatred. "She felt like she was being obliterated,"
a friend remembered. "She'd drop acid and everything would go

black inside her head. Then she'd be terrified, but she wouldn't even consider seeing a shrink. She was really tortured, fragmented. Sometimes she said she felt her mind being completely obliterated by her venom toward herself."

Then came a personal salvation for Nancy in becoming obsessed with others' problems: the prison movement. She gave up drugs and picked up radical politics and violence, finding an intense friendship and a sense of belonging in a small, committed group of comrades, much as DeFreeze had found a sense of personal order he had never known before in the political discussions at Vacaville's Black Cultural Association. Indeed, from what I had to go on that last week in March, it seemed that Nancy's confessional January "Letter to the People" spoke revealingly about her and Cinque: "A revolutionary is not a criminal nor is she or he an adventurer, and revolutionary violence *is nothing but the most profound means of achieving internal as well as external balance.*" Politics seemed to me nothing but an outlet for the borderline insanity of Nancy Ling Perry and Donald "Cinque" DeFreeze.

But what of the other members of the group? That week, in a series of articles, *Chronicle* reporters Tim Findley and Paul Avery sketched out their backgrounds. There was twenty-two-year-old Willie Wolfe, the son of a Pennsylvania doctor and the product of a private school education. Willie had come to U.C. Berkeley after bumming around Europe supporting himself with part-time jobs. One of his courses at the university, black history, had led to his participating in the Black Cultural Association, where he met DeFreeze and it all began. Then there were Bill and Emily Harris, a well-educated couple who had moved to Berkeley from Bloomington, Indiana, and involved themselves in Venceremos, Vietnam Veterans Against the War, and the prison movement. Angela Atwood, the Harrises' close friend, had arrived in Berkeley a few months before them with her husband, Gary Atwood. A year later Gary had returned to Bloomington and Angela had moved in with the Harrises, her political mentors, who included her in their radical study groups. The only two SLA members who had lived in Berkeley for any appreciable amount of time were Patricia "Mizmoon" Soltysik and her lesbian lover Camilla Hall. A militant feminist, it appeared that Mizmoon had introduced Camilla to her radical friends and then, in the summer of 1973, to a black escaped convict, Donald DeFreeze.

But all of these people were only one-dimensional figures in my mind—photographs and lines of copy—compared to my feelings for the warped personalities of DeFreeze and Perry. To me the SLA was Donald DeFreeze—the others were "pilot fish to a shark," as Findley and Avery described them. And if there were other SLA members still unidentified, the fact of their existence gave me little cause for encouragement. My teeth were still numb from the mechanical brutality of the second black assailant, whose identity, along with the murderers of Marcus Foster, was still unknown.

Overall, then, I could envision the SLA only as a small, cultish group of unbalanced people who would resort to anything in pursuit of their fantasy revolution and who could not be satisfied with anything we did. Disturbed by this, and yet encouraged by the events of the past five days, I wracked my wits trying to put it all together and arrive at some conclusion about the SLA's next move.

Nothing today, but I still expect to hear from the SLA soon. They *have* to say something; it doesn't seem there is anything left for *us* to do. There are so many reasons why Patty should be returned, if not immediately, at least in the next few weeks. The last giveaway was much improved and there is $4 million in the bank waiting for them. It seems we have made enough of an effort that they could not possibly kill her and have a friend left in the world. Perhaps they see that if they quit now they will have succeeded in quitting with a rather large group of supporters—something that seemed impossible when all of this began.

I'm just hoping that they like Patty, that they see that everyone is emotionally ready for a finish, especially Patty. But it seems impossible they will release her without further "negotiations" of some kind. I keep trying to think of what new demands they might make. I can't delude myself that they are happy with their victory, or even that they consider it a victory at all. From their point of view there must be no options they are happy with. But what else can they do now but release her? I can think of nothing.

The next morning, March 31, brought two more encouraging signs. The front page of the *Examiner* featured a photograph of Death Row Jeff. Below it was the result of all of Mr. Hearst's secret meetings with the self-proclaimed founder of the SLA, an open letter in which Jeff urged Cinque to start negotiations for Patty's release in the interest of "the poor and oppressed." Later that morning Arnold Townsend read the coalition's report on the PIN program. Not surprisingly, it was highly critical of the operation, but laid most of the blame on Kramer and Maze. I remember listening to a broadcast of the report on KPFA the next day, waiting for them to tear into Mr. Hearst, then feeling relieved when they did not. With the four-million-dollar escrow arrangement in the works, Death Row Jeff's letter in the papers, and the coalition's reasonable treatment of Mr. Hearst on the air the stage was now set for the SLA's response. They did not waste much time.

Less than an hour after the KPFA broadcast, a well-dressed young woman entered the Crete Florist Shop in San Francisco and ordered a bouquet of long-stemmed American Beauty roses to be delivered to *The Phoenix,* an underground newspaper, no later than six o'clock that same evening. The shopkeeper assured her this could be done, but later that afternoon the shopkeeper's car broke down and the bouquet, accompanied by a sealed envelope, did not arrive until the following day.

When John Bryan, editor of *The Phoenix*, tore open the envelope attached to the box of roses he found a greeting card with a cartoon of a stork holding a diaper-wrapped bundle in its beak. "Guess what?" the caption read. Inside the card was half of Patty's driver's license and a two-page communiqué from the SLA.

Most of the communiqué was devoted to the "Codes of War," including a list of crimes the SLA declared punishable by death: surrender to the enemy, deserting a comrade on the field of war, and leaving a team position, among others. But by far the most staggering line of communiqué #7 opened with, "Subject: negotiations and release of Prisoner." Further communications would follow within seventy-two hours, revealing "the state, city, and time of release of the prisoner." It was signed by Cinque.

So momentous was the announcement that no one, not the Hearsts, the media, the authorities, nor myself thought to check the date it was supposed to be delivered—April Fools' Day.

When the news of the communiqué came over the radio, I tried to take it as calmly as possible, as did Diana and Stu Olson. Over dinner that night we discussed possible setbacks: additional SLA demands or perhaps the release date set far in the future. We wondered and worried about Patty's state of mind.

Before turning in I wrote the following:

> For the first time I actually believe it possible that Patty will be released at any moment, but the announcement puts me in an extremely uneasy and unmanageable mood. All of us must take great pains to protect ourselves from another disappointment. We are too quick to grasp at signs of apparent relief— already the media mood is that release is imminent. Van Amberg (of Channel 7) says, "Mr. Hearst spoke with a smile in his voice," and today Mrs. Hearst was publicly happy for the first time, I think.

> But it is impossible to suspend one's thoughts. I find myself thinking of such things as how to make Patty's reentry as gentle as possible, how to handle the press, who to thank, etc. The absurd thought has even occurred to me that Patty may return with my driver's license which I have not yet had a chance to replace. . . . But I'm extremely nervous. . . . I just cannot believe that after all this time, given the kind of people they are, the SLA will just let her walk away.

I got up the next morning and sat out on the patio, waiting and thinking. The house was quiet, the Olsons off teaching school. At 2:15 the telephone rang. It was Bob Joffee, a reporter from the *Washington Post,* and he sounded on the verge of tears.

"Did you hear about it?" he asked.

"About what?"

"Patty says she's decided to stay with the SLA."

In that instant all of my efforts to prepare myself, to brace myself collapsed. I listened woodenly as Joffee described the photograph of Patty holding a submachine gun in front of an SLA flag and paraphrased some of her statements. He said the tape was at the Hearsts's and would not be broadcast until later that afternoon.

Five minutes later I was on the freeway heading north to Hillsborough, my mind locked on the answer to all of the questions that I had gone over and over during the past week and an answer that would dominate my thoughts and actions for weeks to come: the SLA, with their capacity for deception and cruelty, had discovered an option that had not even occurred to me, a ruse so clever that they could keep Patty prisoner, claim that they had acted honorably, and then eventually murder her without having to admit it. After two months of waiting and hoping, it had come down to that. We had lost her.

"All I expect is that you try to understand the changes I've gone through," Patty would say to me on the tape I was to hear that afternoon. But as had been the case with all of her previous messages, I didn't really hear it. I simply could not believe that Patty *had* changed because I had no real conception of what she had been through, what those same two months had been for her: none of us did. From the moment she was abducted, Patty and those of us on the outside had been traveling divergent courses, existing in increasingly separate and, finally, diametrically opposed realities. And although she had repeatedly tried to explain her position, to give us "something to use, some knowledge" of what she was experiencing, all that we heard was her voice, and all that we felt was sorrow and fear mingled with the thin relief that she was still alive.

I was to be many months circling in toward an understanding of how we *really* lost Patty. There were many layers of the complex answer to consider: the facts of her physical confinement, theories of "brainwashing," the nature of Patty's character and her relation to her family and me, the inherent power of the political vision, and the incredible psychosocial intensity of the group of eight people that held her. And yet more important than any single one of these was a layer that should have been easily grasped as it happened—Patty's feelings of being betrayed by her would-be rescuers. Objectively our attempts to retrieve her were for the most part ineffectual, our phrasings often unfortunate, and Patty did not even have the benefit of a clear view of our errors. She saw in our efforts the *deliberate* failure her captors wanted her to see—what they themselves saw: a field of vision that was filtered, selectively magnified, and passionately interpreted by people whose perceptions were such that they could see Marcus Foster as a fascist oppressor and enter into a pact to murder him. Out of this, a very real experience of betrayal was fashioned, an experience that Patty so clearly describes in her first few tape recordings. We heard first her pleading and then her criticism, but so strong was our preconception that she would, regardless of circumstances, hate those who held her and side with us on the outside, that we were, fundamentally, tragically unable to see her advancing disillusionment when we most needed to.

Six months later and with a fresh ear, I replayed those tapes. I was sitting in my Berkeley apartment at the time, my second apartment in Berkeley. Hanging by the windows were our plants and the holders Patty had macraméd for them on Benvenue. A few prints we had picked out together decorated the walls. For three hours I played and replayed those tapes, listening for every nuance, every change of tone and emphasis in Patty's voice, all the signals that I had learned to recognize in her voice during the years we had spent together, all the things I had missed when I had first heard the tapes in her parents' home.

It was Friday, February 8—four days after being taken—that Patty was allowed to record her first message. The first few days had been every bit as harsh as we had imagined—hit in the face with a rifle butt, terrified that I had been stabbed and killed, gunfire, dragged from car to car, and finally thrown blindfolded into a hot, stuffy, three-by-six-foot closet. For ten days she would be unable to eat, and not permitted out of her closet to relieve herself. Her voice was shaky, pathetic in this first tape, as if she would have been unable to record anything any earlier. But even this early there is scarcely a trace of the hatred for her captors that one would expect:

> Mom, Dad. I'm okay. I had a few scrapes and stuff, but they've washed them up. . . . And I caught a cold, but they're giving me pills for it. . . . There's no way that I will be released until they let me go, so it won't do any good for somebody to come in here and try to get me out by force. . . . These people aren't just a bunch of nuts. They've really been honest with me. . . .

> I was very upset to hear about the police rushing in on that house in Oakland. . . . It's really up to you [Dad] to make sure that people don't jeopardize my life by charging in and doing stupid things. . . . It's important that you realize that this is not considered by them [the SLA] to be just a simple kidnapping. . . . I'm telling you now why this has happened so that you'll know, so that you'll have something to use, some knowledge to try to get me out of here. If you can get the food thing organized before the nineteenth then that's okay and it will just speed up my release. Bye.

Already Patty is fearful of a police assault, for from the moment she was taken to the small bungalow in Daly City, not ten miles from Hillsborough, it must have appeared to her that there was a full-scale battle shaping up. Given the precautions the SLA had taken in the Concord house—the gas masks by their mattresses, their loaded weapons always within reach, and the tunnel they dug under the house—as well as their knowledge that the authorities must certainly have learned their identities from the evidence left behind there—Patty must have heard her captors moving about on bare, hardwood floors of other rooms, talking in low voices while standing watch at the windows, breaking down and cleaning their incredible arsenal of weapons, and going through BB-gun maneuvers as they did at Concord. Within a few weeks, perhaps even days, she must have begun to sense that the SLA did not intend to murder her—despite their chilling threats —and that it was a battle with police that she most had to fear. "They're perfectly willing to die for what they are doing," she says of the SLA in a barely controlled voice. "I would *appreciate* it if everybody would just calm down and not try to find me, because not only are they endangering me, but they're endangering themselves."

And so Patty pleads with her father, a man who has always been able to get anything done, to hold back the authorities and meet the SLA demand, though it is not clear whether she was aware of its details and enormity. Probably she was not, for although Patty's voice is accentuated with terror and shock throughout this first recording, there is not a trace of worry that the SLA's demand might be impossible for her father to meet. It was just a matter of organizing "the food thing" by the nineteenth. "Today is Friday the eighth," Patty says, reading into the tape recorder the last line provided her, "and today in Kuwait the commandos negotiated the release of their hostages and left the country." Her voice is almost inaudible.

But then, at some point in the next six days, something happened: one or more of Patty's jailors must have softened, showed her some sympathy, perhaps even warmed up to her, and the divergence between Patty's experience and our dark imaginings began. "These people aren't just a bunch of nuts . . . they've been really honest with me." I remember being struck by these lines, wondering what they could mean and trying to find hope in them—but to little avail. Cinque's horrifying statements about the "execution of the prisoner" and his threats that "the blood will be on your hands only" were too overwhelming.

But while we were certain Cinque and his followers were half-insane, to Patty they did not appear as the monsters we saw.

Cinque was a sociopath certainly, but not an irrational psychotic: he was a man who could be at once warm and supportive among his friends, then suddenly rage with hatred and pull a trigger, a man possessed of a chilling power to terrify and love and manipulate those around him. And Nancy Ling Perry—introverted, troubled, "a dedicated sister who didn't say very much," as Patty described her months later, a person who could write kidding little notes to herself on margins of papers: "It may not look like it but I'm working on the communiqué!" The four-foot-eleven Nancy in person could not bear much resemblance to the fearsome Fahizah who had filled so many newspaper pages. But most important, there were the four SLA members who must have had some natural appeal to Patty—Willie Wolfe, tall, gangly, soft-spoken, and intelligent, "the kid brother type," as a friend described him; Camilla Hall, a strong, talented woman who had written yearning, whimsical poetry and had drawn Thurberesque sketches before becoming "Gabi," a soldier in the SLA; Emily Harris, serious, persuasive, a former junior high school teacher whose intelligence was softened, perhaps, by a touch of melancholy; and finally Angela Atwood, headstrong, spunky, attractive, an ex-sorority girl who was very much like Patty herself. These were the four people who were probably the most comforting to Patty, the ones she tried to relate to and from whom she got something in return—reassurance, sympathy, perhaps just some conversation.

Whatever the case, when the second tape arrived on February 16 the change in Patty's tone was astounding. Her voice was strong, her statements almost matter-of-fact.

Dad, Mom. I'm making this tape to let you know I'm still okay and to try to explain a few things, I hope. . . . First, it was never intended that you feed the whole state. They [the SLA] weren't trying to make an unreasonable request. . . . So whatever you come up with is basically okay. . . . And do it as fast as you can and everything will be fine. . . . I would like to emphasize that I *am* alive and I *am* well in spite of what certain tape experts seem to think. I mean I'm fine.

If everybody's convinced that I am dead . . . it gives the FBI
an excuse to come in here. . . . I'm sure that Mr. Bates under-
stands that if the FBI has to . . . get me out by force they
won't have time to decide who not to kill. They'll just have to
kill everyone. . . . So people should stop acting like I'm dead.
Mom should get out of her black dress. That doesn't help at all.

I really think you should understand that the SLA does have
an interest in my return. Try not to worry so much. Take care
of Steve and hurry. Bye.

Although she was clearly nervous, there were moments on
this tape when Patty almost sounded perky, and moments when
she definitely sounded irritated, especially with her mother's black
dress and her constant invocation to God. There is a story behind
her reference to her mother's black dress that sheds some light on
Patty's attitude.

Six years before, when Mr. Hearst was in the hospital in Los
Angeles with a perforated ulcer, Patty had flown down from
Santa Catalina to see him. When she arrived she found that her
mother was already dressed in mourning. Patty was furious over
her mother's automatic assumption of the proper widow's role at
a time when it was obviously not the most helpful thing to do.
And yet now her mother was back in her black dress doing the
same thing to her. All of us were, as was the entire country.
There were public fasts, public prayer days, tears, and mourning.
Many people saw her death as a foregone conclusion. "Stop acting
like I am dead," she tells us. "It's really depressing to hear people
talk about me like I'm dead. I can't explain what that's like. What
it does."

One of the things it did was give Charles Bates and the FBI
the green light to attack, which made perfect sense from Patty's
point of view. "They'll just have to kill everyone," she says. It
is an indication of how differently we already saw things, that
I mistook her to mean that the SLA would have to kill everyone.
After listening to this tape I remember Mr. Hearst saying, "It
sounds like they think they're surrounded." We were actually re-

lieved that her captors were beginning to feel the pressure of the FBI's investigation, but in reality it was the worst thing that could have happened. The SLA's paranoia continued to grow and Patty breathed and absorbed it.

But by the end of the February sixteenth tape, Patty obviously felt that she had explained her situation, clarified the SLA demand, and reassured us that whatever we came up with would be basically okay. Everything would be fine.

Two days later, on February 18, when her father stepped out on the porch and made his counteroffer, everything must have suddenly blown up around her. That day was the turning point in the entire case. Frustrated over their inability to free their captured comrades—which apparently had been their primary goal in abducting Patty—chagrined that their original demand had amounted to $400 million—from which they backed down immediately—and stung by the denunciations from all sides, the SLA was certain that Mr. Hearst was trying to take advantage of their conciliatory message by offering a "measly" $2 million: three-quarters of which came from the Hearst Foundation, a "tax loophole," and went to a program run by a secretary of state. In two short days they saw their revolutionary demands become part of the system they were bent on destroying. And it wasn't even their program anymore, but "The Hearst Food Program," then "People In Need." But whatever it was called, it was "crumbs to the people" and "corporate trickery." The SLA was enraged. They felt despised, manipulated, backed into a corner, and Patty was locked in that corner with them. "We must combat enemy attempts to demoralize us," they said bitterly on the February twentieth tape. They did this by striking back. "You have always known me," Cinque raged. "I'm that nigger that is no longer just hunted, robbed and murdered. I'm the nigger that hunts you now."

So just as Patty was beginning to feel secure and hopeful, just when it appeared that things had been straightened out, the atmosphere around her changed drastically. The SLA must have confronted her, attacked her father as a man worth "hundreds of millions," a pig, an enemy of the people. And what could she say at a time when she was desperately trying to keep in their good graces, trying to be a person to them, not an object, not a target? That her father was not a pig, that he was not worth hundreds of millions? Patty had neither the desire nor the knowledge to counter their accusations with any force: in fact she had no clear idea of the extent of her father's wealth. I remember her asking me once what I thought her father was worth, but given the perquisites afforded him as a Hearst, the various Corporation write-offs afforded him as the chairman of the board, and the multiple salaries he received, I told her it was impossible to tell. He lived like a man with $10 to $20 million, I said. Whether or not this twenty-million-dollar figure stuck in her head, there can be no doubt that Patty was confused, frightened that in offering only $500,000 (and in carefully chosen tax deductible phraseology at that), maybe her father was indeed trying to get off as cheaply as possible. But she knew it wouldn't work. The SLA's "Intelligence Unit" had researched the Corporation and her father's financial position, knew that $2 million was a pittance, and assailed her with this. Patty found herself trapped between the two sides. "I wish you'd try to understand the position I'm in," she had said on the previous tape. "I'm right in the middle and I have to depend upon what all kinds of other people are going to do."

But now Patty must have felt the two sides closing in on her. So she listened anxiously to her captors, agreed cautiously, and then began telling them what she knew of her father's holdings, listing off his properties, describing the valuables in the house—the collection of Greek vases, the Shah's Persian rug—and naming all the stocks she could remember from her personal seventy-thousand-dollar trust fund. Many of these holdings had long since been sold, Patty knew, and many of her personal stocks did not appear in her father's portfolio; that she would provide such inaccurate as well as accurate items of information is an indication of how relentlessly they must have questioned her, how desperate Patty must have been to convince her captors she was holding nothing back. Additionally, she must have sensed that the SLA did not really *care* if the information she could provide was strictly correct, and so in the February twentieth communiqué all the items extracted from her are listed as "huge Hearst interests." With this exposé of Hearst wealth, the SLA demanded another $4 million within twenty-four hours and then allowed Patty to read only a single line into the tape recorder. "Today is the nineteenth and yesterday the Shah of Iran had two people executed at dawn." The message, the threat, was clear.

If Patty was confused and frightened on the nineteenth, just the events of February 22 alone must have been enough to hasten along a change of attitude that was already taking place. On that morning her father stepped before the cameras and announced that "the matter" was now out of his hands. Next came Charles Gould with the Corporation's offer—$2 million upon Patty's release, $2 million in January 1975, a new tax year. And yet Patty knew that the Corporation had more money than it knew what to do with. She had been with me when her father happened to mention that it had $40 million in liquid capital just sitting in the bank—another huge figure that might have stuck in her head. And her captors surely must have confronted her with a fact they had pointed out in the last communiqué—that the Foundation had to give out each year well over its $1.5 million food program donation just to maintain its legal status as a nonprofit organization. They also must have shown her Attorney General Saxbe's view of the matter that ran under the headline, "Saxbe: Execute them!" And finally the crowning blow. After Peggy Maze's careless remarks about "culls" being given out and Ludlow Kramer's confident pronouncements about the $1 million donated to PIN and his predictions that contributions would eventually exceed Hearst money twenty to one, at eleven o'clock that same morning the food riots erupted in Oakland.

Things could not have gone worse if we had tried. And had we tried? Over and over the SLA pointed out to Patty how her father had intentionally sabotaged the food program with no regard to her safety. Soon they began to explain and predict that the rest of us would fail her too—her mother, her sisters, her friends, her fiancé. For the next fifteen days little was said or done on our side to dispel this impression that was forming. PIN struggled along, the FBI still maintained they knew nothing about her abductors—an obvious lie to Patty—Mrs. Hearst, in her black dress, continued to invoke God, and Mr. Hearst continued to refuse to give any defense or justification of his efforts that Patty might have been able to hang on to. Added to this, the rest of us, Willie, Patty's sisters and friends, and I, were afraid anything we said might upset the fragile situation, and we had said nothing. Aside from my press briefing when I first arrived in Hillsborough, Patty had not heard a single word from any of us for over three weeks.

In view of this, it could not have been long before Patty began to feel, with the peculiar power of prediction, that she was being abandoned. During this time her captors had political discussions with her and gave her things to read on the torture and brutality of the prison system. In early March she was transferred to a "special security unit"—which probably corresponded to the SLA's moving from the Daly City house on to yet another "safe house"—and instructed in the use of a 12-gauge shotgun with which to protect herself in case of a police attack. Told of the authorities' notorious lack of concern for the lives of hostages during the Attica Prison uprising and the Marin County Courthouse shoot-out, surrounded by paranoia, by seven people who now felt they were protecting her as well as holding her, and not having heard from us for weeks, it is not surprising that Patty sounded much changed on the March ninth tape. Now there were no more pauses as she tried to collect her thoughts, no rustling of her notes in the background as she went from point to point. This time she read a speech, her tone bitter and accusatory. Significantly, her message had no ending provided her by the SLA, but ran into the next speech, forming an integral part of the communiqué. And yet there were moments when she would falter, as if she could not believe, did not *want* to believe that the outside world had turned its back on her.

Mom, Dad. I received the message you broadcast Sunday. It was good to hear from you after so much silence. But what you had to say sounded like you don't care if I ever get out of here.

I don't believe you're doing everything you can, everything in your power. I don't believe you're doing anything at all. You said it was out of your hands; what you should have said was that you wash your hands of it. . . . I don't know who influenced you not to comply with the good faith gesture. . . . I know you could have done what the SLA asked. I mean I know we have enough money.

Whether consciously or not, the news media has been assisting the FBI in what is now an overt attempt to set me up for execution. First, by promoting a public image of my father as a bereaved parent who has done all he can to meet the demands of his daughter's kidnappers. . . . Second, [it] has created a public image of me as a helpless, innocent girl who was supposedly abducted by two terrible black escaped convicts. I'm a strong woman and I resent being used in this way.

Mom, I just hope you can be stronger and pull yourself together from all these emotional outbursts. . . . You've got to stand up and speak for yourself. . . . I wish God would touch your heart and get you to do something concrete to help me.

I'm starting to think that no one is concerned about me anymore. I wish I could hear from the rest of the family. I'd like to hear what my sisters have to say about Dad's decision. . . . Steven, what do you have to say? Willie, I know you really care about what happens to me. Make Dad let you talk. You can't be silent.

I really want to get out of here and I really want to get home alive. . . . I realize now that it's the FBI who wants to murder me. Only the FBI and certain people in the government stand to gain anything by my death.

After listening to this tape I remember Mr. Hearst saying, "She'll come home, everyone will gather around her in a flood of tears, and it will all be forgotten." Although he was hurt by Patty's attack, he really believed that; all of us did.

A week later I appeared on KQED, having made the emotionally difficult decision not to appeal directly to Patty by saying how much I loved her and how desperate we were for her return. Not wanting the SLA to see the distraught condition we were in, I directed my comments to her captors and the business between us. Further contributing to what must have seemed to Patty our distance from her was Randy's refusal to have Patty's sisters and Willie appear publicly, fearing as he did for their safety. Their silence, in the face of Patty's request that they speak out, must have been another blow to her confidence in us. A final blow was Mrs. Hearst's choosing to accept, at this, the worst possible time, another term on the U.C. Board of Regents. Since Patty had asked her mother to say something for herself, accepting the Regents post must have seemed to Patty like a bitter act of defiance. It was the last straw. If Patty was slipping on the March ninth tape, by the last PIN giveaway two weeks later, we had lost her.

On April 2 the SLA stated that the release of the prisoner would be announced within the next seventy-two hours. That night at the Olsons, after weeks of balancing, shuffling, and weighing what I thought was every conceivable possibility, after reading and rereading the backgrounds of the known SLA members, talking with Dr. Hacker, and spending hours with Patty's friends trying to assess the psychological effects of her imprisonment, I wrote, "For the first time I actually believe it possible that Patty will be released at any moment."

Fourteen hours later I was on the freeway to Hillsborough, stunned by Bob Joffee's call and consumed with hatred for the seven people who had victimized us all and were going to murder Patty.

When I pulled into the Hearsts' driveway the crowd of newspeople gathered around my car. Unlike other times, when I was besieged with shouted questions and had to shove my way through, the newspeople were subdued, almost quiet. They too were in a state of shock from the news of Patty's message. A few of them asked me questions: Did I believe it? Did I think Patty had been brainwashed? What was my reaction? But none of them badgered me for answers. Carolyn Craven, a newswoman from KQED, hugged me sympathetically, then I made my way through them to the kitchen door.

I have little memory of what happened after that. I have the feeling that I saw Emmy, that she said something to me, but I can't recall what it was. I think I heard the tape by myself in the library, though there may have been one or two other people present. But it was nothing like the previous gatherings when a new tape arrived. The house seemed full of people, but it was absolutely silent.

In her message Patty announced that she had been given the name Tania "after a comrade who fought alongside Che (Guevara) in Bolivia." "I embrace the name with the determination to continue fighting in her spirit."

It was truly Tania speaking, not Patty. Her voice was a calm, detached monotone as she listed the crimes of her father, a "corporate liar," and those of her mother, whose acceptance of a second term on the Board of Regents "as you well knew, would have caused my immediate execution had the SLA been less than together about their political goals." Her parents, she said, were concerned only with money and power and would never willingly surrender either. The corporate state which they supported was about to murder black and poor people "down to the last man, woman and child." The energy crisis was a hoax, a means to get public approval for the construction of nuclear power plants to be manned by a small class of "button pushers." All of the lower class and half of the middle class would be unemployed within the next three years. The extermination, the removal of these unneeded people had already begun "in the same way that Hitler controlled the removal of the Jews from Germany."

In one part of the tape she greeted Remiro and Little, from

"an environment of love," to them in "the belly of the fascist beast." In another section she talked to me:

> Steven, I know that you are beginning to realize that there is no such thing as neutrality in time of war. There can be no compromise as your experience with the FBI must have shown you. You have been harassed by the FBI because of your supposed connections with so-called radicals, and some people have even gone so far as to suggest that I arranged my own arrest.
>
> We both know what really came down that Monday night, but you don't know what's happened since then. I have changed, grown. I've become conscious and can never go back to the life we led before. What I'm saying may seem cold to you and to my old friends, but love doesn't mean the same thing to me anymore. My love has expanded as a result of my experiences to embrace my comrades here, in prison and on the streets, a love that comes from the knowledge that no one is free until we are all free. While I wish that you could be a comrade, I don't expect it. All I expect is that you try to understand the changes I've gone through.
>
> It is in the spirit of Tania that I say, "Patria o muerte. Venceremos."

8

WHEN THE TAPE WAS OVER someone turned off the recorder and handed me the photograph of Patty that had accompanied it. Dressed in dark overalls and a knit cap, she was posed wide-stanced, holding an automatic rifle in front of a red flag with the seven-headed cobra emblazoned across it. The person who handed me the photograph did so without comment. I don't remember who it was. After a moment I put the photograph down and made my way out of the library and into the large entrance hall.

There was a fairly large group of people gathered there— a couple of servants, some members of the family, a few people from the *Examiner,* and John Lester, the press liaison, who was standing solemnly by the front door. The atmosphere was much the same as it had been when I had first arrived at the Hillsborough home two months before—low voices, expressions of shock and disbelief, and that particular kind of anguish one senses in onlookers at the scene of a fatal accident, a confused pain that separates each person with his own thoughts and feelings. As I was starting up the stairs, Lester approached and asked if I would have anything to say to the press. "A little later," I heard myself tell him, then continued up the stairs.

I went into what had been my room during the first month of the kidnapping, closed the door, conscious of how quietly I closed it, and sat down on the bed. In a film the scene would have cut at that point, perhaps picking me up where I would be a few days later in a Mexico City hotel room, talking with the French Marxist, Regis Debray, playing Patty's tape for him and explaining how it had devastated me; or perhaps years later, as in *Citizen Kane,* an old man sitting in a wicker chair in a solarium, shaking his head and telling the eager young journalist how it had been with Patty and the Hearsts and the kidnapping. At that point any cut would have been appreciated. But the scene did not cut, and I sat in that small room thinking of the photograph of Patty, her gaunt face, her hollow eyes staring off into space, thinking about how they had dressed her up like a lifeless manikin and posed her in front of the flag, thinking of that until I wanted to put my fist through something.

A half hour later, after the Hearsts had made a statement, John Lester consulted his watch, then leaned out the front door. "Thirty seconds," he called out. Standing behind him I heard his announcement echoing through the press corps as they began making final adjustments on their equipment. Then the television lights flared up. "Ten seconds . . . okay, Steve." I followed Lester out the door, walked down the steps, and stood in front of the ring of microphones. Except for the click of camera shutters and the rustle of a slight breeze through the pines along Santa Inez, it was strangely quiet.

"It really seems that if the SLA wants the truth to be known," I began, "they must ask Patty to leave, at least temporarily, and speak her mind. If only she speaks to me that would be enough." I said a few more things, then realized I was repeating myself and stopped. "I can't think of what else to say. I want to tell Patty I love her just as much as ever. I think she knows that I can accept whatever she has chosen even though it may be hard for me. . . . But to accept what has happened today in the manner in which it has been given would be to just sell her out. . . . That's the way I feel right now. . . ."

I stood there for a moment—no shouted questions this time as it was clear that I couldn't handle them—then turned and went back inside. Someone stopped me in the entrance hall. "That was a good statement, Steve," he said. I told him I didn't think it would do any good.

I stayed at the Hearsts' that night. Despite the tension between us, which had been heightened by a recent magazine article in which I had been quoted as referring to Mrs. Hearst as a "rubber stamp" for the Reagan faction on the Board of Regents—"Don't bother to spend much time around the house," Mr. Hearst had told me a few days earlier—I was in no condition to drive elsewhere and they were in no condition to send me packing.

At 3:00 A.M., a few lights still burning in the campers and mobile units outside, I sat down on the bed and began writing in my journal:

Wednesday, April 3

Today was in many ways the most crushing since the beginning. Perhaps not emotionally, since I am still functioning somewhat, but certainly in a more profound, objective sense. The situation has turned irrational and although I have to keep trying, I have given up a good measure of hope.

I told Lester today that the pain is not so much over Patty's "rejection" of us, but over the new danger she seems to be in, the likelihood that she is being used in some way. But it is really more than that. It's the utter confusion I feel. I know Patty is suffering terrible mental strain, but I cannot any longer tell what is in her mind. It is heartrending to think of her mental state—the deception, fear and encouragement that must have been used to put her where she is. And the fact that not only are they using her, but are degrading her as well.

I clutch at straws and try to believe that this is some weird prelude to her release. But what really seems to be the case is that they are using Patty as an instrument of propaganda, while at the same time either setting her up for death, or for continued incarceration, or for participation in some action. It is really hard to grasp what may be their plans, if indeed they have any. . . . After today's tape there is no longer any doubt that at least two of these people, Perry and Cinque, are psychotic. . . .

Indeed. After Cinque announced on the tape that three people—Robyn Steiner, the ex-girl friend of Russell Little, Chris Thompson, a former resident of the Chabot Road house, and Colston Westbrook, the coordinator of Vacaville's Black Cultural Association—had been declared enemies of the people and were, along with all members of the ruling class, "to be shot on sight at any time and at any place," he suddenly, almost schizophrenically changed gears, his voice becoming choked with emotion as he read a message to his six children—"Daddy wants you to understand that he can't come home because you and the people are not free. To you, my children, even though I may never see you again, know that I love you." He then played the "SLA national anthem," a jazz-rock instrumental called "Way Back Home." It might as well have been taps. As I listened to it, I had the sickening feeling that Cinque was saying a final farewell. And then Nancy Ling Perry who, in her breathy, spaced-out voice, came close to delivering the general field marshal's eulogy—"Cinque is not a God, nor is he from God, nor does he have an extreme ego problem. . . . The word 'Cinque' means the seventh prophet." She spoke bitterly of the other prophets who had been murdered by the pigs— Malcolm X, Martin Luther King, and George Jackson—and now "once again the people have brought forth another prophet and leader," she announced. "The bringer of the children of the wind and the sound of war. . . ."

"Tape From Patricia—I've Joined the SLA," read the morning headlines, "Parents Say They Don't Believe It." It was something of a comfort to read that *very* few people believed it. "I think she's just pretending to go along with them so she won't get killed," said a fifty-year-old mechanic in a man-on-the-street interview. The authorities' position, as stated by U.S. District Attorney James Browning, was that Patty "was under some duress—someone holding a gun at her or the like." But if that was the prevailing opinion, there were others. "I have a very serious concern that the girl is dead," said Vincent Hallinan, one of the trustees of the four-million-dollar escrow account. FBI chief Charles Bates did not agree: "I have no information that she has been killed. I must act on the theory that she is still alive." Mae Brussell, a so-called "conspiracy expert," had quite another theory. "The script from the beginning," she explained, "was to have a nice, rich, white princess kidnapped. The whole plot for the paramilitary takeover of the United States might come out if the truth is revealed about this kidnapping." Meanwhile, posters of Patty in her SLA garb began appearing on telephone poles and kiosks along Telegraph Avenue in Berkeley with the caption, "We Love You, Tania!" In bold red letters the *Berkeley Barb* proclaimed, "Patty Free!" while an astrologer for the *National Star* declared that Patty's chart "indicates that she fell in love with one of her captors and is very happy."

With the arrival of what was called "The Tania Tape" no one could anymore be sure of anything concerning Patty and the SLA. The kidnapping was over, we had been told, the "action terminated"; now, in place of the pandemonium of working, planning, dealing, we had only the anguish of our bewilderment. Moreover, when Mr. Hearst had tuned in radio station KSAN the day before and heard his daughter described as "Tania, the ex-Hearst," there was nothing for him to do, no new demands to meet, no announcements to make, nothing. But perhaps that was just as well. After fifty-nine grueling days of PIN, prison meetings with Death Row Jeff, trips to New York, streams of advisors, law enforcement personnel, and community leaders; after hundreds of false leads, crank calls, and extortion attempts Mr. Hearst's resources—financial, physical, and emotional—were finally exhausted. He had pretty much come to the end of himself. After making a brief statement to the press that afternoon, his voice strained with bitterness and grief, he began making arrangements to fly the family to Las Cruces to recuperate. "The Hearsts," said a friend, "feel like they've been kicked in the stomach. There's just no more dealing left in Randy."

So whereas I had been physically and emotionally battered, as well as discouraged from taking an active part in the negotiations for Patty's release during the first month of the kidnapping, now it was Mr. Hearst who had taken a beating and was utterly discouraged. He had used his personal influence, his money, and the Corporation's power to try to free Patty, but it had all failed. Almost by default, then, the next series of maneuvers was pretty much left up to me, the second string.

On April 5 I drove down the San Francisco peninsula to the home of Jeanetta Sagan, a small woman of boundless energy who had been in the Italian underground during World War II and was currently an officer in Amnesty International (A.I.). Headquartered in London, A.I. is a nonpartisan, humanitarian organization working for the release of political prisoners and the abolition of torture throughout the world. It was my second visit to Mrs. Sagan. I had been referred to her the week before by Bob Joffee, my hope being that she might be of some help in contacting foreign governments that might offer the SLA political asylum. At that first meeting Mrs. Sagan had made it clear that neither she nor A.I. could involve themselves in any negotiations for Patty's release, but then had struck upon another idea. Regis Debray, the Marxist theoretician whose books had been found in the burned-out Concord house, was in Mexico City and so was another one of Mrs. Sagan's close friends, Joan Baez. In fact, Debray and Baez had been friends for some time and were staying at the same hotel. "Regis will do anything for Joanie," Mrs. Sagan had told me, "and he's wanted to visit the U.S. for years, but has been refused a visa because of his politics."

It had seemed like a perfect opportunity. If Baez could persuade Debray to help us in our negotiations with the SLA, perhaps

I could persuade Mr. Hearst to pull a few strings and get him a visa. Moments later, Mrs. Sagan was on the phone to Joan Baez who promised to get in touch with Debray. A half hour later Debray himself had called. After a lengthy conversation in French, Mrs. Sagan hung up and told me that Debray was cautiously noncommittal, but that he had not vetoed the idea. I immediately called Mr. Hearst.

"Who the hell is this guy again?" Mr. Hearst asked.

"Regis Debray," I told him, then began sketching out Debray's background—French, Marxist, a South American revolutionary—but that's as far as I got.

"We need a goddamn South American revolutionary mixed up in this thing like a hole in the head," Mr. Hearst cut in. "It'll just bollix up the whole thing. Besides, if it gets out that I helped this guy into the country it'll neutralize any use he might be, which I think is none."

I tried to persuade him otherwise, but to no avail. I hung up the phone feeling pretty deflated. "Don't you give up, Steven," Mrs. Sagan half-lectured me. "Don't ever give up. During the Occupation we had people lost for years and we got them back. For now we can just keep Regis in mind in case something else comes up."

What had come up four days later was communiqué #8— "I have been given the name Tania after a comrade who fought alongside Che in Bolivia," Patty announced. Tania and Che Guevara, the well-known Cuban revolutionary and confidant of Fidel Castro, had been killed in 1967 on the eastern slopes of the Andes mountains when Bolivian troops tracked them down and ambushed Che's small band of guerrillas. Months earlier the troops had captured the messenger between Che and Castro, a young French Marxist who also knew Tania, Regis Debray. Now Patty had claimed the name of Tania and I had an introduction to Debray, who was released after four years in a Bolivian prison. The coincidence seemed incredible.

Before driving to Mrs. Sagan's house on April 5, I stopped by the Hillsborough home and told Mr. Hearst of my plans to fly down to Mexico City and talk with Debray. "I guess it won't do any harm now," he said, "but why don't you give Dr. Hacker a call and see what he thinks first."

Out of politeness I called Hacker in Los Angeles.

"Sure," he said. "It sounds like a good idea. . . . But why did Randy want you to call me?"

I explained that Mr. Hearst and I had had our differences and that he didn't have all that much confidence in my ideas.

"Yes," Hacker said in his thick Viennese accent, "I have gotten that impression."

When I arrived at Mrs. Sagan's we drove over to Joan Baez's home in nearby Woodside. She had just returned from Mexico a few days before. Located off a country road, her redwood home was warm, sunny, and unpretentious, very much like the woman herself. She served us tea and we talked for a couple of hours about what Debray could and would do to help. Joan explained that he was extremely wary of being associated with the politics of the SLA and did not want to be put in the position of having to make pronouncements on the situation. "But if you handle it right," she told me, "I think he'll help you." When I left she gave me a warm hug and wished me luck. I thanked her and Mrs. Sagan for all they had done, then drove to Berkeley to spend the night at the Swantons'.

Later that night, the Swantons in bed, I looked through a book on Tania that Mrs. Sagan had given me. When I was moving, when I was busy, I was all right. When I was alone, when it was dark and quiet, I began sinking again.

Friday, April 5   2 A.M.

I just looked through the book on Tania, trying to feel a little bit of the revolutionary frame of mind, but the psychology of the whole thing frightened me—the emphasis on conversion, the total submersion of the self in the cause—"The old life is buried in the past." I try to grasp how much of this very real and powerful religious force was present in Patty's voice, and how much she was merely parroting. My finding out may not help much, but any understanding I can gain has to be better than the utter bewilderment I have felt in the last two days. In the delirium of looking through the book it struck me how much the picture of Tania on the cover resembles Patty. . . .

Forty-eight hours later I was looking out my window at the Chateau Royale Hotel in Mexico City, nervously awaiting the arrival of Regis Debray. I had called his room when I checked in, around six o'clock in the evening, but got no answer. It worried me. For the past few days I had been scrambling madly around, scraping up the $300 for the plane ticket, reserving a seat on the flight, getting a Mexican visa, and then suddenly I was sitting in that hotel room with no assurances that Debray would even try to help us. He would, Joan had said, *if* I handled it right. But she did not say how. I remember thinking: If Debray doesn't know much about the kidnapping how can I possibly explain the whole thing to him? I got out my portable tape recorder and the last tape and sat on the bed. After trying his room again, then sort of staring out the window at the park across the wide boulevard—a festive scene with balloon vendors and mariachi music, families, kids, and tourists strolling under the strings of lights decorating the trees that lined the plaza—I pushed the cassette into the recorder, turned it on, and went weirdly back into the kidnapping.

I got only halfway through Patty's statement, then had to turn it off. I had thought that I could handle it, that I had toughened somewhat, but listening to her diatribe was almost as bad as the first time I had heard it, in some ways worse. There was an unmistakable element of free will in her voice, a calm willingness to say those things that I had been too shattered to really hear before. She had not simply been forced to read her speech. And yet colliding with this, while I could almost believe a misinformed anger at her parents, it was impossible to believe that she was actually convinced of the nightmarish scenario she described—the mass unemployment, the wholesale slaughter of the poor down to the last man, woman, and child, and the removal of the unneeded by a small class of button pushers, all of this to take place within the next three years. She couldn't possibly believe that, and yet she sounded as if she did. "Tell the people, Dad, that all of the lower class and at least half of the middle class will be . . ." I had to turn it off and go take a shower.

I was still agitated when I dressed, so I decided to go down to the hotel dining room, which didn't help my mood much. Dimly lit with flickering electric candles, the dining room was only half full—mostly American tourists chattering excitedly about taxi rides to Taxco, good buys, great bars, and long hikes up the pyramids. Innumerable white-jacketed waiters and busboys stood against the mosaics awaiting the tap of a fork on a plate, while a lone guitarist lurked around searching for eye contact and another rendition of "La Paloma." I sat at a corner table with a nearby post for company.

At 11:30 I finally got through to Debray. A few minutes later he knocked on my door. A good-looking man in his mid-thirties, Debray looked like someone who *had* spent four years in a Bolivian prison. His narrow French face was creased and weathered and his expression deadly serious. I don't remember him smiling once during our meeting. Debray was also in a state of total disarray, one tail of his rumpled, unbuttoned dress shirt hanging out, his hair disheveled, his large moustache going off at strange angles, and his eyes red rimmed and bloodshot. As it turned out I'd caught him just after he had taken two sleeping pills. He spent much of the time shaking his head, rubbing his face, and fighting to stay awake.

After a rather awkward introduction, Debray told me that he had kept abreast of the case by reading newspapers and magazines. It was apparent that he had been distressed by what he had read. Heartened by this, I filled him in on some of the latest developments, sometimes groping for a better word or phrase because of his difficulty with English, then brought out the tape recorder and put on the last communiqué. I hoped that it would speak for itself. It did. Debray listened intently to Patty's statement, asking me to stop it in parts, nodding seriously at my translation, but then began to fade as Nancy Ling Perry launched into her rap on "Cinque, the seventh prophet," and finally waved his arms impatiently midway through Cinque's shoot-on-sight orders.

"It's enough," Debray said. "I have nothing more to learn from this tape."

In a perverse sort of way I was disappointed that he had not made it to Cinque's "Save the children" plea with the SLA national anthem playing in the background, knowing it would finish him. But it wasn't necessary.

"I cannot approve of a kidnapping of this kind," Debray said. "It is one thing if it is a police torturer and the people see the purpose of it. But with this kidnapping I am disgusted." He told me that from everything he'd seen and heard, the SLA had made a caricature of good and valid revolutionary struggles throughout the world. "Bad imitators," he called them. He was particularly scornful of Patty's conversion. "No one is made a revolutionary in two months," he said. "This is more religious than political."

We talked for over an hour before Debray pulled himself wearily out of his chair. "If you think it will help," he said, "I will write a letter to Patty."

I told him I thought it would, feeling greatly relieved. His offer was more than I had hoped for.

Debray wrote the letter the next morning in his room, occasionally stopping to think or ask me about a phrase, then bending back over it again. When he finished he explained that he could not, in good conscience, address the letter to Tania and that he had postdated it "Paris, April 12." By then he would be back in Paris and his involvement in the case could not embarrass the Mexican government. He also asked me to call him before the letter was published so that he could consult with the leaders of the Socialist Party, fearing that the press might use it to attack the party in the French elections, which were drawing near. "I very much hope your fiancée will be safe," he said as we were shaking hands good-bye. "I hope to talk with her someday."

I was extremely impressed with Debray's letter, the way it subtly challenged the SLA to let Patty surface and prove her conversion:

To Patricia Hearst
    I just received a visit from your friend, Steve. It is at his

request . . . that I take the liberty to intervene in a situation in which the spirit, methods, and intentions are obviously foreign to me.

Steve let me listen to your last message in which you say you have exchanged your name with that of Tania. . . . It is because Tania was a comrade and a friend that I want to speak to you. . . . The only purpose of this message is to contribute to the clearing up of any ambiguity of your real situation, and to relieve the anguish of your friends who fear for your safety and your life. . . . I ask you only to assure me that you have consciously and freely chosen to take the name and follow the example of Tania. If such is indeed the case, we can do nothing but respect your decision—no matter how questionable it may seem. . . .

If there is a reason of security for yourself or for those in your company that impedes you from appearing personally in public, I am sure that . . . you will find a way to deliver to an anonymous intermediary, without needless publicity, irrefutable proof of your free and conscious choice. This intermediary can be any common friend of Steve and you.

Good luck, Patricia,
Regis Debray

After a two-hour wait on standby, I finally caught the last plane back to Los Angeles, not having set foot outside the Chateau Royale once since I checked in. After another long wait in Los Angeles, I caught a commuter flight to Oakland, climbed into my VW, and promptly ran out of gas. But it didn't bother me much. Although I was thoroughly worn out, my mission had been successful. I had Debray's letter and in the next few days I hoped to elicit similar statements from other leftist leaders, a chorus of influential voices that would also challenge the SLA to give proof of Patty's change of heart. With this in mind, on April 10 I drove into the Tenderloin and parked in front of Glide Church.

Cecil Williams was hardly impressed with my plan. He sat behind his large desk, idly tapping a pencil on the edge of it, then leaned back in his chair. "Steve, I really don't think Angela Davis would have much influence on the SLA," he said. "She's not even in town now and I seriously doubt if she'd be willing to get involved."

I asked him if there wasn't someone who might have some influence with them, someone we could appeal to.

Williams was uncomfortable. I had the feeling that he was trying to let me down easy. He hesitated a moment, then told me what was on his mind. "Steve, I think you should prepare yourself for the possibility that Patty and Cinque have a thing going," he said gravely. "These things are possible. Especially when you have a charismatic leader like Cinque with a lot of . . . of vitality." He meant virility. "Women," Williams went on, "especially white women find something irresistible about a black leader. I know about these things from personal experience, Steve. . . ."

Vincent Hallinan, the craggy seventy-seven-year-old radical attorney, was not in the habit of letting anyone down easy. He had been in and out of jail on numerous occasions for his courtroom outbursts, had recently been waylaid by two muggers in an alley and had beat hell out of both of them, and was aptly described by an associate as a man "who didn't take any shit."

"Steve," he said forcefully over the phone, "Cinque is psychotic and Patty is dead. I think you'd better brace yourself for that. I've been working with criminals for fifty years and the first thing they do is get rid of the witness. Another letter from Death Row Jeff isn't going to change that." Hallinan went on to tell me how disgusted he was with the radical community's paranoia about the SLA. "Every leader in the Bay Area's got goddamn bodyguards," he said angrily. "It astounds me that they can be so fearful of these people. Christ, how dangerous can half a dozen juvenile delinquents be with every cop in California looking for them?"

Hallinan gave me the phone number of Raymond Procunier, head of the Department of Corrections, through whom I could get in touch with Death Row Jeff, but it was clear he thought it was a waste of time.

My next call went to John McLean, the AIM representative, who was back in St. Paul meeting with Dennis Banks and Russell

Means. "They're already thinking of coming out with a statement," McLean told me. "I'll ask them to get back to you this afternoon." A few hours later they tried, but ended up talking to a very confused woman in San Francisco. I had given them the wrong telephone number.

Meanwhile, I was sitting in Charles Bates's office on the sixth floor of the Federal Building. By then there were strong suspicions in many quarters that the FBI actually had the SLA surrounded and were on the verge of an assault. I knew that one of these quarters was Glide Church, having heard that Cecil Williams was ready with a secret contingency plan to avert bloodshed. When a shoot-out threatened to erupt, Williams was going to lead a group of citizens between the two forces and try to bring about a "viable solution," whatever that meant. But as well-intentioned as he was, I knew that if things reached the point where the SLA and the FBI had each other in their gunsights, Williams's group of citizens would be ducking for cover within a matter of seconds. Because of this I had gone to Bates's office to ask him, to plead with him to hold his men back and give the SLA a chance to respond to Debray's letter. "I don't know how close you are to the SLA," I told him, "but if you could just give them some time to . . ."

"Steve, we are conducting this investigation as we always have," Bates interrupted, "with Patty's safety foremost in our minds."

As usual Bates was absolutely unreadable and to all appearances quite confident that the SLA would soon be brought to justice. But behind his cool exterior he was painfully aware of the fact that all over the Bay Area his best agents were bumping into each other and chalking up an impressive string of blunders. Along with the Oakland police, they had failed to notice—or at least to do anything about—Patty's name in the notebook found in the Concord house in January; although Camilla's first name and East Bay Regional park patches had also been found at Concord, the FBI raided Camilla Hall's rented house three days after she had abandoned it on February 19 in order to join her SLA comrades. Then, in March, they had just missed a perfect chance to capture Camilla red-handed. This last blunder began in late February when agents discovered that Camilla had a savings account in the Bank of America almost directly across the street from FBI headquarters in Berkeley. Informed of this, the bank manager put a hold on Camilla's account, assuring the agents he would contact them if she tried to withdraw her funds. It didn't work out that way. On March 1 Camilla walked blithely into the bank, closed her account, and stuffed $1,565 into her Levi's, remarking that she was nervous "carrying this much money around Berkeley." The teller had failed to notice the hold on Camilla's account, and although at that time there were up to 300 FBI agents working on the case, not one of them had been assigned to watch the bank.

Although the story of this incident had not broken yet, Charles Bates must have known that when it hit the papers he would have some fast explaining to do. But what he could not know was that in weeks to come there would be more such stories, all of which drew analogies between the FBI and the Keystone Kops. In fact, while we were talking that day in his office, there was another one sitting directly under him just waiting to go off. For three long months the FBI had been scouring the entire state for the blue VW that had been seen the night of the kidnapping, unaware that an FBI secretary had bought it from a used car dealer. She had been driving it to work for weeks and, while Bates was talking confidently with me about the investigation, the car was parked in the garage six stories below his office. And finally, as we were to discover later, had Bates looked out of his office window that day he could almost have seen a one-bedroom apartment on Golden Gate Avenue in which eight people were holed up, Patty and the SLA, not twelve blocks away.

In short, Charles Bates was literally sitting on a mountain of evidence, had "the best agents in the field," the finest scientific equipment available, and yet time after time his men had been made to look hapless and bumbling by the SLA. Of course none of us knew this at the time, and in a way it is to Bates's credit that he did not show the teeth-gritting frustration he must have felt because of it.

"I know you probably can't tell me anything," I remember saying to him toward the end of our meeting. "But I want you to know that if anything breaks in the next few days I *can* be trusted."

"I know you can, Steve," he said, one hand shaking mine, the other opening the door. I thanked him for his time, knowing that he wouldn't trust me to go down to the corner and buy him a hamburger.

For his part, Mr. Hearst did not fare much better with the Bureau than I did. While they apparently trusted him, it was still not policy to discuss anything but the general outlines of the investigation, and, for the most part, Randy did not press them. But sometimes even he would lose patience with the FBI's closed-mouth approach.

"Do you or don't you know where Patty's being held?" I remember Mr. Hearst asking Bates one evening.

"If the investigation proceeds as . . ."

"If!" Mr. Hearst cut in. "If a goddamn frog had wings he wouldn't bump his ass on the ground! Do you know where the girl is being held?"

"Not at this point, no," Bates replied. "But I can assure you . . ."

So that's all we had to go on, Charles Bates's calm assurances and Attorney General Saxbe's rather inane statements from Washington, the latest of these being that "The lid is off the case" and that the SLA was "operating by the book," neither of which we paid much attention to.

It is ironic that while Saxbe was hardly considered a man of penetrating insight insofar as the case was concerned, his comment that the SLA was operating by the book proved far truer than anyone suspected at the time. Among the stacks of material taken from the Concord house was one book in particular, Carlos Marighela's *For the Liberation of Brazil* and its key chapter, "The Minimanual of the Urban Guerrilla." Marighela founded a Brazilian terrorist group, and in 1968/1969 his forces had robbed more than seventy-five banks of well over a million dollars and had kidnapped U.S. Ambassador Charles Burke Elbrick, forcing the release of fifteen rebel prisoners. Before being shot dead by Brazilian police, Marighela had produced his famous how-to book on guerrilla warfare. In Joseph Remiro's copy of the minimanual found in the house, the most pertinent passages had been carefully underlined. It was all there in black and white, the SLA's next move and Patty's trial by fire:

> Within the framework of the class struggle [are] two essential objectives: A) The physical liquidation of the chiefs and assistants. . . . B) The expropriation of government resources. . . .
> The most popular model is the bank assault . . . serving as a sort of preliminary examination for the urban guerrilla in his apprenticeship. . . .

By the second week in April I knew that time was running out, that the SLA was bound to make a move in the next few days. Fearing this, on April 10 I drove to TV station KQED to tape a question and answer session with news director Joe Russin. My purpose was twofold: to assure the SLA that a plane out of the country could be arranged for them, and to predict, and, therefore, take the steam out of, any future actions they might be considering.

For weeks, since Mr. Hearst's first meeting with Death Row Jeff, there had been a lot of discussion about offering the SLA safe passage out of the country—one of Mr. Hearst's acquaintances had even offered a jet that could be ready to take off on six hours' notice. But knowing that the SLA would automatically reject any offer we made at that point, Mr. Hearst was of the opinion that we had to wait for them to demand it. So we waited, and we waited until April 10, when I decided to present the offer to the SLA. It was a last ditch effort, and I planned to be as calm and cautious in my statements as possible. But just prior to the taping session Marilyn Baker buttonholed me in a corner of the newsroom and began grilling me about Patty's and my "dope connections," her theory being that we had bought grass from Nancy Ling Perry while she was working at "Fruity Rudy's" juice stand in Berkeley.

"You're totally wrong, Marilyn," I told her. "You're way off."

Controlling her anger, Marilyn then told me what she wanted me to do during the interview. I was to ask Patty what we had for dinner the night she was kidnapped. "If she sends back the right answer we'll know what the story is," Marilyn explained.

Now I was controlling *my* anger. I asked her if she had considered the possibility that even if the SLA allowed Patty to respond, they might force her to tell them what we had for dinner that night. Moreover, if Patty sent back the wrong answer, to signal that she was being held against her will, and we made this public, as I was sure Marilyn would, the SLA might do away with her on the spot. "So if she says we had Beef Wellington, when it was really a tuna casserole, we don't say anything, right?" I asked. "Or do we pretend that she has gone over? What's the point other than satisfying idle curiosity?"

At this Marilyn reddened, then huffed off.

By the time Russin and I took our seats in front of the cameras I was still angry and it showed in the interview.

"If Patty were even a temporary convert," I said, "it would be of infinite propaganda value to have her say that in public and not in a room full of machine guns. . . . The most frightening thing on the last tape," I continued, "is the impression that Cinque is saying good-bye, that he's on a suicide mission and seems to like it."

Then I was suspicious of Patty's claim that she had joined her abductors, Russin said.

Like everyone else, up to that point I had been tiptoeing around the SLA for two months, treating them like dangerous children, bending over backward not to upset the general field marshal. Up to that point, but no further. . . .

"This whole thing is a cruel hoax being played on her," I said. "It seems strange that the SLA are the only ones trying to save the Hearst Corporation its four million dollars. If the SLA is not planning to kill her themselves, they're planning to get her into a situation—perhaps with the FBI—in some confrontation where she might very well be killed."

The "situation" I had mentioned was already in the works.

That same afternoon two women entered the Continental Rent-A-Car agency in San Francisco. One of them identified herself as Janet Cooper, using identification stolen from a former key member of *Venceremos*. She rented a green Hornet. In the following two days these same women rented three other cars, getaway cars. Meanwhile some other SLA members, and perhaps Cinque himself, entered a bank on Noriega Street and made a note of its layout and procedures. On April 11 and for the next three evenings, a few blocks from the bank, a resident noticed a green Ford station wagon in the same spot, idling for a moment, then speeding off. Though curious, the man did not report this to the police.

The next day, April 12, I gave *Examiner* editor Tom Eastham the postdated letter from Debray, then returned to KQED to talk further with Russin, the station's resident cynic.

KQED is something of a counterculture television station, its ramshackle offices located next to a railroad spur in the industrial area, its staff hardworking, dedicated, and extremely informal— secretaries in ponchos, newscasters (of every race, color, sex, creed, and age) in everything from three-piece suits to work shirts and Levi's. People were on top of it there; they were concerned and informed. It was a good place to go for information, for "feedback," as Cecil Williams would call it.

On this particular morning, however, sitting in a large, empty studio, lights and electric cords hanging from overhead scaffolding, the feedback I got from Russin depressed me. Like Hallinan, Russin believed that the SLA had used the announcement of Patty's conversion as a way to bury her. "All they have to say," he told me, "is that Tania is off with Combat Unit Eighteen taking part in another action." He then produced from memory a list of sixteen prime SLA suspects the FBI had on file and asked me if I recognized any of the names. I did not. We talked awhile about the new ring Patty was wearing in the SLA photograph. Patty's hand was wrapped awkwardly around the weapon so that the ring was in plain sight. Then Russin mentioned that he had a woman friend who had once been approached by Mizmoon and described her as "an aggressive lesbian, pretty kinky"—"bull-dykes," as Marilyn Baker had repeatedly characterized them.

The speculation about odd sex complications in the SLA never failed to crush me, but this morning I was particularly vulnerable, sunk with the growing realization that all of my attempts to encourage Leftist leaders to speak out and question what the SLA was doing were in vain. An hour earlier I had called William Gagan, Joseph Remiro's attorney, and had told him about the Debray letter, which was at that moment being set in type at the *Examiner*. Gagan was not optimistic. From what he had seen of the two SLA soldiers he doubted that the appeals of anyone from the established Left would give them pause, even someone they respected like Regis Debray. Though discouraged by this, I told him that I was planning to write a letter of my own to the two men, asking for any suggestions they might have about getting through to the SLA. "Well, I guess it's worth a try," Gagan said. I told him I'd bring it by his office on Monday.

After leaving KQED and running some errands, I drove to the Swantons' to spend the night. Nothing that Russin, Hallinan, or Williams had said was something that I hadn't already grappled with myself, and while it disturbed me, edging in from the back of my mind while I listened to them was a more immediate fear—that in Patty's and my relationship there were flaws, weak spots that the SLA might have exploited, might have blown out of proportion in an effort to turn her against me. "I have changed, grown," she had said to me on the last tape, "and can never go back to the life we led before. . . ." I kept thinking of that.

When I arrived at the Swantons', I found that Nate had dropped by. Afer a quiet dinner the four of us stayed up until 2:00 A.M. talking about the life Patty and I had led before, trying to focus in on the ways the SLA might have conceivably gotten to her. It was not an easy thing to talk about, not easy to dissect our relationship and analyze its weaknesses, but it was all we could do to try to get inside Patty's mind.

"Just the dynamics of her situation—not really knowing what's happening on the outside and being manipulated from the inside—would get to anyone," Scott said. "People *can* change under those circumstances." Scott had done his senior thesis at U.C. on thought reform, a reeducation technique used by the Chinese and North Koreans, and went to some length to point out that no one, "not even John Wayne," was totally resistant to a concentrated form of group pressure. At this Mimi became somewhat defensive of Patty.

"You only knew her six months," she reminded him. But later that evening she expressed a fear that had been worrying her since the March 9 tape in which Patty had declared: "I'm a strong woman and I resent being used in this way."

Given the feminist makeup of the SLA women, Mimi felt that if there was any one way in which they could have gotten to Patty it was probably sexism. "Patty really did live your life so much more than you lived hers," she told me, then talked about all the ways that Patty had tried to make my things her own, even to the extent of wearing my Boy Scout shirt, and using my old monogrammed billfold and book bag. "You were the one who always decided what to do, where to go, and even who your friends were," she said. *"Your* old friends." She added that while I could not be called a sexist in the common sense, there were times when I didn't take Patty seriously enough. "Sometimes you just didn't listen to her opinions, didn't respect them," she said, "and I know that bothered her."

Nate listened to this quietly, then suggested that what Mimi was talking about was actually my paternalism. "Weed was definitely a benevolent despot," he said, mentioning some phrases that often slipped into Patty's speech. "My father does that too . . . Steve's just like my father when it comes to gadgets." Even at the time, Nate had thought it pretty telling.

It was. As I thought back on it there was no question that Patty and I had fallen into parent/child roles a little too easily and a little too frequently. "I like it when you teach me things," she would tell me when I'd point something out to her. Or, "No, no, no! . . . Make me," she'd say when I'd remind her of, say, a paper she was supposed to be working on. And if she didn't do the paper and her grade dropped a notch because of it, the way she would hang her head rather sheepishly and say, "I know, I know . . . I've been bad."

Nate also suggested that because I was a "protective figure" for Patty, "the guy who had given her a home away from home"— "You take such good care of me," Patty would sometimes say—I must have been drastically deflated in her eyes the night of the kidnapping. "I mean she knew that you couldn't stop them from taking her," he explained, "but to hear you yelling and crashing around helplessly must have been pretty traumatic." Mimi added that for those first two weeks in Hillsborough after the kidnapping it must have appeared to Patty that I had slipped into the background behind her father, "behind the man who was supposed to be afraid of you because you were a grad student, an intellectual"—something that Patty had once told me.

By the end of the evening we had picked Patty's and my relationship apart. Putting together everything I heard that night, it seemed remarkable that Patty had not walked out on me our first week on Benvenue. But then compared with all the positive things we had together, our problems were relatively small, things that would have eventually worked themselves out. We were extremely happy together, "almost disgustingly so," as Mimi put it. "And Patty was really coming into her own," she said. "The way she used to tease *you*—'Oh, Steve is always doing that,' or, 'Just give Weed a new tool and he's happy all day'—that sort of thing."

Because of these reminders, instead of being dismayed by the weaknesses in our relationship, by the end of the conversation that night I felt reassured of its strengths. There were, indeed, cracks, which Patty's captors could widen, but not ones that were deep enough to explain her words on the April 3 tape.

"I can see her getting discouraged with you," Mimi said, "or really exasperated that you haven't been able to do anything, but not to the point where she's going to turn her back on you. . . . I really don't believe any of that garbage on the last tape. . . . Really, it didn't even sound like her."

But like all of us, Mimi was sick with worry about what was happening to Patty—what was in her head, why she *hadn't* sounded like herself on the last tape, and what the SLA had in store for her next.

After Nate left, Mimi made up a bed for me on the couch, then before going into the other room she said, "I wish Patty'd hurry up and get back. I'm getting tired of mothering you, Weed." I could tell from her voice that talking about Patty and me had upset her, that she was close to crying.

The next morning I began working on the letter to Remiro and Little. I finished it the following day, Sunday, April 14.

Russ and Joe:

Patty's friends and I have been in a very strange way since the last tape. It is, perhaps, not realistic to expect any direct help from you . . . but I would appreciate any advice or opinions you may have to offer on what I have been doing and what the SLA may be doing. . . .

First, I hope that you can understand that I am sick with worry about Patty's safety, and that nothing else means much to me now. It is not of much importance to me if what I say pleases the public, the FBI, the SLA or the Hearsts—I have no side I feel I owe allegiance to. . . . I am speaking honestly when I say I think that the SLA seems to have lost direction and are playing a cruel joke at Patty's expense. . . . I can't believe Patty is already dead, as do many others, but on the other hand I can't seem to envision any circumstances in which the SLA will release her.

I very much appreciated the concern you showed for Patty's well-being in your earlier letter. . . . I don't think Patty and I will forget your help, or the help of the many people who have tried to straighten things out. . . . Again, there may be nothing you can do or are willing to do now, but it does seem important to me to convey some of my feelings to you.

Good luck to all of us.

The next day, Monday, I got in my car and headed for

William Gagan's law office. That same morning across the bay in San Francisco, John McLean and Jack Webb were about to leave for Webb's bank, the Hibernia Bank on Noriega Street in the Sunset District. Ironically, the Hibernia Bank chain had been founded by the great-grandfather of Patty's closest childhood friend, Irish Tobin. Almost casual in their view of urban violence, both men were armed, each carrying a .38 revolver. As McLean recalls it, "We were just out the door, it was about 9:15, when something came up—Jack got a phone call or something, I'm not sure. Anyway, we decided to go to the bank the next morning. . . . Man, it's not hard to imagine what would have happened if we hadn't put it off until the next morning. . . ."

Although Webb and McLean postponed their visit to the bank that Monday morning, eight other people did not. At 9:45 two cars pulled up outside, the Ford station wagon and the green Hornet. At 9:50 five people ran single file to the bank door, Patty in the lead. A customer, not knowing that Patty was directly behind him, slammed the heavy entrance door in her face, knocking her down on the sidewalk. Mizmoon, Camilla Hall, Nancy Ling Perry, and DeFreeze spilled past her. Patty stumbled into the bank picking up some spilled cartridges. Then, brandishing carbines, which they had removed from beneath their coats, all took up positions in the middle of the lobby. Perry shouted, "SLA! SLA! Get on the floor!" Then Cinque, "First motherfucker doesn't get on the floor gets his head blown off."

"She wasn't scared, I'll tell you that," said the bank guard, sixty-six-year-old Edward Shea. "She looked as though she knew what she was doing. She had a gun and she looked ready to use it."

DeFreeze quickly disarmed Shea and shouted for everyone to get on the floor. Alerted by his shouting, bank manager James Smith peered down into the lobby from his upstairs office, then tripped the silent alarm which set off the bank's automatic cameras. He witnessed the entire robbery. "It was done with such a precisionlike manner that they seemed to have a knowledge of the bank, knew where to go and what to do."

With DeFreeze covering the door, swinging his carbine back

Dr. Marcus Foster, Oakland superintendent of schools, who was assassinated by the SLA, November 6, 1973. (*Bill Crouch,* Oakland Tribune)

Headquarters of the SLA, 1560 Sutherland Court, Concord, California. Authorities discovered this "safe house" after a bungled arson attempt, January 10, 1974, less than twenty-four hours after the arrest of Russell Little and Joseph Remiro. (*Kenneth Green,* Oakland Tribune)

Russell Little and Joseph Remiro as they are led to court, March 1974. A year later a Sacramento jury found them guilty of Dr. Marcus Foster's murder. (*Lonnie Wilson,* Oakland Tribune)

Street view of our apartment, 2603 Benvenue, Berkeley.

Agents check the front entranceway of our apartment. Arrows point to bullet holes made by SLA gunmen. (*UPI*)

Composite drawings of the three prime kidnapping suspects, released by the FBI on February 8, 1974.

Three faces of Donald DeFreeze.

Police mug shot of Emily Harris, September
1975.

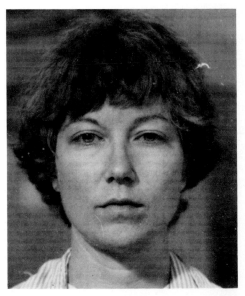

Patricia Mizmoon Soltysik ("Zoya"), one of six SLA members who died in the shoot-out with Los Angeles police, May 17, 1974. (*UPI*)

Angela Atwood ("Gelina") as an Indiana University student, 1967; she died May 17, 1974. (*Black Star*)

Camilla Hall ("Gabi"), as a groundskeeper for East Bay Regional Park District, September 1973; she died May 17, 1974. (*Wide World Photos*)

Nancy Ling Perry ("Fahizah"), former cheerleader and political conservative, who worked actively in Senator Barry Goldwater's presidential campaign, was sought in connection with the assassination of Dr. Marcus Foster. She died May 17, 1974. (*UPI*)

William Wolfe ("Cujo") on a camping trip in Utah's Uinta Mountains in 1972; he died May 17, 1974. (*Wide World Photos*)

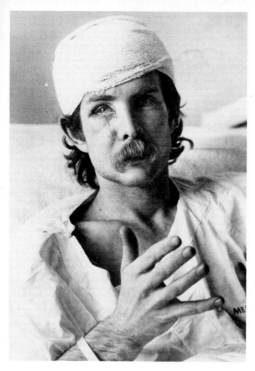

Two days after the kidnapping, I am interviewed at Cowall Hospital by Jay Bosworth, Patty's brother-in-law, a reporter for the *San Francisco Examiner*. (*UPI*)

Saturday, February 9, I leave the hospital to stay with the Hearst family. (*San Francisco Examiner*)

Paul Fischer, News Director of KPFA, reads the SLA "Arrest Warrant" for Patricia Campbell Hearst, February 7, 1974. (*Clem Albers,* San Francisco Chronicle)

Appearing on the front steps of their Hillsborough home, Mr. and Mrs. Randolph Hearst tell the press, in renewed pleas for Patty's safe return, that they have "no real desire to prosecute if she is returned unharmed." (*UPI*)

The first disastrous attempt to distribute food in hope of winning Patty's freedom, Friday, February 22. Pictured are people crowding the Hunters Point distribution site, in San Francisco. (*Wide World Photos*)

Dozens of people were injured and arrested at the West Oakland Food distribution site as rioting broke out. (*Kenneth Green,* Oakland Tribune)

While inspecting coffee and snacks sent up by Hilton Hotel room service, Indians of AIM guard closed doors, behind which their leaders are meeting with Mr. Hearst to discuss the mechanics of the two-million-dollar food program. (*San Francisco Examiner*)

Representatives of three of the activist groups asked by the SLA to monitor the food program hold a press conference Sunday, February 17, at Glide Memorial Methodist Church, San Francisco. From left to right are Yvonne Golden of the Black Teachers Caucus, Rev. Cecil Williams, minister of Glide, and Dennis Banks of the American Indian Movement (AIM). (*UPI*)

Peggy Maze of Washington State's "Neighbors In Need" is shown at the Hearst Building with several "People In Need" (PIN) volunteers; they are taking donations for food, trucks, warehouse space, and volunteer work. Ms. Maze arrived in San Francisco Tuesday, February 19, 1974, with Washington's secretary of state, A. Ludlow Kramer, to organize the two-million-dollar "People In Need" program. (*San Francisco Examiner*)

Oakland woman and her daughter, "Sugar Momma," get PIN food, distributed peacefully several days after the violence of February 22. (*Don Lau*)

A. Ludlow Kramer (*right*), director of the PIN program, at a February 27 news conference. At left is Arnold Townsend, chairman of the Western Addition Project Area Committee. (*UPI*)

Clifford "Death Row Jeff" Jefferson, convicted murderer who helped found the SLA. (*UPI*)

Attorney Vincent Hallinan, one of three trustees chosen to control the escrow account set up by the Hearst Corporation, is holding a letter from Folsom inmate Clifford "Death Row Jeff" Jefferson. In the letter, Jefferson appeals to SLA to begin "negotiations" for Patty's release. (*Wide World Photos*)

A few days after the April 3 tape from Patty, which announced her intention to "stay and fight," posters of approval began to appear throughout Berkeley. (*UPI*)

At the Hibernia Bank robbery, Monday, April 15, 1974:

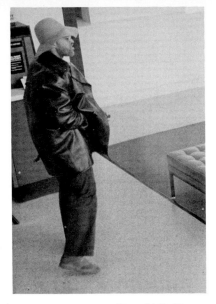

Donald DeFreeze

Mizmoon Soltysik

Nancy Ling Perry

Camilla Hall

Patty Hearst

U.S. District Attorney James Browning holds photo allegedly showing Patty holding a weapon, as an SLA member holds a weapon on her. Charles Bates of the FBI looks on. (*UPI*)

Colston Westbrook, former coordinator of Vac ville Prison's Black Cultural Association (BCA holds a press conference to read a personal letter Cinque. Westbrook, "Peking House" resident Ch Thompson, and Robin Steiner, former girl frier of Russell Little, were all listed by Cinque on t April 3 tape which contained the "death warrant (*Don Lau*)

Christopher Brother Thompson, former friend of Nancy Ling Perry, Mizmoon Soltysik, Willie Wolfe, and Russell Little. In the April 3 tape, Cinque announced that Thompson was a "paid informant to the FBI . . . and is to be shot on sight." (*San Francisco Examiner*)

Popeye Jackson (*left*) with Caesar Moore and Sleepy Bailey of the United Prisoners Union and the disbanded radical organization Venceremos ("We Shall Win"). (*San Francisco Chronicle*)

Mel's Sporting Goods store, scene of the shoplifting incident on May 16 that involved Patty and the Harrises and led to the gun battle at Fifty-fourth Street the following day. The SLA van was parked in the lower left part of the picture (in place of the sports car), when a scuffle broke out in front of the store between Bill Harris and store employees. (*Russ Reed*, Oakland Tribune)

Tom Mathews, allegedly kidnapped by Patty and the Harrises as they fled from the shooting at Mel's Sporting Goods. He was held by the FBI for twelve hours and then released. (*Wide World Photos*)

The holocaust of May 17, 1974, in which six SLA members died in a fierce gun battle against hundreds of Los Angeles police. Pictured here, a police officer carrying a submachine gun runs into position to protect firemen. (*UPI*)

Eight hours after the battle. (*San Francisco Examiner*)

Polaroid group picture found in the burned-out ruins at Fifty-fourth Street. Clockwise from upper left: Emily Harris, William Wolfe, Donald DeFreeze, William Harris, Camilla Hall, Nancy Ling Perry, Angela Atwood, Patty. (*Wide World Photos*)

Los Angeles Police Sergeant Charles Loust points to a grid that charts the locations of the six bodies. On the table are weapons found in the rubble: four 30-caliber machine guns, six 12-gauge shotguns, six handguns, and two pipe bombs. (*UPI*)

Five days after her capture, Patty leaves the San Mateo County jail, accompanied by a federal marshal, en route to San Francisco for her bail hearing, September 23, 1975. (*UPI*)

and forth, barking orders, and Patty in the middle and Camilla covering the far end of the bank, Mizmoon and Perry vaulted the tellers' windows and began emptying the drawers of cash.

"We're from the SLA!" one of the robbers shouted. "This is Tania Hearst!"

At one point Patty was said to shout, "Get down or I'll blow your motherfucking heads off!" According to Smith her rifle was pointed at the customers on the floor and she looked "ready to let go if there was the slightest problem."

There was not. It was over in less than four minutes, the cash drawers emptied of $10,960. But as the bandits were on their way out, a customer was on his way in. Nancy Ling Perry crouched and let go a burst of gunfire shattering the glass doors and hitting the man in the hip. Ducking outside, Cinque fired another burst, hitting a passerby in the stomach. The bandits piled into the station wagon and roared away followed by the second car, which contained the other four SLA members, leaving two elderly men bleeding on the sidewalk and 1,500 pictures of the assault in the bank's cameras.

I waited for Gagan to finish reading my letter to Remiro and Little. He turned to the second page and continued reading, his fingers drumming on the desktop. A moment later there was a light rap on his office door and his secretary entered with a sheaf of papers for him to sign. "There's been a robbery in San Francisco this morning," she said. "A bank holdup. The robbers claimed they were from the SLA."

Gagan and I exchanged glances. "That sound to you like the kind of thing the SLA would do?" he asked.

I shook my head. "They've got every cop and FBI agent in the country looking for them and they're going to go out and rob a bank?" I said, or something to that effect.

This was not the first time we had heard reports of this kind. Grocery store robberies, small-time burglars, even a couple of kids who blew up a telephone booth had claimed they were from the SLA. This was undoubtedly more of the same. Gagan's secretary left the room and he continued reading my letter.

Reports of possible SLA involvement in the robbery continued pouring in all afternoon, but law enforcement officials weren't saying much, especially Charles Bates. I called him the moment I got back to the Swantons'. "We don't know any more about it than you do," he said. I hoped that wasn't true.

That evening I was at Berkeley radio station KPFA, my closest source of updates on the robbery. By then there was no doubt that the SLA had committed the bank robbery. The teletype machine rattled off the bulletin: Five photographs from the bank's cameras had been made public, one a picture of Patty in a dark wig, holding a carbine. "Accounts still muddled," said the message.

Accounts of the robbery, and Patty's role in it, were still muddled the next morning, and the authorities were doing nothing to clear up the confusion. I was frantic. At ten o'clock I hurried into Charles Bates's office hoping to get some information, something to go on. All I got was the runaround. Bates had the photographs all right, but he was "not at liberty" to show them to me. "It's too early to tell much of anything," he said, and yet a San Francisco detective had already been quoted in the morning papers as saying one of the photographs had caught Patty smiling as the first passerby was shot. Bates couldn't discuss that, he said, and sent me upstairs to U.S. District Attorney Browning's office. Browning would tell me no more. "You cannot see the photographs," he told me. "You're not a lawyer. You wouldn't understand."

I exploded. "What the hell do you mean I wouldn't understand!?"

"I'm not saying you can't see them sometime, but not at this time."

Failing that, I practically pleaded with the man not to issue a warrant for Patty's arrest. "At this point she is considered a material witness and no more," he said, then slid one of the photos of Patty across his desk to me. She was standing in front of the tellers' window, her rifle pointed toward the floor, her head turned to the side. "Is that Patty?" Browning asked. I told him yes, of course it was. "Will you sign it . . . and be willing to appear before the grand jury as a character witness?" I signed the back of the photograph. Halfway down the stairs I realized what Browning had done. The photograph I had signed would eventually appear in court. "Let the record show that said photograph has been identified and signed by Steven Weed," Browning would say. The bastard was already building his case against her.

Moments later I was heading down the freeway toward Hillsborough, my bewilderment engulfed by hatred for the SLA and the fear of what they might try next. If they succeeded in making people believe that Patty had willingly taken part in the robbery, they might then feel free to disappear with her or to involve her in another crime in which she might very well be killed. I could contain my rage no longer, and, when John Lester had called and suggested that I make a statement at the house, I had accepted, hoping to make the statement before the Hearsts returned from Las Cruces. I wanted it to be simple and direct, uncomplicated by the tensions that had developed between us.

After pushing my way through the crowd of newsmen, I was sitting in the entrance hall thinking about what to say, Lester posted by the front door as usual, when the Hearsts pulled in. The tension between Mr. Hearst and me was almost palpable. "It is not a good idea to say anything," he told me firmly. "Wait and study it."

I told him that I had already studied it, that we had been waiting for two months and it had gotten us nothing.

"Well, just make it clear that you are speaking for yourself only," he said and turned away.

Lester gave me the nod and I stepped outside.

"Last Thursday I said I thought the SLA would set Patty up. I'm sure they were somewhat disappointed when the bank guard didn't shoot her by accident." I said, "I don't think we should be surprised to get a tape from Patty in a few days explaining the significance of her first revolutionary action of robbing a bank. And when that fails to convince people, we should expect the SLA to try another action like yesterday's—except next time they may not be so clumsy as to have a picture taken with guns trained on Patty." I stopped to get my voice back, then continued. "I cannot understand the inhumanly cruel way in which she is being treated. Anyone who has sympathy to give should extend it now. . . . She is sick and exhausted and bewildered and is dealing with a group that is not going to let her out alive. . . . They are playing a suicidal game . . . but I am still trying to believe there is still hope. . . ."

After my statement I went back inside and sat alone in the hall. I was staring at the floor, already fearful that I had gone too far, when Mrs. Hearst broke away from a group of people in the living room and marched up to me.

"I do not want you making any statements in front of this house," she said angrily.

I told her that I had already made it.

"If you want to make a statement, you go up to KQED!"

"I've already made the statement," I told her again.

At this point Lester entered and she wheeled toward him. "Why doesn't anyone tell *me* about these things!?" she demanded, then turned back to me. "If Patty gets killed, it's your fault! You're killing our daughter!" I hardly even heard her. Lester looked on uncomfortably as she continued her tirade. "She's our daughter and if she gets killed in some future raid, it's your fault! I want you to remember that!"

9

Wednesday, April 17

Stayed at Ed's last night and have regained my balance somewhat. Ed staggered in around 2 a.m. with yet another swingle
girl on his arm. "Does it hurt very much to talk about it?"
she asked, then asked me to talk about it. A nice girl though.

Tomorrow I hope to enlist Cecil Williams' help in putting together a prison proposal with the $4 million in escrow. I'm
hoping that the lure of $4 million for the prison reform move-
ment might persuade the SLA to let Patty surface. If it doesn't
I'm afraid nothing will. . . .

The only bright spot in a perfectly shitty day was hearing that
Joe Merritt, the hustler who tried to con Cecil and me that
night at Glide, was arrested today. After ripping off every
radio and TV station in the Bay Area, as well as Charles Gould

and the Examiner, the idiot actually called the Hearst home and tried to con [John] Lester with the same story about splitting from the SLA with some tapes from Patty. The way Willie tells it, a cop dressed up like Lester parked his car on San Pablo Ave. and, following Merritt's instructions, stuck his head under the hood having left a bag of money on the back seat. Merritt tiptoed up and grabbed the bag and a swarm of dog catchers, postmen and winos grabbed him—undercover FBI agents. The tape he was going to leave was a recording of a song called "My Baby's Daddy Is A Millionaire."

Three weeks before, Joe Merritt had scared the hell out of me with his call. "This isn't some bullshit shakedown," he whispered, as if at any moment I might hear a burst of machine-gun fire in the background and the crash of his body over the phone. "We're talking about your woman." Although he was extremely convincing at first, I was pretty certain his story about defecting from the SLA with two tapes from Patty was bogus—he didn't want any money, just $875 "to get outta here." Still I didn't dare call his bluff, not knowing who he was or what repercussions his arrest might have if it got back to the SLA. Because of this, all I could try to do was keep him on the phone, keep him talking on the outside chance that something might come of it. Nothing did. When Merritt told me how Patty was supposedly being transported to another SLA hideout—in a chauffeured Rolls-Royce covered overhead by a helicopter—I knew the guy was just another con artist. Driving back to Berkeley that night I realized that it was only because I had been so shaken by the call that I had even considered following Merritt's whispered instructions: "put the money in a paper bag and leave it in the parking lot at Sixty-first and San Pablo." It was almost laughable. And yet three weeks later I found myself in pretty much the same position with the SLA.

After Patty's announcement that she had chosen to "stay and fight" with her comrades, which seemed as unbelievable as Merritt's story, I was afraid that with no new offers to reject, no challenges to answer, the SLA might just drop out of sight, go underground, taking Patty with them. Again, all it seemed we could do was try to keep them talking, keep them on the line with the offer of $4 million for the prison reform movement. As with Merritt's call, I thought there was an outside chance something might come of it.

The idea of drawing up a prison proposal seemed obvious to me. As the case wore on, it had become increasingly clear that the prison system was the key to the SLA's origins, philosophy, and rage. If they had a soft spot it had to be the plight of their "comrades behind the walls." Their communiqués were filled with references to "California's concentration camps," "strip cells," and "political prisoners." Reinforcing this were the newspaper articles that traced the SLA's roots back to the Black Cultural Association at Vacaville. Meanwhile, since March 28, there was $4 million just sitting in the bank, $4 million that could be used for defense funds, bail funds, class action suits, prison publications, whatever the SLA wanted, *if* they released Patty. When I approached Vincent Hallinan with the idea, he thought it was a good one. "Even if the SLA rejects the offer," he said, "it will show them up for what they are—gun-toting punks who could give a goddamn about the prison situation." And finally, it seemed that drawing up a satisfactory proposal would be a relatively simple matter. I was hard put to see how any of the prison reform leaders could refuse to endorse it. After all, who could turn his back on a four-million-dollar donation to the Cause? With that question my education began.

On April 18, I drove to Glide Church to sound out Cecil Williams on the idea. Compared to the nine days following that visit, the two hours I spent at Glide were calm, quiet, and productive.

Glide was a madhouse as usual, the place dripping with all manner of crises. The three offices adjoining Williams's inner sanctum were crowded with community organizers, advisors, people who had drifted in off the street, and a sprinkling of sports celebrities doing volunteer work. Doors banged open and shut with frenetic comings and goings, phones jangled, shouted orders volleyed back and forth across the room, and the posters, flyers, and sign-up sheets fluttered on the bulletin boards as people hurried past.

It was the first week of Mayor Alioto's big crackdown on the Zebra mass-murder case that had been terrifying residents of the city since a fifty-three-year-old white man was shot dead on the street for no apparent reason. Since the first murder in November, twelve other whites had been killed and six wounded, by black fanatics it was theorized. At Alioto's order, any black man even vaguely resembling the police composites was being stopped, questioned, and sometimes searched, a policy which immediately produced loud cries of police harassment and racism. As usual, the Reverend Cecil Williams was slightly to the left of the center of the storm, his office keeping open a special line for complaints about police brutality. There was also another open line that jangled with bomb threats against Glide for its stand on Operation Zebra. Williams's secretary, sometimes referred to as "Jan the Eurasian Bombshell"—which is an apt description (conversations would falter and eyes would drift when she breezed by)—was keeping a careful tally on all such threats. "Remember what happened to that nigger church in Alabama," one caller snarled. Jan hung up and scratched another mark in the bomb column. I don't know where the figure stood when I arrived. All I knew was that just stepping into Glide was enough to make me sweat.

When I entered Williams's office he was in the midst of half-a-dozen urgent conversations. I waited for him to finish, noticing his African dashiki hanging behind his desk like a judge's robe, then approached him. No sooner had we exchanged hellos than a black kid moved between us, trembling with shock and trying to explain how he had been grilled by the police for five hours. The boy had a bad stutter, his words stretching out into incomprehensible lengths, and I couldn't understand a word he was saying. But Williams seemed to. He put a reassuring hand on the boy's shoulder, was nodding and listening sympathetically, when another crisis suddenly hit the fan. A man rushed into the room and shouted, "There's a guy on top of the building across the street and he's gonna jump!"

256

Everyone stampeded for the door. I followed.

Sixteen floors up on the building across the street a man was hanging out of a window. I braced myself for a suicidal plunge. "Hell," somebody said after a tense moment, "that's a damn window washer." It was. Considerably relieved, I was starting to turn back toward the door when I noticed an unusual amount of activity centered around a Rent-A-Car agency across the street.

"FBI agents," Williams told me. "That's where the SLA rented one of the getaway cars."

I watched the agents scurrying around for a moment, then started to tell Williams about my idea for a "prison proposal" when his doorman/bodyguard moved up beside us. He recognized me, having insisted upon checking my VW for bombs the night Joe Merritt had called; he nodded, then leaned close to Williams. "We hear there's some strange stuff going on at a flophouse on Leavenworth," he said in a low voice. "People carrying in a lotta guns and tools. The guy below said he heard a lotta heavy thudding and bumping around upstairs and called in." Williams told him to check it out.

Back inside, I again renewed my efforts to explain the proposal, but was not particularly successful. Williams tried to listen while carrying on a conversation with Yvonne Golden of the Black Teachers Caucus across the room—my head turning back and forth between them—then told me to talk with Louis Sawyer, the head of Glide's Prison Project. As I was looking for Sawyer I bumped into Vic Washington, the Forty-Niners' star running back who was answering one of the crisis lines.

"You looked kind of weak on TV the other night, Steve," he told me. "Your legs were shaking."

I told him I guessed they were.

"You just take care of your body and it'll put your mind back together," he said.

It was good advice and I thanked him for it.

"Yeah, just take care of the old body," he repeated as I continued my search for Sawyer. I found him sitting behind a desk, shuffling through a stack of papers.

A thoughtful black man in his forties, Sawyer listened to my idea patiently, then told me no, politely. "There are terrible problems in the prisons," he said, "just terrible, and no amount of money can solve them." I was to hear many variations on this theme in the next nine days.

"But four million dollars wouldn't hurt, would it?" I asked.

Sawyer sort of smiled and shook his head. It was obvious that he thought me naive, idealistic, and woefully uninformed, which, unfortunately, was somewhat true. And then, to my growing frustration, he began explaining some of these problems, constructing the argument that since $4 million would not solve *all* of them, we shouldn't even bother with it. But there was more to it than that. When the PIN program had exploded, some of the pieces had fallen on Cecil Williams and Glide, and Sawyer was extremely wary of getting either involved in another such fiasco.

"Isn't there anyone, anything you can suggest?" I asked him.

Sawyer mulled it over, then took out a scrap of paper and wrote down a list of names. He told me that Glide would endorse the proposal if and when I could get the other Bay Area prison reform groups to support it also. At the time this seemed fair enough to me, and only later did I discover that the rivalries among some of these groups was so intense that their members probably wouldn't sit in Candlestick Park together, much less agree to put their signatures on the same piece of paper.

"Good luck," Sawyer said as I got up to leave.

Before making the rounds of the various groups on Sawyer's list—at least the people on it who were not in prison—I wanted to talk with Colston Westbrook, former sponsor of the Black Cultural Association (BCA) who had operated inside the walls, and who had also been introduced by Cinque himself a few weeks earlier:

Colston Westbrook: male, black, age 35, brown hair, brown eyes, 5' 8", 210 pounds, Berkeley language instructor, resident of Oakland, is a government agent, worked for CIA in Vietnam as interrogator and torturer . . . now working for military intelligence while giving cross assistance to the FBI. . . .

Along with Robyn Steiner and Chris Thompson, Westbrook was to be shot on sight.

When I first tried to phone Westbrook at his Berkeley apartment I was greeted by a tape-recorded message: "I am not dead yet, but am fully dressed [armed] and looking forward to a reunion with my old brother, the General Field Marshal." Despite his recorded bravado, Westbrook was not all that anxious to meet with Cinque again, "dressed" or not. It was only after he had come out of hiding that I was able to arrange a meeting with him.

I got out of my car in front of the University Village, a rather dilapidated collection of buildings that had once been an army housing project, ducked under clotheslines, stepped over broken toys and rusting bicycles, and knocked on Westbrook's door. Someone peered out at me through a peephole, then I heard the snap of two deadbolt locks. A plump, gnomish man wearing a knit cap, Westbrook opened the door and showed me into his cluttered apartment—books, papers, and baby toys everywhere. The locks were new, he said, as was the police band radio, and his neighbors had been great about keeping an eye out for his safety, one of them having called the police when they didn't see that *he* was the man looking under the hood of his car. "I gotta check for bombs every time I go anywhere," he explained, then plopped down on the sofa next to his wife, an attractive woman from the Cameroons. "My main squeeze," Westbrook called her. His second squeeze was their beautiful and enormous eight-month-old baby who bounced on his mother's lap throughout our conversation.

After some preliminary talk about his field at U.C., interracial communications and how "this SLA thing" had fouled up a lot of his projects—"Everybody's suspicious of me now"— Westbrook began telling me about his days with the BCA from 1972 to 1973. He said there were about twenty different groups meeting at Vacaville at the time—the Black Muslims ["Don't fuck with the Muslims. They control themselves and they control others."], a bridge club, Alcoholics Anonymous, Indian groups, Chicano groups, and others he couldn't remember. But the BCA was different, an organization of eighty "black cons with nothing to lose."

"Our sergeant at arms was a guy called 'The Ripper.' He was doing time for dismembering some women somewhere," he told me. "Another dude, a little guy they called 'Killer Blood,' had even the hardest inmates terrified of him. And then there was the Chabot Road crowd, the visiting Self-Taught Commies from Berkeley, who liked to stir things up. . . . Yeah, it was a real hot group."

The first of the Self-Taught Commies—"STCs," Westbrook called them—was Willie Wolfe. On a couple of occasions West-brook had given him a ride to some of the Friday night meetings and described Willie's initial reaction to the BCA as "wide-eyed and grossly naive." " 'Goddamn,' " Westbrook said, imitating him, " 'look at all this shit, blacks and revolution in a prison!' . . . Man, Willie could hardly wait to get back to Berkeley and tell his friends about his big discovery.

"I remember him sitting in the meetings," Westbrook went on, "the college kid in his Mao cap, smoking a big cigar and just soaking it all in." But if Willie seemed wide-eyed and naive to Westbrook, his first impression of the BCA was also essentially correct—blacks and revolution. Each meeting would open with the entrance of a color guard carrying the flag of "The Republic of New Africa"—the internal colonies (ghettos) of America— the hundred members would stand, sing the New African national anthem and raise their fists in salute. It was not long before some of Willie's Berkeley friends began signing their names on the BCA visiting list and raising their fists with the others—Russell Little, Robyn Steiner, Dave Gunnell, and Jean Chan of Peking House on Chabot Road.

When I asked Westbrook how all of this could have taken place inside a state prison, he said that while some of the meetings got out of hand—at a year-end banquet he remembered some of the inmates "balling a couple of the visiting women right under the stage"—to all appearances it *was* a Black Cultural Association, the agenda listing such activities as inmate poetry readings, guest lecturers, films, and discussions. But that was Friday nights, the cultural programs. On Wednesday nights the meetings were divided into small rap groups or tutorials where the members "really got down."

One group, led by Dave Gunnell and the STCs, was supposedly a political science tutorial, but Westbrook knew different. It was Mao, Che, and guerrilla warfare. In an effort to break up Gunnell's group, he assigned all its members, except Gunnell, to another group dealing with the problems of the black family. The new group was to be chaired by an inmate who was eminently well suited to discuss these problems, and one who had impressed Westbrook with his serious, well-prepared approach to the subject, Donald "Cinque" DeFreeze. "He hated whites and Uncle Toms," Westbrook told me. "I thought he could handle them."

For three months DeFreeze *did* handle them, as well as recruit some fellow comrades. Then, in December 1973, he was transferred to Soledad State Prison. The following March he simply walked away from the prison's minimum-security area and made his way to the house on Chabot Road.

"After DeFreeze was shipped to Soledad I got out of the BCA for a while," Westbrook told me. "I needed a rest from all the hassles with the Chabot Road crowd. Then the next thing I know, DeFreeze is a field marshal and I'm on his hit list for being a CIA agent." He laughed at the idea of his alleged CIA/FBI connections, but did not deny them. Westbrook was a colorful character and I got the feeling that he enjoyed being something of a mystery man in the case. "Not even my old lady knows everything about my background." He laughed.

His wife looked over at him. "You just better not wake up laughing in the middle of the night, or I'll know you *are* an agent!"

Westbrook laughed again, but a little too heartily. As I left, I heard the deadbolt locks snap shut behind me.

My talk with Colston Westbrook about the BCA had produced in me much the same reaction as the reality of the BCA had produced in Willie Wolfe—"Goddamn, all this shit in a prison, blacks and revolution!" The stories about "Killer Blood," the STCs, the ritualistic opening ceremonies, the inmates having intercourse with some of the visiting women under the stage were at once fascinating and disturbing. But later that night, after reading George Jackson's *Blood in My Eye,* the same book Patty had referred to on the March ninth tape, I was simply disturbed. The fascination had gone out of it, and the reality of the rage, bitterness, and desperation of an articulate black inmate who had died, who had in fact predicted his death at the hands of prison guards, sunk into me. Jackson opened my mind and made more understandable, though not acceptable, the actions of another inmate I had quite literally dreamed of killing, Donald David DeFreeze. Like Jackson, DeFreeze had been born in the ghetto and arrested time after time. But unlike Jackson, DeFreeze had escaped from prison bent on destroying all prisons and the society that had produced them and crowded them with men like himself. He had accepted as truth the vision George Jackson had described in the preface to his book:

> We must accept the eventuality of bringing the U.S.A. to its knees; accept the closing off of critical sections of the city with barbed wire, armored pig carriers criss-crossing the streets, soldiers everywhere, tommy guns pointed at stomach level, smoke curling black against the daylight sky, the smell of cordite, house-to-house searches, doors kicked in, the commonness of death. . . .

It is neither my place nor my intention to discuss here the dead-end conditions of America's prisons and the "cons with nothing to lose" they help create. But it is my place simply to say that there is something very frightening and very powerful taking place behind those walls of which I was unaware before all this began. As Louis Sawyer had told me at Glide, "There are terrible problems in the prisons and no amount of money can solve them." And yet I had also been right—$4 million could not hurt the situation which, after reading Jackson's book and talking to Westbrook, seemed to me so utterly hopeless. Because of this, and my desire to at least embarrass the SLA and provoke a response with the four-million-dollar offer, I decided to continue trying to win support for making the escrow money available to the prison movement.

My next few days were spent fighting traffic all over San Francisco as I tracked down the first four people on Sawyer's list, presented them with the proposal, then went outside and collected the parking tickets off my windshield. By the time I pulled up at a newsstand on Union Street, I was tired and discouraged with my results—two for the proposal and two leaning toward rejection.

John Maher, the dynamic leader of the Delancey Street organization, didn't think the offer would have any effect on the SLA. "You've got to use a more masculine approach," he said. "Ram it to them. Put the four million dollars on their heads. That's the only way I can see of dealing with them." Still, he said he'd endorse it. Willy Holder of the Prisoners Union said the same. A soft-spoken man with a southern accent, Holder was extremely sympathetic. "I'll do anything I can to help," he told me. "It must be hell on you." Ron Silliman, a savvy young guy who headed The Committee for Prisoner Humanity and Justice, had to get back to his people before committing his organization to anything. Velia Hancock of the Vacaville Project said the same. Neither of them looked promising.

I dug twenty cents out of my pocket and bought a *Chronicle.*

"I don't even read the damn thing anymore," the old vendor said. "Nothing but murders in there these days. Zebra murders, death warrants from that SLA group, and now this latest thing."

He pointed out a front-page story about an incredibly brutal murder that had taken place right across the street from Ron Silliman's Portrero Hill apartment. A man claiming to be from the SLA had tied his victim to a chair and had hit him with a hammer until his head was partially knocked off, then had raped the man's wife repeatedly before setting their house on fire. I had just that day returned from Silliman's house and had passed two or three places where police were searching young blacks in the

Zebra dragnet. The city was a very strange place to be in at the time; "The City of Fear" the headlines called it and they were not far wrong.

A half hour later I was just stretching out on Ed's couch when the telephone rang. Ed answered it, then handed the phone to me. It was Mr. Hearst calling to remind me again not to come around the house since I felt it necessary "to divulge private matters to cheap-shot reporters." He was referring to an article that had used me as a source on the live-in "swamis." "Hell," Mr. Hearst said angrily, "I didn't go around telling everyone about your being afraid of cameras at first. But now it looks like you've become a damn lens louse. . . . All you can do is complain about not being listened to around here!"

More upsetting than Mr. Hearst's anger over the article, for which I apologized (though I hadn't yet read it), was his belittling what he thought was in it: "Your Be-Kind-to-Prisoners thing," he called it. The conversation ended with my saying I'd try it anyway, and that I'd let him know what happened.

I felt as if I were catching it from all sides. After trying to get some sleep, which was impossible as my head was swimming with explanations to Mr. Hearst—I even tried writing down a couple of apologies—pleas to the prison people, and thoughts of Patty, I got up and drove to the Hyatt Regency to meet with another reporter, Ms. Andy Port. I had agreed to the interview only after Charles Gould had called to say that Port was interested in doing a sympathetic portrait of Patty and the family. I thought she had the Hearsts' imprimatur and saw it as a chance to make up for whatever I had said to the "cheap-shot reporter" about the swamis. It didn't quite turn out that way. "Spent the evening talking with Andy Port, an attractive young reporter for *Newsday*," my journal began,

> and then had dinner with her on the 26th floor of the hotel. The view was unreal and the restaurant posh, totally incongruous with the rundown storefront offices I had visited earlier in the day. . . .
>
> I managed to get pleasantly high on the drinks and wine, or at

least at first it was pleasant. After dinner we sort of staggered back to Andy's room. I was enjoying the feminine companionship and really didn't want it to end. We ended up watching an old Ronald Reagan movie that bounced off my eyes, and another movie that made so little impression on me that I cannot remember its name. By then I was feeling very strange. As had happened before during the last two months, two or three drinks was enough to put me in a very weird state—the unmanageably pressing feelings of frustration and non-comprehension that crowd into my head. I kept thinking about Patty and the tension and energy that must surround her. . . . I have always been a pretty good drunk, never maudlin, but tonight I felt as if one more drink or one more thought would be enough to make me burst into tears.

By the time the movie ended I had sobered up enough to realize that I had talked much more openly to Andy than I had intended. I also realized that the girl was dead tired and had been keeping me company out of sympathy and opportunity, rather than any particular enjoyment. I left feeling slightly foolish, slightly sad and a little used, despite Andy's friendly good-byes. . . .

I also left Andy's tape recorder full of raw material for an article that would prompt another angry call from Mr. Hearst. But this time I couldn't blame him. I was primarily to blame. I had not yet learned that in the competition for "exclusive interviews" and "new angles" in the case, honesty is not always the best policy as far as the press is concerned.

It was around two in the morning when I walked out of the Hyatt Regency and into the underground parking lot below Union Square. As I rounded a corner I came face to face with a very tough-looking guy in a leather jacket. The garage was pitch dark and deserted and I was still unsteady on my feet. The man frowned at me, then approached. I braced myself. "Are you Steve?" he asked. I told him I was. There was a moment, his face began to contort, then he said, "I think I'm gonna cry." I thought he was. He took my hand and pumped it sympathetically. Although I was somewhat embarrassed, I felt very good about his concern and sympathy. A mugger with a heart of gold. He wished me luck and I walked to my car feeling a little bit better.

The next morning I was knocking on the door of John McLean's Haight-Ashbury apartment building. Next to me was a thicket of barbed wire to slow up the police if they decided to raid the White Panthers' headquarters next door. Behind me a couple of kids were jumping up and down on the roof of an abandoned car and throwing rocks at their friends hiding behind some trash cans. A nice neighborhood.

Dressed in his usual beaded denims, his long red braids wound with strips of leather, McLean cracked open the door, peeked out, then let me in to what looked like the interior of a wigwam, arsenal, used-magazine store, and arboretum—bows and arrows leaning against the walls, rifles and lances here and there, stacks of papers and old AIM newsletters piled on the floors, plants of every description hanging by the windows, and a fairly large tree growing out of a tub in the living room, such as it was. McLean fed his angelfish, then introduced me to Hector, a muscular, but gentle Indian from the Tarahumaro tribe. "His father is a very powerful brujo," McLean said, "a sorcerer in contact with the spirits." Hector nodded at this and told me that since Patty and I had "mingled blood" the energy between us was such that his father's medicine would aid me in my attempts to free her. Somehow his optimism cheered me up. He certainly sounded more convincing than the swami from Nutley, New Jersey; and John McLean sounded even more convincing than he.

An extremely articulate man in his forties, McLean was deeply imbued in the Indians' ways and beliefs, his Scottish father having been born in 1854 and raised by the Sioux. Before I got down to the purpose of my visit, the prison proposal, McLean told me of a "vision" he had had the night after Patty was kidnapped. In a low, resonant voice fogged with cigarette smoke, he said he had fallen into a troubled sleep that night of February fifth. His vision began with a phone call summoning him to a house where he was to make up some phony passports. "I used to do a little of that," McLean explained. When he arrived at the house, he was met by strangers who showed him into a room. "There was a young woman sitting in a wooden straight-backed chair in the middle of the room with her hands behind her," he said. "She looked frightened and bewildered and I knew that her hands were tied. . . ."

McLean was a spellbinder, calm, quiet, authoritative. It was as if we were sitting around a campfire surrounded by mesquite and the distant silhouettes of long mesas.

"Setting my equipment down slowly," he went on, "I took my pistol out of my waistband, had them untie the girl, then backed out of the room with her. I drove her to her father's home and was offered a large sum of money, but told the man I only wanted enough money to outrun the cyanide bullets. . . . Later I was driving north toward Nevada and it was snowing heavily. My car stopped and it continued to snow." He paused, then went on. "I couldn't get out of the car and it kept snowing until everything was white, absolutely white." McLean lit another cigarette. "I take that to mean that I will die, that the circle will close. But I have no choice . . . I am going to find Patty," he said and he believed it. Two weeks to the day after his vision, McLean had been called to represent AIM on the PIN coalition and had worked selflessly. He said he had contacts in the underground and that he was certain that he would eventually make contact with Patty. There was something of Carlos Casteneda, or Don Juan himself, in McLean. While his "vision" was probably a dream or a fantasy, I had a strange feeling that if anyone found Patty, McLean would. He had that kind of mystery and power.

"But to the matters at hand," he said, stepping back into the twentieth century.

Hector served us tea and tiny sandwiches, then sat cross-legged on the floor while McLean and I discussed the wording of the proposal and whether AIM would sign it.

When I left his apartment Hector walked me out to my car. McLean had told me that Hector was his wife's bodyguard. He also let it be known that Hector was a black belt in karate and carried a "piece" on him at all times. "He has killed men in battle," McLean said. I didn't know what to say, but was just glad to have him on my side.

The next morning, to ground myself in reality and try to relax after three days of racing around frantically, I dropped by the Swantons'. As luck and coincidence would have it, Scott had some news that sent me off again.

On November 9, three days after the Foster assassination, Scott had walked out of a Berkeley paint store and almost into two members of a gang that had just robbed a bank. A half hour later he was picking them out of a police lineup. He had pretty much forgotten the incident until April 18, when he was summoned to appear as a state witness at the trial of Earl Satcher, a well-known prison/political heavy and ex-Black Panther who was suspected of masterminding the bank assault.

"It was only then," Scott told me, "thinking back to the robbery that it struck me how similiar it was to the SLA assault— a black ex-con, four white women, and two men hitting a bank."

Scott had mentioned this to the district attorney who then showed him one of Satcher's cards. "The Tribal Thumb," it read, and below it was a two-headed dragon. The D.A. told him that Satcher had known DeFreeze in prison and it was the FBI's guess that Satcher's Tribal Thumb had robbed the bank to finance the purchase of a safe house in Berkeley. "But the story doesn't stop there," Scott told me. "The woman I picked out of the lineup is a Rumanian girl named Hedy Sarney who lived on Channing Way and knew Mizmoon, Camilla Hall, and Chris Thompson." He said that Hedy had pleaded guilty to a lesser count and was out on bail. "She claims to have been held against her will by Satcher and the others," he said. "More or less kidnapped. She lives just down here on Adeline Avenue."

Hedy was still living on Adeline when I found her, sharing a flat with five other people in a rickety wood-frame apartment building, a tenement actually. Although fearful of reprisals by other members of the gang, she sympathized with Patty's plight and reluctantly agreed to talk with me. Her story was a frightening one, beginning with her introduction to Earl Satcher and his friends, Joe Monaco and Janet Hashemi, in a Berkeley beer parlor. She said that after chatting with Satcher a while he showed her one of his Tribal Thumb cards and asked if he could visit her sometime. Hedy told him yes. Four days later her new apartment became the temporary headquarters of the Tribal Thumb, and she found herself their prisoner. Hedy's deposition, which she made two months later to appeal her conviction, speaks for itself:

> Satcher asked me whether I had ever thought of joining a real revolutionary guerrilla group—no rhetoric, no bull. I didn't answer, and he began talking faster and faster. Then he said they were going to rob a bank in order to buy a house for their commune in Berkeley. I was stunned and didn't know what to say. . . .

> Later that night when all of us were together again they began to play some tapes about prisons and the Third World. They talked more about conditions in prison. I began to get scared about what I was getting into.

> The next day was Tuesday and I got up to go to school. Earl stopped me. He said that school was a waste of time and that I would learn what I needed to know from them. . . .

> I spent the whole day walking around in a daze. They never left me alone for a minute. I felt like I was in a prison. When I said that . . . Earl called me a reactionary and began to beat me. He called Joe on the telephone and told him to come over with a gun. . . . When Joe came [over] they talked about killing me. Their plan was to stab me and leave me in the street somewhere. At that time the "machete man" was in Berkeley, and there were a lot of stabbings, so people would think that he had killed me. Earl punched me some more. They asked me to write a suicide note, but I refused. They put a knife to my throat and threatened to burn down the house. I still refused. Then they wrapped me in a blanket and set fire to it. I was too frightened to move or say a word, but they must have thought that I was very brave because they put

the fire out and Janet Hashemi embraced me and called me a comrade. . . . Earl said that he was going to stay with me for a week. . . . He said that if at the end of the month I wanted to leave they would let me go. . . .

They spent days talking to me about prisons. I was in a daze and did not eat for days. I dreamt about running away. The next day Joe and Earl planned the robbery. By that time I wanted to go through with [it]. I thought that once it was over they would buy the house . . . and I could leave them.

On Friday, November 9, we robbed the Bank of America. My job was to go behind the counter and take the money from the tellers' drawers. I did not have a gun. After leaving the bank I went back to the van, undressed and got under the covers. A few minutes later the police entered the van and arrested us. . . .

Although I felt a real affection and sympathy for Hedy Sarney, after reading her deposition I had to wonder how an intelligent twenty-six-year-old woman could fall under the sway of the likes of Earl Satcher. She had not been kidnapped, but met her captors over a pitcher of beer in a crowded bar. Hedy herself was at a loss to explain how she had been at once fearful and mesmerized by Satcher and his group. "Earl knew how to control you with fear and guilt and his arguments," she explained, getting agitated just talking about it. 'Just look at this, just look at that,' he'd say about the ghettos and the prisons. . . . After a while I felt like I was in a dream. I wasn't sure who I was or what I wanted anymore. . . .''

But after talking with Hedy that day, it became apparent that the dream had begun much earlier, in 1970 to be exact, when she moved into the 1900 block of Channing Way in Berkeley, where it was all happening. As she described it, I began to get a feeling for the people, the interconnections, and the atmosphere of that scene.

"It was like a self-contained community," Hedy said, but from her description it sounded vaguely make-believe, almost like an *Our Gang* on a counterculture, radically political level. There were block parties to raise bail funds; "food conspiracies," where everyone chipped in to buy goods in bulk quantities directly from the producers; "phone trees"—something like a chain letter, each person calling two other people when "something was coming down," usually the cops; political movies, discussions, men's groups, women's groups, potluck dinners, and a neighborhood patrol to keep the block free of rip-offs. There was even a club-house of sorts, a small, poster-lined shack behind one of the ram-shackle houses on Channing Way where coffee was served and one could go to rap, crash, get information on rides, medical and legal aid, or just come down off a bad trip. "Everybody on the block knew each other," Hedy told me. "Everyone was into something." Indeed.

On the face of it, the scene on Channing seemed pleasant enough. But there was another side to that scene. For some of its residents it fostered dreams of peaceful communalism and universal brotherly love; for others, visions of necessary violence and armed struggle against fascist, racist, sexist Amerika. What began, developed, and in many cases ended in death, in prison, and in the shattered lives of the people on that street is a story, a horror story in itself.

It was late 1970 when Hedy first moved to Channing Way. She was attending classes at nearby Grove Street College at the time. Located on the Berkeley/Oakland line in a predominantly black area, the college was essentially a counterculture institution, its walls covered with murals of Malcolm X, Che Guevara, and others, its courses emphasizing ethnic studies. It counted among its alumni Huey Newton and Bobby Seale who had founded the Black Panther Party a few years before. In years to come Grove Street College would also have the dubious distinction of counting two key SLA members among its students, Joseph Remiro and Patricia "Mizmoon" Soltysik.

Hedy met Mizmoon within weeks of her move to Channing Way, and later she met Camilla Hall who was also living on the block. Describing Mizmoon as dreamy, romantic, but fiercely outspoken, Hedy recalled an image in one of Mizmoon's poems of her hacking her way through a jungle with a razor-sharp machete. But whereas Mizmoon had a bitter, angry side—the result, perhaps, of an unhappy love affair with a student who had left her only months before Hedy arrived—and was basically bisexual, Camilla Hall was a "natural lesbian" who was happy and outgoing. "She'd kind of breeze into a room and cheer everybody up," Hedy told me. A few months after they met, in early 1971, Mizmoon and Camilla became lovers, moving into an apartment together and taking part in the real beginning of the Channing Way scene, a time when people were getting to know each other and the block was becoming organized politically and socially.

But it was during the following year, in 1972, that the paths of the other future SLA members began to converge. In the fall of that year, Chris Thompson appeared on the scene and began seeing Mizmoon, whom he had met, along with Hedy, at Grove Street College. Not surprisingly, Camilla was deeply hurt by Mizmoon's interest in the young black man and soon moved to an apartment of her own. But that did not end it. With Thompson came others and among them a series of connections and interconnections which would captivate both Mizmoon and the woman who had given her that name in a love poem, Camilla Hall. In fact if there was one central figure in the SLA's formation it was Chris Thompson—"male, black, brown eyes, height 6'3", Berkeley resident, government agent, paid informant for the FBI," Cinque announced on the April 3 communiqué.

Thompson had lived in the Chabot Road house in 1971 with Dave Gunnell, Jean Chan, and Willie Wolfe before leaving for New York for six months. When he returned to the house in the fall of 1972 he enrolled in Grove Street College and began operating a food stand called "Harlem On My Mind" next to the Berkeley campus. Among the other food stands that lined Bancroft Avenue was "Fruity Rudy's" in which Nancy Ling Perry worked. The two became friends, and Thompson introduced her to the Chabot Road crowd—which now included Russell Little and his girl friend Robyn Steiner—and in doing so he became the conduit between Grove Street College, where he met Remiro, the Channing Way scene, and the "Peking House" on Chabot Road.

Meanwhile, during that same fall, when Patty and I were just settling into our apartment on Benvenue, four other people pulled into town—Gary and Angela Atwood, and a few months later their friends from Bloomington, Indiana, Bill and Emily Harris. Almost before they unpacked their bags the Harrises became involved in various political activities—the United Farm Workers Union, Vietnam Veterans Against the War, and Venceremos study groups, where they met Remiro, Willie Wolfe, and through them the others.

By early 1973, then, almost all of the SLA members had met each other and were traveling in the same radical circles. The only odd man out in this was Gary Atwood, who found the Harrises' politics extreme and his marriage to Angela rapidly deteriorating. In the spring of that year, after many arguments, tears, and finally pitched battles, Angela moved in with the Harrises who quickly became her political mentors. "Angela and the Harrises had joined with some people I didn't know," Gary said later, "in a sort of 'encounter group' where they discussed personal and political problems." With reconciliation an impossibility, with Angela calling him a "sellout," Gary returned to Bloomington that summer, unaware that an escaped convict had moved into the scene, functioning as a catalyst that would harden his wife, the Harrises, and their new friends into gun-toting revolutionaries— Donald "Cinque" DeFreeze.

Hedy had a vague memory of DeFreeze's arrival. In the spring of 1973 she heard that Mizmoon had moved to an apartment on Parker Street and was living with a black man introduced to her by someone in the Chabot Road crowd. "Sin," she thought his name was spelled. Later that summer she was told that Mizmoon had moved out of the Parker Street apartment, but wouldn't tell anyone where—probably to the small house on Sutherland Court in Concord which was rented in August.

Although the SLA was now only a few months away from its first "operation," most of its members continued their above-ground activities—target practice at the Chabot Gun Club, visiting prisoners, attending BCA meetings and VVAW study groups, and taking an active part in the Chino Defense Committee (a group that had formed around four Venceremos members arrested for the murder of a Chino Prison guard, shot dead during the escape of a Venceremos inmate). But at the same time, and on another level, Cinque and his followers were holding supersecret meetings in the Concord house in which they discussed future actions, armaments, methods of obtaining false identification and renting safe houses. Throughout the summer these discussions continued, intensified, and finally gave birth to "The Codes of War" of the Symbionese Liberation Army. The time for discussion was over. What followed was the actual renting of safe houses, the deployment of surveillance and intelligence teams, and war-game maneuvers with BB guns in preparation for their first attack on "the ruling class oppressors."

It was only at this point, when a "target" had been chosen, that the SLA soldiers began dropping out of sight. Nancy Ling Perry quit her job at Fruity Rudy's. Mizmoon quit her job at the Berkeley Public Library. Willie Wolfe moved into a small apartment with Remiro. Russell Little moved out of the Chabot Road house and joined Cinque, Mizmoon, and Perry in Concord. In October of that year, Hedy remembered hearing that Camilla had finally decided to meet Mizmoon's new friends, but was worried because it might be "a little dangerous." At about the same time that Nancy Ling Perry told her parents to "think of me as dead," Mizmoon ordered hers to destroy all their photographs of her, and Angela told friends that she wouldn't be seeing them anymore. "I'm into my own thing now," she explained. . . . Less than a month later Marcus Foster was gunned down and the first SLA communiqué was sent to radio station KPFA. The day it was delivered, Hedy was being handcuffed and led to a police van along with Earl Satcher and the rest of the Tribal Thumb.

Although Hedy didn't think there was much, if any, contact between Satcher and DeFreeze, she did mention another name that startled me. While Satcher was being held in the San Francisco County Jail, he met another black inmate who had just been arrested on drug charges, had played an important role in Chino Defense, had had his own defense committee in which the Harrises and Perry had been active, and who would represent the United Prisoners Union on the People In Need coalition, one Wilbur "Popeye" Jackson. With this bit of information everything—Chino Defense, Venceremos, the BCA, the Chabot Road house, the Tribal Thumb, and finally the SLA—all of it had come full circle. Popeye Jackson, head of the United Prisoners Union, was the next name on Louis Sawyer's list of prison reform leaders I planned to visit.

Hedy's mention of Popeye was not a coincidence, rather it pointed to a weirdly inbred Bay Area subculture of ex-cons, escaped cons, white radicals, militant feminists, embittered Vietnam veterans, misfits and losers, all of whom saw themselves—*see* themselves, for it still exists—as fighting in "the belly of the fascist beast," inspired to self-righteous rage by George Jackson's cry—"People are already dying who could be saved, generations more will die or live poor butchered half-lives if you fail to act. Discover humanity and your love in revolution. Pass the torch. Join us, give up your own life for the people!"

Before I left Hedy that day, she asked me not to reveal certain parts of our conversation to anyone. She was afraid of people thinking her a snitch. She was serious, she said. Someone from the movement might murder her.*

On April 21, I parked near Capp and Eighteenth Street in the Mission District—a predominantly black and Latin neighborhood—and walked to a small community center where the Popeye Defense Committee was holding a rally. I could hear the shouts and wild applause of the hundred or so participants three build-

* After almost a year of appeals, Hedy Sarney was convicted of armed robbery and went to prison. She and the other members of the Tribal Thumb refused to testify against Earl Satcher; he was found innocent and is free today.

ings away. This was Popeye's last big boost before his parole board met to decide whether his previously mentioned arrest on dope charges was sufficient cause to send him back to prison where, I might add, he had already spent twenty of his forty-six years. Although the charges had been dismissed against him, just having been arrested, guilty or not, was enough to have his parole revoked. To me this policy sounded somewhat questionable. To his defense committee it sounded like more "fascist, police state bullshit," which is what one of the speakers was saying as I entered the building.

I stuck my head in the main hall to see Popeye and a few others standing on the stage, then went into a small kitchen to wait for him, scribbling down some notes about the prison proposal in my journal. After some more shouts and applause from the main hall, Popeye and a dozen others of his supporters entered the kitchen. When he spotted me, recognized me, Popeye suddenly became agitated, cursing to the people around him and doing his best to avoid me. I almost had to corner him. In fact, I *did* corner him.

"What do you want?" he demanded suspiciously. "I got nothing to say to you."

As I explained the proposal, he listened with his eyes riveted on mine, as if he were searching for something. Only later did I learn that Popeye and some other people thought I was an FBI informer. Because Popeye knew that the FBI had found marijuana in Patty's and my apartment, Popeye immediately made the endemic paranoid assumption rampant in the Berkeley underground that I must be working for the FBI in return for their not bringing me up on drug charges. It is a sardonic twist on Popeye's suspicion of me that he became suspected of playing ball with the Hearsts and the police authorities as a result of Randy's successful manipulations to keep Popeye out of jail despite his parole violations. The vengeance wreaked on Popeye was more than mere suspicion; he was murdered.

"Just let me explain the proposal to you," I told him.

He hesitated, then, "Okay," he said curtly. "C'mon upstairs."

As I was following him up the narrow stairway, I was suddenly aware of someone following me and turned to see a big, slovenly white guy in hiking boots and greasy Levi's, a reporter for the *Daily Californian*. He turned out to be a perfect caricature of the Berkeley right-on, more-radical-than-thou, I-can-dig-it mentality. He followed us into the upstairs room, totally uninvited and pulled up a chair between us. I wanted to tell him to get lost, but didn't want to get involved in a confrontation that might tip Popeye the wrong way. He looked dangerously close to exploding as it was. When I told him that Delancey Street and the Prisoners Union had agreed to sign the proposal he exploded, his every other word *fuckin'*.

"Those fuckin' sellouts!" he shouted. "They're all fuckin' capitalists! They exploit the people, get fuckin' rich, and fly all over the fuckin' country! Then they fly down to Mexico for a fuckin' vacation!"

"Right on, Popeye," the reporter said, then scribbled down Popeye's comments in his notebook.

"I just want your advice," I told him, "your help in using the four million dollars for the movement."

"You're talkin' about Patty Hearst and the SLA," he said. "I don't put nobody in front of myself. Not no Patty Hearst, not nobody. Not even my own son!"

After more shouting, Popeye finally ran out of "fuckin's" and told me to take the proposal to Arnold Townsend and the Coalition to see what they thought about it. "I ain't gonna be fronted off by no fuckin' proposal 'til I know where it's at with myself!"

"Right on, Popeye," the reporter said, raising a fist with a Bic pen sticking out of it. I told Popeye I'd get back to him.

I was on my way to my car when I ran into Mark Swartz, a reporter for KPFA, and a friend of his, a girl named Chris. Swartz specialized in prison reporting, had received a couple of letters from Remiro and Little, and knew the prison movement inside and out. He was friendly, helpful, and an important man to talk to at a time when I was finding it difficult to talk with Popeye Jackson—"the tension maniac," Willie had called him.

Swartz and I fell into a conversation, were standing on the

sidewalk, when a squad car cruised by, both officers giving us the onceover. Moments later they had backed up and were asking us for our identification. I produced mine, and after being politely informed that his press badge could be revoked, Swartz grudgingly produced his. Chris, however, said that she didn't have any identification with her. At this one of the cops went to his car, radioed in her name to headquarters, then returned with the news that she had thirteen dollars' worth of outstanding parking tickets. "I'm afraid you'll have to come with us," he said. Chris had no such intentions. She began putting up an argument; I was trying to intervene on her behalf when a second squad car pulled up. Glancing past it, I saw the community center disgorging a lot of angry Popeye supporters. They were heading our way.

"Is it worth it?" I asked one of the cops, nodding toward the approaching crowd. "You're going to start a riot if you're not careful."

The cops ignored me and were starting to take Chris to the car when two more squad cars pulled up, their lights flashing. The next thing I knew we were surrounded by a large crowd. Shouted epithets, orders from the cops to "back off!" and the grating voice of the radio dispatcher filled the air. Then suddenly from out of nowhere, Popeye came barreling through the crowd. "What's goin' on here!?" he shouted. "What's she bein' busted for!?"

A face-off between Popeye and a very large sergeant ensued. "Get back on that curb!" the sergeant ordered. Popeye stood his ground and the sergeant moved right up to him. There was no physical contact between the two men; the whole confrontation looked like something out of a cartoon—their faces inches apart, their necks straining, and little specks of spit flying as they yelled at each other. "Back on that curb or you're under arrest!" the sergeant shouted again. A moment, then suddenly out came the handcuffs and Popeye was against the squad car, then inside it.

Five minutes before, I had been standing on the sidewalk talking quietly about my prison proposal, and now I was surrounded by a near riot, having precipitated an altercation that could send a man to prison.

"Fuckin' pigs!" the crowd yelled as the four squad cars pulled away. "Let's go down there!" "Down to the pig station!" people started shouting. I caught sight of Arnold Townsend, moved up to him, and suggested that just he and I go down to the station and try to straighten things out. Neither he nor anyone else wanted any part of the idea. They were all piling in their cars to go down and confront the pigs.

"Popeye's old enough to know better," the desk sergeant told me when I made my way through the crowd and up to him. Next to me, the first cop who had pulled up was filling out his report. I asked him why they had needed four squad cars for a parking ticket violation.

"Well, the first car was mine," he said, "and the second car was a back-up unit . . ."

"Yeah . . ."

"And the third car was on Zebra patrol," he went on. "And the fourth car was my commanding sergeant's car. That makes four."

I stood there stupidly for a moment, watched him bend back over his report, then gave it up and sought out Popeye's attorney who had just walked into the station. After assuring him that I would be willing to help in any way I could, that the whole thing was a stupid misunderstanding, I headed out the door. As I was walking down the steps I passed Popeye's wife, who was crying about him going back to prison. She glared at me as though I had intentionally set him up for the bust. There was not much I could say until I appeared before the bench on Popeye's behalf. I walked to my car, was digging out my keys, when I was approached by an officious, humorless young black woman.

"Some people saw you writing down names in that notebook at the rally," she said coldly. "I want to see those names."

The whole situation had been so weird that I was somewhat giddy and made a feeble attempt at a joke. "I hate to talk with people without being introduced," I said. "What's your name?"

She didn't think it was funny. "I want to see those names," she repeated.

I very much wanted to tell her what she could do with those names, but then it was more important that I dispel her and others' suspicions that I was an FBI informant. I opened my car, took out my notebook, and handed it to her. She scanned the pages one by one, as though she was searching for a code, then handed the notebook back to me. "Okay," she said, then turned and walked away.

Two days later I was down at the Hall of Justice talking with the D.A. who would prosecute Popeye's case, a very severe young woman who looked as though she had not smiled in twenty years and did not anticipate smiling in the next twenty. I suggested that under the circumstances it might be best for all concerned if the case was dismissed. She told me she would take the matter under advisement and then showed me to the door. As I was heading for the exit, I passed two off-duty cops and their girl friends in the hall. "That's Steve Weed," one of the cops said loudly after I was by them. "I think I'll gross him out." Gross me out, I thought to myself, hearing their girl friends giggling and trying to shush him. "You deviant," the cop called out. "Get yourself a real woman." Instead of being angry, I smiled to my-self. It was somehow comforting to know that I was not the biggest idiot around.

A half hour later I was at the AIM headquarters talking with John McLean and a rather motley crew of Indians who had been called there to discuss my prison proposal. Unfortunately, most of them had been caught unawares at a local beer joint when McLean had called and were three-fourths drunk, which made the discussion a bit difficult to get off the ground. Now and then an Indian guard stationed by the door would shout "That's it!" to some unintelligible remark that had been made inside. I remember hanging my head and watching a flea hop around on the linoleum floor. By the time the flea had disappeared, the party had decided that they could get behind the proposal and disbanded, making jokes about drunken Indians.

The next morning McLean and I headed for Jim Queen's makeshift office on Portrero Hill, the scene of several boisterous coalition meetings. We made the mistake of bringing along a couple of six-packs of Colt 45, hoping it might smooth out any differences that might arise. As with the Indians the day before, the discussion on Portrero Hill was a bit difficult to get off the ground.

Arnold Townsend, his tough assistant, D.W.—"a venomous bastard," Peggy Maze had called him—and Jim Queen, a community organizer, could all "dig that [my] woman was in the box," but wondered why, very pointedly, I had not taken matters into my own hands from the very start. "If it was my woman," they kept saying, "it'd be no holds barred." After trying to explain the utter confusion of the first weeks of the kidnapping, I gave up and started talking about the prison proposal. But they wanted to talk about the raw deal they got in the PIN program, the way the Establishment had only come to them when one of its "princesses" had been ripped off, and "why weren't you into the PIN program from the beginning? If it was my woman. . . ."

It went like that for most of the afternoon. Every time I nodded yes to something that had been said, hoping to gain their confidence and support, D.W. would cut me off with, "No, that's not it!" and shake his head in disgust. At one point, when he seemed totally exasperated with my ignorance, he drew a little diagram of the bank robbery on the back of a matchbook cover and handed it to me.

"Which X is in the best position?" he demanded.

"This one." I pointed.

"Right. That's Cinque, the pivot man. Dig?"

I stared at the matchbook cover not digging it at all. Finally McLean leaned over to me and explained what D.W. was trying to say: Cinque was not only the leader, the pivot man in the robbery but of the whole group, and if I wanted to get anywhere with the SLA I had better start thinking about what motivated Cinque.

All that in one little diagram, I wondered.

D.W. took the matchbook out of my hands and burned it to destroy the evidence.

I thought it was about time for me to be going. I told Townsend I would get back to him. "After you talk to Popeye," he said firmly.

"Popeye told me to talk to you," I said.

"Well, go back and tell him you did."

Chronicle reporter Tim Findley worked the action on his Walther .380 and showed me how to load it. It was the same kind of weapon that had killed Marcus Foster, but that wasn't why he was showing it to me. He had it just in case the SLA decided to put an end to his career as an investigative reporter. He had received a lot of threats lately.

Findley had reached me by phone at the Hyatt Regency while I was being interviewed by Andy Port. I had been avoiding him and most other reporters for days, but the gruff, gravel-voiced Findley had a lure—poems, letters, notes, and scrapbooks of the SLA that had been pirated from the Concord house before it had been cordoned off. He was trying to tie up all the loose ends of the SLA mystery, he said, and wanted me to look through the material to see if anything caught my eye. I went to see him the day after my visit to Portrero Hill.

Findley and his wife lived in an attractive redwood home perched in the densely wooded hills above Sausalito. I parked my car on the narrow road and walked down the stone steps to the house. Findley greeted me at the door in Levi's, boots, and a work shirt, looking more like a cowboy than a reporter. But he was a reporter and a first-class one at that. He was also angry, an emotion with which he had considerable experience. Abe Mellinkoff, the *Chronicle*'s city editor, had recently remarked, "In all my years as city editor, only two reporters have quit in a huff—and both of them were Tim Findley." Findley's latest exit had been precipitated over Mellinkoff's refusal to run one of his stories on Mizmoon and Camilla for fear it might endanger Patty's life. "The word came down from Randy," Findley told me, sighting down the barrel of his Walther .380. "But the hell with it." After introducing me to his wife, who had just stepped in, Findley led me to his work alcove and pointed out the cartons of SLA material. "Dig in," he said.

I dug in, for about three hours. Much of what I saw that day was the work of the SLA "Intelligence Unit"—stacks of neatly typed profiles on business leaders, newspaper clippings from society and business pages pasted on construction paper, crudely drawn diagrams of time bombs, electric blasting caps, and trip wires—all of it resembling a high school sophomore's civics project. "Stakeout of a Restaurant," read the title of one of the many surveillance notes. "There are three of us. Osciolla's room is the twenty-four-hour cafe. Pay phone is the hall closet. Cin's room is our base. The corner lamp is the bar where targets are drinking." And I could see them playing commandos with their BB guns, ducking into rooms, pretending to call each other from make-believe phones, checking their watches, and then crouching out of a doorway and dropping the imaginary targets with BB gun fire. . . . Incredible, preposterous, except for images of Marcus Foster face down in a parking lot. . . .

But more than anything else it was the personal notes, the scribbled lines, the unsent letters to home, and the poems that had the greatest impact on me. The people became real, frighteningly real.

Written in red ink in Angela Atwood's journal:

Men are bombarded with fuck propaganda. No matter what your problem, fuck it away. Fuck away anger. . . . There are so many of my people who suffer so. They don't have the luxury of this kind of worry. I am mad that we all have so little and have to grab for what we can get! . . . Scream! Throw shit all around! But would the others in the house think I was crazy? Would they understand? . . . I need to direct this anger, get something out of it. Oh scream, fuck, paper, words. Fuck! Shoot, shoot, shoot!!!

From Nancy Ling Perry's notebook:

i am here inside this body all alone. Of course. i do not show myself anywhere. i am a phantom, i think. i wonder if i am or if it's because i see phantoms. If i draw a picture of myself as soon as it's finished shall i tear it up into many peices? When you come, come alone. . . .

Uterus normal in color. Could be from wanting sex and not getting it. Try masterbating, lady. Do you know the reality of things or nerves?

A portion of Remiro's letter to his mother:

I helped burn entire village and kill all animals and leave those alive in mourning and starving. Hitler would have had orgasms in the 101st. Now I look at the police and see them in the same frame of mind as the army I was in. . . . This letter is mostly addressed to you, Mom, because Dad has never been interested in listening to me. . . .

Little's notes to himself:

Don't interrupt. That's what I was going to say. . . . Bullshit. Asking for recognition. Don't mouth ideas, actualize them. Think of myself last. . . . Listen to myself. Have confidence in my own ideas, enough to argue about them. Here are the reasons for, here are the reasons against. . . . Think! Think! Think!

One of Mizmoon's poems, dated August 21, 1973, the formal beginning of SLA:

My committment must be total
My pistol aim must bring death . . .
No nice girl
No nice, groovy young woman
An angry, vicious, deadly revolutionary Woman
I am to be feared.
I mean death
To the class who are our oppressors . . .

I thought of Patty surrounded by these people with their as-sassination games, their sick introspection, their mania for plan-

ning and secret codes; all of it bonding them together like a per-
verted encounter group, a psychological snakepit, upon which they
depended for their sanity. I remembered Harris's words on "The
Tania Tape": "To purify our minds of the bourgeois poisons. . . .
Part of the revolutionary process in which we are engaged involves
the constant redefining of thought, word, and action. . . . We
must deal with the [bourgeois] enemy within." I thought of them
planning the bank robbery with her—renting the cars, diagraming
the bank's layout, working the timing down to the second. And
then that moment when they moved into the bank and what incredible exhilaration they must have felt afterward, counting out
over $10,000 in their hideout. . . . Then Hedy Sarney's words
came back to me: "You don't know what it's like to have eight
people always coming at you and you can't get away. After a
while it was like living in a dream. I wasn't sure who I was or
what I wanted anymore. . . ."

The next morning, April 24, I was sitting in the basement
cafeteria at the Hall of Justice listening to Popeye rant and rave.
"They're crazy," he said of the SLA. "They're a fuckin' suicide
squad and they're gonna get burned for sure. You can't go after
the enemy like that. They got no tanks, no airplanes, not a fuckin'
thing. There ain't no way out of it for them. No way."

For all his wild mau-mauing, Popeye knew far more than
he showed and was far more complex than I had originally
thought. He fully understood the power of U.S. District Attorney
Browning's SLA grand jury and how it might be used to "come
down hard on the Left." Moreover, he understood that the four-
million-dollar escrow arrangement was actually nonbinding; that is,
it could be successfully contested, which I had just discovered myself after talking with Hallinan the day before. As far as the prison
proposal was concerned, Popeye said he might endorse it if Delancey Street and the Prisoners Union were out of the picture, but
he had to show it to his people first. I could bring it by Glide that
night, where he was speaking out against Operation Zebra. I told
him I'd be there, then left.

I was leaning against the wall of the elevator when the
doors swished open and I was face to face with a group of re-

porters, not knowing that a new tape had arrived at the Hall of Justice, where it was about to be played for the press.

"Jesus, how'd you know it was coming here?" one of them asked.

"What do you mean?"

"The new tape from Patty. What's your reaction to the things she said about you?"

I told him I hadn't heard it yet, then ducked a few more reporters who had hurried up, and drove to McLean's apartment.

There were a few Indians gathered in front of a tiny Sony TV when I walked in. On the screen the newscaster was describing the tape as "Tania's statement on the SLA bank robbery and the efforts of her fiancé, Steven Weed, whom she calls a sexist, ageist pig." One of the Indians patted me on the back as I sank down into a chair. The photo of Patty holding the carbine flashed on the screen as the tape played over it. "Greetings to the people. This is Tania," Patty began. She announced that she and her comrades had "expropriated" $10,662.02 from the Hibernia Bank to ensure the survival of the SLA in their struggle with and for the people. Then came her comments on my efforts:

> To the clowns who want a personal interview with me— Vincent Hallinan, Steven Weed, and the Pig Hearsts—I prefer giving it to the people in the bank. . . . As for my ex-fiancé, I'm amazed that he thinks that the first thing I would want to do once freed, would be to rush and see him. I don't care if I ever see him again. During the last few months Steven has shown himself to be a sexist, ageist pig.
>
> Not that this is a sudden change from the way he always was. It merely became more blatant during the period when I was still a hostage. Frankly, Steven is the one who sounds brainwashed. I can't believe that those weary words he uttered were from his heart. They were a mixture of FBI rhetoric and Randy's simplicity. . . .
>
> I have no proof that Mr. Debray's letter is authentic. How could it have been written in Paris and published in your

286

newspaper on the same day, Adolf? I hope that the last action has put his mind at ease. If it didn't, further actions will.

To those people who still believe that I am brainwashed or dead, I see no reason to further defend my position. I am a soldier in the people's army. . . . Patria o muerte, venceremos.

The screen was now filled with Patty's face, then it cut back to the newscaster. McLean turned off the TV, came over, and put a hand on my shoulder. For the next twenty-four hours, I traveled on automatic pilot, just went through the motions.

That evening at Glide Church I gave one of Williams's assistants the revised prison proposal. Behind him the main hall was jammed with people, Popeye up on stage haranguing the crowd about police harassment.

The next morning at Hillsborough I was mobbed by reporters as I made my way up the front steps and entered the house. I talked briefly with Mrs. Hearst, who was surprisingly cordial, almost sympathetic now that I too had been vilified by Patty, then gave a copy of the proposal to Mr. Hearst.

He scanned it quickly, then shook his head. "The trustees aren't going to go for this thing," he said. "We'd look like damn fools, wouldn't we, if she came out just long enough to collect the four million dollars, then went back."

By then I was so worn down, so weary of the whole idea that I was almost relieved by his reaction. Popeye Jackson was definitely relieved. "Right on. Right *on!*" he said when I called to tell him not to bother taking it before the UPU. It seemed that everyone was glad that I was finally giving up.

The Swantons were not home when I pulled up to their apartment that evening. I let myself in and found a note on the dining room table—"Steve, there's some hamburger in the fridge. Help yourself. Mimi."

I started to get out some eggs for dinner, but then put them back and sat on the couch. It was all sinking into me then. I had known when I denounced the SLA that they would answer in kind through Patty. I had predicted it publicly, had wondered what words she would use. "Steven has shown himself to be a sexist, ageist pig," she said, and yet only three weeks before it was: "I wish that you could be a comrade." The timing and motivation behind these words were so obvious, so transparent, that I couldn't take them seriously. It almost didn't matter what she called me. And she was still alive, at least there was that. But what else was there now that it was clear that Patty's statement was less a product of coercion than disorientation, that the SLA had done something horrible to her mind? But how? And what was happening to her now? And what could I possibly do? I could think of nothing, could not even tell what I was feeling sitting there—confused, crushed, depressed, suicidal? I listed the adjectives. "The main trouble," Mimi had said a few days earlier, "is that I just miss Patty."

On the wall next to me was one of Patty's photographs that she had mounted and given to the Swantons. I remembered her working on it, remembered her sitting on that same couch with me three months before, talking about our forthcoming marriage. . . . Despite all that had happened, all that she had said on the tape, more than anything else it was a terrible loneliness that I was feeling that night. As strange as it sounds, I just missed Patty.

The next morning Charles Gould called. "There are so many possible reasons for what Patty's doing," he told me. "They may have a gun to her head or they might have threatened to kill one of her friends if she didn't go along with them. . . . I think you should bear that in mind, Steve," he said gravely. "There's no telling what they may force her to do."

10

⌇⌇⌇

THE .380 WALTHER HELD SEVEN SHOTS and I fired three of them, one bullet taking some wood off one of the posts, the others puffing the dirt behind the suspended target. For thirty yards on either side of me people were squeezing off shots on the firing line or giving into impulse and just blasting away cowboy style. The uneven barrage of gunfire was deafening and, as far as I was concerned, a bit unnerving. I didn't like the shooting range much, but as I had told Jack Webb, I really wanted to find out firsthand what a fascination with guns was all about. My appearance at the Daly City shooting range went a little deeper than that, however.

Two days before I had been talking with Webb and John McLean and had mentioned Charles Gould's call. "Things are getting a little strange," I told them. "The Hearsts have hired two armed security guards to patrol the house around the clock." Mc-

Lean nodded. An off-the-wall group like the SLA was capable of anything, he said, and in view of this he didn't think it was a good idea for me to be knocking around the ghettos of San Francisco alone and unarmed. It was then that Webb offered to lend me a pistol.

The thought of packing a gun around struck me as a little melodramatic at first, but on the other hand it was common knowledge that I was splitting most of my time between the Swantons' and Ed Stow's apartment—certainly the SLA knew that from Patty —and having a pistol within reach when some stranger knocked on the door at 2:00 A.M., which reporters were wont to do, might make me feel a little more comfortable. I took Webb up on his offer. "I'll take you out to the range," he said, "and show you how to use the Walther." The next day, while visiting my mother in Santa Rosa, I filled out an application for a gun permit.

The .380 was a very fine piece of machinery and it fit neatly and perfectly balanced in my hand. But it did not guarantee accuracy. "You're pulling," Webb told me. He was sitting on a wooden bench behind me, next to his "old buddy" Billy from down the street, a cheerful nineteen-year-old boy who was slightly retarded. "Squeeze," Webb said, then nodded for me to finish the clip. I raised the pistol and fired the last four shots. It was easy to see how someone could get into firearms—their craftsmanship, precision, and power, the kick, the explosion, and the bullets splintering wood or socking into the dirt. But how could anyone be more fascinated than *afraid* of them—it was so easy to imagine the bullets ripping and tearing into human flesh; I could *feel* it with each shot I fired.

"Cease firing," came the command over the range's loudspeakers. "Breech your weapons." The firing stopped. "Retrieve your targets."

Billy ran out and got our target, and I sat down next to Webb who was clicking magnum shells into a .38 revolver. He told me he had a friend on the force who had been charged by an armed robber and had shot the man two times. "But the guy just kept coming," Webb said. "The third shot put the guy away, but after that my friend went to magnums. They'll stop a guy in his tracks."

Billy came up and showed us the target. I had just nicked the edge of it with one shot. The rest had gone high and to the right, according to Webb. He stood up and walked to the firing line with Billy. "We're using magnum loads here," he told the shooters on each side of him, then handed the pistol to Billy. Although the boy was extremely careful and knew much more about firearms than I did, when Webb placed the gun in his hand, I scooted down the bench so that I was directly behind him, then braced myself as he began pounding away with the .38. He put four bullets in the target.

When I arrived at the Swantons' that evening, I found Scott tightening the screws on an extra lock he had fastened to the front door. "For psychological reasons," he explained a little too casually. "Mimi's kind of freaked out." While this was true, Mimi was also more than a little irritated with him about an interview in that day's *New York Times* in which he was quoted as saying that Patty might indeed be susceptible to a "flip-flop conversion." Mimi considered this a serious breech of faith in Patty's character. "You just didn't know her that well," she told him over dinner that night. Scott had evidently been hearing this all day. "Look, both of you had better face the fact that it *is* a possibility, a *distinct* possibility," he said, then finished his meal in silence.

As I look back on what Scott said that night, I now realize that he was coming to a conclusion that neither Mimi nor I could accept. Namely, that for whatever the reasons, and regardless of how impossible it seemed, in a very real sense, and in her own mind, Patty was no longer the same girl we had known and loved. She was Tania, a soldier in the SLA.

For weeks the media had been filled with theories and speculation along these lines, and after the last tape even the Hearsts seemed persuaded by them. Patty was brainwashed, they said. "Whatever that means," I remember thinking after reading the quote. If it merely meant that Patty had been driven to a state of irrationality, had temporarily lost herself in the process of being manipulated and degraded, then I could agree that she was "brainwashed." But I could go no further; my confidence in Patty's strength of character was such that I simply could not believe that *she* had changed in a significant way. But starting with the night of April 29 my confidence took a serious beating, then collapsed altogether, leaving in its place a fear and obsession that would consume me for the next two weeks.

It began with a phone call.

"Wes Davis," Mimi said, holding her hand over the receiver. "I think he's that guy who's really into brainwashing. Scott saw him on the news and thinks he's a little rabid."

Scott was right. When I rang the doorbell to Davis's apartment the next evening, I was greeted by a man who had dedicated his life to alerting the Western world about the dangers of "Cheng Feng,"—the Chinese form of "brainwashing" or "thought reform." A clean-cut man in his early thirties, who had spent some time in Vietnam, Davis began talking excitedly about Cheng Feng the moment I stepped in the door and was still talking Cheng Feng when I walked out that door four hours later. His apartment was filled with books, case histories, and scholarly journals on the subject, half of which he read out loud to me. If he was a little rabid, he was also extremely well versed in the area and was quite confident in his analysis of Patty's mental state. "She's been put through a systematic process of thought reform," he told me, "the glue that holds Communist China together." Then out came a book on the subject and off he went for a couple of pages. "The Communists feed on human material," he said, thumbing to another section, "and they've learned how to mold and shape this material to their own ends." Then it was back into the book and, "Okay, now listen to this. . . ."

Although I felt that Davis was a little too eager to squeeze Patty into the Cheng Feng mold. ("She has to come back," he told me at one point; "she's pivotal to the West's understanding of this process.") Most of his arguments were painfully well documented. Brainwashing, he explained, often begins with a "conveyor belt system," keeping the prisoner awake, totally controlling his sources of information, his communications with himself, and forcing him to take part in criticism/self-criticism sessions where silence is forbidden. "Patty's denunciation of you and her parents is typical," he told me. "At first she was forced to say something against her beliefs, which created some psychological dissonance. That dissonance was the first step in fundamentally changing her beliefs." The way Davis saw it, Patty had gone from being a "member of a ruling class family," to "I am a symbolic warning [to all ruling class families]," and finally, after being convinced that she had been betrayed, to Tania. Unfortunately it made some sense.

By the end of the evening, as Davis was picking out some books on the subject for me to read, he confided that he was certain that the SLA had studied thought reform techniques and might even have been trained by Chinese or North Korean agents. Although both of these suggestions struck me as giant steps into the realm of anti-Communist paranoia, I was disturbed by the thought that from what I knew from the tapes Patty's confinement did seem to approximate the various stages of the Cheng Feng process. "A person can be totally disoriented in twelve hours," Davis told me, "and fundamentally changed within a matter of weeks."

I asked him what he meant by "fundamentally."

"There are POWs in North Korea today who still refuse to come back," he said.

Mimi was still up when I returned to the apartment, and, as I told her about my discussion with Davis, I became progressively more disturbed by what he had said. Finally, hoping somehow to disprove his theories, I got out my tape recorder and pushed in Patty's last communiqué. We listened to it over and over that night, playing, then rewinding and replaying certain sections: "To the clowns who want a personal interview with me, Vincent Hallinan, Steven Weed, and the pig Hearsts, I see no reason to further defend my position. I am a soldier in the People's Army." I shut off the recorder and Mimi sat back and shook her head. "It isn't Patty," she said. "The phraseology, the intonation, it just isn't Patty." Whether or not Mimi was just trying to be reassuring, that was precisely what I was afraid of, that it wasn't Patty.

It was around 2:00 A.M. when Mimi went to bed. I put away

the recorder, sat on the couch, just staring off into space, then picked up my journal.

My confidence in Patty's eventual return and the reestablishment of our relationship has always been unshakable, but just now, after playing her tape and imagining a completely changed Patty sitting next to me, I'm afraid I wouldn't even know how to reestablish contact. Probably all I could do would be to ask her to tell me everything that had happened to her.

But what could I say? I practiced all kinds of things to say—sweet things, tolerant things, pleas to understand, pleas to remember, questions to ask—but none are very good and it's all beginning to look horribly futile to me now.

That night I dreamed of a cavernous, gray room filled with people crowding around tables, laughing, talking, and calling across the room to each other. I felt trapped, suffocated. I was trying to get through them, sidestepping and pushing past the bodies, and then it became registration at U.C. and I was searching for Patty. I went from table to table, but no one would tell me where she was. Then a kid I used to know in grammar school came up and whispered that Patty had transferred to another school. I asked him where, what school? He backed away and said that she didn't want to see me anymore.

On Friday, May 3, the four-million-dollar escrow account expired with no word from the SLA. There was, however, "a new development in the Hearst case," as the radio announcer put it later that same afternoon. The abandoned SLA hideout on Golden Gate Avenue had just been discovered after a tenant downstairs had complained to the manager about a steady stream of cockroaches from the apartment above.

The one-bedroom apartment was filthy, littered with rotting food, discarded clothing, and makeup kits, the bathtub filled with an acid mixture to destroy SLA documents, and the walls covered with slogans, poems, and a large seven-headed cobra. "There are some juicy SLA clues throughout this safe house," said one message. "However, remember that you are not bulletproof either, Charlie

[Bates]." Above the bathtub was written, "Cyanide crystals have been added to this 'home brew' so, pig, drink at your own risk!" But most upsetting was Patty's handwriting: "Patria o Muerte, Tania."

Using sniffer dogs, investigators determined that she had indeed been in the apartment, probably for over a month, but under what circumstances was not yet clear. Two small sponges, evidently parts of a crude blindfold, carried Patty's scent. When I heard the reports, I realized that I had been passing the Golden Gate apartment almost every day on my way to John McLean's.

A few days later I drove to Hillsborough, having been asked by Duane, the agent-in-residence at the Hearst home, to come down and identify something found in the hideout.

Duane pulled a stained, blue bathrobe out of a tagged plastic bag and handed it to me. "Is that Patty's?" He nodded at it. I had seen Patty in that bathrobe a hundred times—cooking breakfast, lounging in front of the TV, studying in our bedroom—and yet it didn't look the same. It was not as I remembered it, but then, perhaps, nothing was. "I think so," I told him. Duane stuffed it back into the bag. "We'll send it off to Washington to see what those stains are," he said.

Before leaving I picked up some mail that had been sent to me there and read it when I got back to Berkeley. Most of the letters were the usual, hysterically religious prayers, appeals, and denunciations, and the usual threats from semiliterate political fanatics from both ends of the spectrum: from the Ku Klux Klan to SLA supporters. But there was one letter in particular that made me laugh giddily at first, then left me subdued:

Dear Weed:
First off, why don't you get yourself a haircut? You look like something that just crawled up out of a cave and saw the light of day for the first time.

Secondly, you refer to this gang of thieves as smart, and intelligent. Let's face it. It's a gang of rag-a-muffins, snotty-nosed
rag-a-muffins led by a few hardened criminals. Or homosidal
maniacs. Have you ever seen a maniac who is smart?

Thirdly, you were a rotten influence on the Hearst girl. Be
honest. That University of California is a hell hole to begin
with. It was once a wonderful town to be in. The only way
you'd get me there now would be by pistol point. It's a veritable dung-hole, filled with all kinds and sorts of human confusion and hellishness. A seething inferno of veritable evil.
And nothing more.

You took her there, exposed her to a lot of bearded nuts who
probably filled her mind with all kinds of crapola. Then she
simply went over—head first into the inferno of suggestion
and romantic adventure.

Well, she's really adventuring now with the alcoholic "field
marshall." Ye gads.

What next?

I don't think anything good is going to come out of this. I
believe they will start making all kinds of mistakes and will
end up in a hail of bullets. And another venture into illusion
will be over with.

That's the way life goes—at least the side we peer through
darkly.

Why is it that man must take every wrong step until he stum-
bles on the right one?

Sincerely,
An Onlooker

Despite the comedy of the letter, I hadn't wanted to be reminded of what I myself had been trying not to think of for some
time: that the SLA was inexorably moving toward a suicide confrontation. "It's becoming harder every day to envision a good end
to all of this," I wrote that evening. "Things have gone too far.
I remember early on almost superstitiously promising myself that

it would be over by page 40 of this journal, and thinking what an impossibly long wait that seemed. I'm on page 140 now, which is why I thought of it, and I wonder how many more pages I will have to fill."

It was May 7 when I wrote that, and, before the worst part of it was over, I would fill thirteen more pages in that green notebook, some entries scribbled down illegibly, some pages left blank, the events of those days to be added when I had recovered from them enough to write.

The next afternoon in San Francisco, a cashier at Woolworth's told reporters she was absolutely certain that she had seen Patty Hearst and Camilla Hall. They had been in the store for over an hour, she said, and before they left she overheard one of them say, "We've been spotted. We better leave." The cashier called the police and the six o'clock news carried the report.

When I turned off the television my hands were shaking. I tried to tell myself that it was probably just another so-called Patty sighting. I tried to be logical about it, but logic wouldn't hold. Just the thought that it might be true, that Patty had been walking freely through a department store not fifteen miles away was enough to pitch me into bitterness and depression. And there was nothing I could do, no plans, no proposals, nothing. I felt utterly dead-ended. For the first time I could truthfully say that the thought of being rejected hurt more, at least momentarily, than my fear for her safety. I needed to get away for a while.

An hour later I called the Hearsts to tell them I was thinking about flying down to San Diego and I gave them my telephone number there. My timing could not have been worse. Mr. Hearst had just read Andy Port's *Newsday* article, had had a few drinks, and was furious.

"What the hell is it with you?" he shouted. "You get up there with some girl on the twenty-sixth floor of some hotel and just bubble like a yeastcake. All this crap about Anne being kicked out of school and you liking Catherine more than Patty did. I don't want you coming around here even to pick up your mail! You just aren't housebroken!" He slammed down the receiver.

That was it. I made reservations on the morning plane to San Diego.

The commuter flight to San Diego was packed with Shriners, hats, tassels, and all. Somewhere over Santa Barbara one of them plopped down in the seat next to me and grinned widely as his friend snapped a picture of the two of us. "Thanks, sport," he said and slapped me on the back.

Betty Trimble picked me up at the airport. She and her husband, Ridge, an old Princeton roommate, were both doing their residencies at one of San Diego's hospitals. For three or four weeks they had been urging me to come down and get away from it all, and finally I was ready to accept their offer. In the week following my arrival, I didn't really get away from it, but I did find I was able to relax, recover, and do the reading and thinking I needed to do. The Trimbles were almost always at the hospital, popping in for dinner perhaps, and I was left alone in the big upstairs bedroom, reading on the waterbed, occasionally putting down my notebook to sit in the sun on the patio, or putting on my jogging shoes to run down to the beach.

I had a lot to think about, the obsession with Patty's rejection to work out. For two weeks now the public imagination had called out for a choice between two alternatives. "We're taking a poll here," my friend Ed had been told by a teller at his bank a week before. "Do you think Patty Hearst has joined the SLA or do you think she's being forced?" Neither answer had any significance for me. It was absurd to think of her "joining" the SLA the way one "joins" the Republican party, but at the same time it was hard to believe, listening to her voice, that she had made the last two tapes and participated in the Hibernia bank robbery out of simple fear for her life. It was "something in between" I had told an interviewer two days after the "sexist, ageist pig" tape of April 24; "she's had to accommodate somehow to survive." But I rebelled against calling this accommodation "brainwashing," the third,

298

tentative explanation that a few such as the Hearsts held to, for I had strong suspicions that it was in fact a pseudo explanation, that in most people's minds there was no meaning to back up the term. And if there was, it was some vague *Manchurian Candidate* fantasy of Pavlovian conditioning, drugs, and hypnotic trances.

It was, then, that week at the Trimbles' that I began to discover and dig into the works that gave me some understanding of psychological conditioning and the effects it might have had on Patty's situation. For the first time since I had begun to ponder Patty's imprisonment and conversion, I was able to achieve some intellectual underpinning for my speculations. I read studies of foreign civilians who had been caught inside China after the communist takeover and who had been detained and "reeducated." I read and was gripped by two outstanding works in the field: Robert Lifton's *Thought Reform and the Psychology of Totalism,* and Edgar Schein's *Coercive Persuasion,* along with an articulate autobiographical account by a couple so reeducated, *Prisoners of Liberation.*

As I read I began to learn what the crucial techniques of coercive influence were: total control of the information reaching the target, and forced and intensive self-examination, with the emphasis on confession and the production of guilt.

The total "shaming milieu" (as Lifton calls it) is crucial to the process. The prisoner is immersed in an apparently morally infallible environment. For a prisoner already physically and psychologically weakened, it is almost impossible to resist. In the face of relentless accusation and self-analysis, feelings of guilt (most commonly the social guilt of having been favored with accidental good fortune and having neglected the less fortunate) wipe away the possible defense of resentment ("I deserve this treatment"). Perhaps the most outstanding feature of thought reform is the total personal exposure of the prisoner that can at once be devastating and exhilarating in the possibility it provides for catharsis and extreme intimacy with others.

As I read and learned, I began to feel not only the power of the method, but the *vulnerability* of the human personality—of our self-image—when it is deprived of emotional and social supports. I felt how illusory is the fixity of self and our belief in the permanence of our ethics and loyalties. My obsession that Patty had "freely renounced" me . . . us . . . and that she was unalterably changed began to modify as my understanding grew.

In the midst of my reading, I had the opportunity to meet with Dr. Hacker in Los Angeles. If Patty was to return to us, what were the chances of her recovery?

Dr. Hacker could not say for sure. He tapped the whiskers out of his electric razor in the bathroom adjoining his Beverly Hills office, then slapped some lotion on his face. "There are well-known cases in which airline stewardesses have been held captive by hijackers and have later refused to testify against their attackers." Hacker cited other such examples, among them the case of a Swedish woman who, after being held hostage during a bank holdup, wanted to marry one of the robbers. "Even some of the Israeli students who survived the Maalot massacre expressed admiration for the courage and determination of the Palestinian commandos," he told me.

As for the chances of Patty's eventual recovery, Hacker could only point out that being kidnapped is the most terrifying and profoundly disorienting experience a person can endure. "Even in prisoners of war there was at least some degree of psychological preparation for the possibility of enemy capture," he said, "and some reason for it, namely war." But in a kidnapping there is nothing but the feeling, the irrationality of having been singled out to face the possibility of death *without* reason or meaning. Because of this, he explained, identification with one's captors is not only a typical, but a "normal" survival reaction that often parallels the dynamics between parent and child. In order to keep alive the captive often tries to please his captors by imitating them, reassuring them, and in some cases even helping them exact the ransom successfully. "It is there that the captive/captor distinction begins to blur," Hacker said. "First there is the feeling that 'We're all in this together,' which may then lead to 'It's us against them.' " In Patty's case "them" being the FBI and the police who might endanger her life by staging an assault. "Her almost cheerful tone on the second [the February sixteenth] communiqué," Hacker observed, "indicates that this kind of identification with the SLA, and their fear of the police, was beginning to take place." But to reverse this process, he said, which culminated in Patty's conversion to the SLA, depended not only upon the time and the circumstances of her return, but her state of mind and the way in which she is treated by those she had left behind. "And given the extraordinary nature of this case," Hacker said, "that is impossible to predict."

Later that evening, Dr. Hacker and I had dinner with a woman friend of his, whose voguish appearance and bearing alone were enough to raise my spirits somewhat. After dinner we sank into her enormous white Cadillac and roared up the Pacific Coast Highway in search of a place for me to stay. Thus began one of the strangest nights of my life.

Hacker's woman friend squealed away from every stoplight like a teen-ager with daddy's car, then suddenly hit the brakes and bounced us into the parking lot of the first motel we came to. Set against the eroded bluffs between Santa Monica and Malibu, the "Cliff House" looked like the epitome of the lonesome motel. There were no other cars in the parking lot, and some of the units above the restaurant-bar had been boarded up with plywood and crisscrossed two-by-fours. After nosing around, we noticed a faint glow in one of the restaurant windows, trooped over to the door next to it, and knocked. Behind us we could hear the roar of the ocean and the occasional rush of a car that whizzed by at sixty miles per hour—like a projectile hurtling by in outer space, I thought. The place had that kind of ends-of-the-earth feel to it.

After a moment a young woman opened the door for us, then took a seat behind a small, glowing bar. Above her a television was on but the sound was off. Except for the rattle of ice cubes in the glasses as she made our drinks, the room was silent. It was an enormous room, draped with faded streamers and fishnets, the floor crowded with bamboo cocktail tables, and in one corner a large bandstand lined with plastic plants and displaying a complete set of musical instruments that looked as if they had been collecting dust since the Tommy Dorsey days.

Dr. Hacker and his friend had a couple of drinks to keep me company, then said good night and left me alone with the woman behind the bar. She made me another drink, said it was on the house, then turned up the sound on the TV. Dick Cavett was interviewing Jan Morris, the famous historian and transsexual. I felt as if I were entering the "Twilight Zone."

Around 1:00 A.M. a few people began drifting in: a hale and hearty fellow named Frank who bartended at a bar called Jumbo's on Sunset Strip, two ancient Japanese women, a couple of hippies, a millionaire from Burbank who wanted to know if I cared to go for "a buzz to Santa Catalina" on his yacht, and an elderly couple who kept calling "Clifford, Clifford" at their toy poodle as it ran up and down the bar lapping drinks out of ashtrays. Clifford was partial to whiskey, I was told, but it got the better of him and he fell off the bar around 2:00 A.M.

The Burbank millionaire was the only one to recognize me, though he didn't say so directly, or ask what I was doing in the Cliff House at two in the morning. "Frank," he said, "this is my friend Steve from San Francisco." Frank nodded, slapped a hundred dollar bill on the bar, and called out for drinks for everyone. "I was the dumbest guy on the block in Boston," he said, "but I'm a fucking genius in L.A." The millionaire broke up and then began telling nautical jokes about "twin screws" and the like. I asked the lady bartender where the bathroom was, and she said it was down the hall, next to the phone. "You can't miss it," she said. I couldn't. The telephone was set like a deformed pearl in a huge, pink, glowing shell.

I was back on my barstool a few minutes later when the late night movie was interrupted by a news bulletin. I caught only the last part of it—"Emily Harris . . . Thirty shots fired." Then it was back to the movie. No one seemed to have noticed it. The bartender was polishing a glass, Frank was laughing with the millionaire, and the others were drinking quietly. I asked the bartender if she could show me to my room, suddenly feeling quite sick. I was too drunk to know if I had actually heard the bulletin or merely imagined it.

I had not imagined it. Ten miles away the front of Mel's Sporting Goods was stitched with bullet holes.

At four thirty that afternoon, while Emily Harris was paying for thirty-one dollars' worth of camping equipment, one of the store's employees, Tony Shepard, saw Bill Harris stuff a two-dollar cartridge belt up the sleeve of his hunting jacket. Tony notified the owner, Bill Huett, then armed himself with a pistol and a pair of handcuffs. He followed the Harrises out the door and confronted them. A scuffle ensued, the two men wrestling on the sidewalk, Emily jumping on Tony, biting, kicking, and scratching as Harris pulled out a pistol. Then Huett and another employee rushed out to help. Tony got one of the cuffs on Harris's wrists, then saw the pistol. "Bill, he's got a gun!" Tony yelled. Huett grabbed it, while the second employee tried to pull Emily off Tony's back. In the next instant there was a burst of gunfire, then a second burst that shattered the store's windows. It was Patty, apparently, who had done the shooting. Standing next to a red van across the street, she let go a third volley that ricocheted all around the group. "You better get outta here!" Harris shouted, then broke free, picking up his sunglasses and a package as he and Emily raced for the van. Huett ran back inside the store for a shotgun but found his wife bleeding from a glass fragment that had struck her in the forehead. Another fragment had torn into his arm and the second employee, now feeling pain, found the ball-point pen in his breast pocket bent in half by a hollow-point bullet that had lost its force on a ricochet through the glass windows.

In those same seconds, outside, Tony had rolled behind a cement lamppost for cover. Leaning around it, he fired two shots at the trio and the woman put several slugs into the post in response, then ducked into the van. As it roared away through the shopping center parking lot, Tony ran to his car and took off in pursuit.

He followed them for eight blocks, then saw the Harrises get out of the van with rifles in hand and approach a couple sitting in a Pontiac. The two people climbed out of the car and hurried toward a nearby house. Bill Harris spotted Tony and pointed his rifle at him. Tony jammed his car in reverse and backed out of range as Patty and the Harrises took off in the Pontiac. Moments later Tony was back at Mel's phoning the police. "She was either very good, very lucky or both," he said of Patty's marksmanship. "It's a miracle no one got killed."

At twelve o'clock that night, while I was sitting at the bar in the Cliff House, Patty was sitting in a blue Ford van with the Harrises at a drive-in theater, occasionally giving a reassuring pat to Tom Mathews, a seventeen-year-old boy they had kidnapped six hours before.

A few weeks later I talked with Tom Mathews and learned what had happened during the twelve hours he had spent with Patty and the Harrises. The following is a transcription of the notes I took during our conversation:

Of all the people I've met who have had anything to do with this case, Tom Mathews seems the least affected by it all, unperturbed enough to have slept through half of what most people would consider an unusual ordeal. "I had a game to play the next day," he said, "so I was trying to get some sleep."

Tom's memory of the whole incident seemed to be entirely dependent upon asking him the right questions. It was hard to get him to elaborate on his own.

Emily Harris rang Tom's doorbell around seven at night to look at and test drive his van, that was out front with a "for sale" sign. She drove him around the corner where Patty and Bill were waiting. "We're from the SLA and we need your car," Bill said. He didn't really point the automatic rifle at Tom, but sort of cradled it confidently. Harris: "Don't do anything flaky or we will hurt you." Harris said they didn't want to hurt civilians, but would if they had to. They were nervous, of course, but evidently not overly so, considering the recent shooting at Mel's. Harris: "Do you know who this is? This is Tania." Tom said that every other word they used was *pigs*.

Emily drove, dark hair, not smiling as in her pictures. Didn't talk much. Stopped at a couple of stores to get a hacksaw to cut Harris's cuffs off. Tom: "I realized they weren't going to hurt me. I felt they were my friends in a funny sort of way. I would have even gone and gotten the hacksaw for them." Tom said he didn't buy their violent revolution bit, but implies he was sympathetic with them on some level. "We're trying to help blacks and Chicanos, particularly blacks," they said, "who have been oppressed. We're trying to overthrow the government."

They went to a drive-in where, ironically, *The New Centurions* was playing, saying they were to meet up with their friends at 12:00 midnight: the rest of the SLA. Evidently all three of them actually watched the movie. Harris would get excited and say, "Shoot that pig." At one point Emily went to the snack bar and came back with a pile of hamburgers, and there was some confusion about distributing them. Tom thought it was a bit strange for revolutionaries to be sitting in a drive-in arguing about who got the burger with relish.

Patty was pissed about speculation that she had been tied to her gun in the robbery. Also pissed at her mother for thinking she was brainwashed, but hateful of her father for the way he intentionally screwed up PIN, distributed lousy food, and had done everything as a tax write-off. She said she had been tempted to call him a "fucker" on the tapes but was afraid it would not be broadcast.

Tom thinks the politics made her hate her father, presumably that she had begun to see him as an oppressor. Talked about being against gun control, that it was only a plot to leave the police in power, that Nixon had already overthrown the government, that he was getting ready to call out the troops and declare martial law, that E. Howard Hunt and the Plumbers unit killed Kennedy. Patty: "Go look it up in the library."

But despite all this oddly paranoid talk, Tom thinks that overall they behaved quite normally. I prodded him for any hint of erratic behavior on their part, but he couldn't think of any. They acted like soldiers, wore hiking boots and did not seem happy or sad—just something they had to do. Called each other comrade. At one point Patty told Tom that she'd only tried to fire warning shots at Mel's. "It was a good feeling to see my two comrades make it across the street safely. It's lucky I wasn't reading the newspaper."

To Tom, Patty and Bill seemed closer and more a couple than Bill and Emily. Patty was comforting Bill as his wrist hurt from the handcuffs. Tom cut off the cuffs with the hacksaw since the others couldn't manage it—got a hug from Bill in return and "a kiss on the mouth from Patty."

They talked about Mel's. They thought they had made a stupid mistake. Emily said they shouldn't have gone into a gun shop because the security was too tight. Bill joked about how stupid it was for them to get the cuffs on him when he was supposed to be a general. I could not get from Tom the exact delivery or attitude Bill had about this joke.

Harris talked a bit to Tom about baseball, but it seemed to Tom like he was just making conversation. Patty: "I wish I had a cigarette." She was proud of her shooting. To Harris: "I did a good job, didn't I?" Harris: "Hell, yes, you did." Bill was definitely the most gung ho politically. Patty would agree with him and add things. Harris also seemed to make most of the decisions and seemed to be the strongest to Tom, though it was Emily who seemed to be most aware of the practicalities of their situation. Patty apparently had little if any authority in the small decisions that were made moment to moment.

Patty seemed slim, skinny, but attractive and in good health and had "nice teeth." Of the three, Tom much preferred Patty. She said she was indeed kidnapped and said it was ironic because a few days before she had dreamed she was going to be kidnapped. At first she had screamed, but then she realized she wasn't going to be hurt and thinking back on it she said, "It was stupid of me to scream like that."

They laughed about the Golden Gate apartment and the FBI's consternation, but started getting nervous at 12:00 when their friends didn't show up. Emily insisted that they wait until 1:00 A.M. Finally they left saying that they had another place to meet tomorrow. Stopped at a couple of places to spend the night— seems they had some friends to stay with but they were not home or something. Tom did not know where they were because he was under a blanket in the back. From time to time Patty would pat him on the head and ask if he was okay. Finally one of them said, "Let's go up on the hill" (Outpost Drive in the Hollywood Hills), where they parked and tried to get some sleep. At 6:30 in the morning the two girls posed as hitchhikers, commandeered another car, and relieved the driver of $250. They left Tom in the van about 7 o'clock.

Tom said they seemed dedicated, that he definitely saw their point of view, but not to the point of wanting to join. Patty talked about FBI agents walking around with $50,000 in a suitcase trying to find out where she was, like bounty hunters. She really seemed to think that her father was paying people to kill her, that he wanted her dead. But it was hard to get from Tom whether she thought he *actually* wanted her dead, or if she was just referring to the overall effect of the reward money.

All of them seemed quite taken with the idea that Patty was the number one most wanted person in the U.S., that the police wanted more than anything else to see her dead. They told Tom that he had better watch out if the police came, because if they found out that Tania was in the van they would try to "blow all of us away," hostages included.

I was in pretty bad shape by the end of our talk. We had started in good cheer, but I had gotten progressively more disturbed by the details, by the reality Tom had to offer. When I left I was so preoccupied, was doing battle with myself over the same old issue—Is she still a victim, or did she just turn on us?—that I made one of those twenty-minute freeway turnoff mistakes that you can do only in L.A. I had asked Tom if my name had ever been mentioned and he said no, it hadn't come up once. My head kept spinning all the way back to Westwood.

But that night at the Cliff House I was simply and miserably drunk, following the woman upstairs, holding onto the railing and fighting off what has been aptly described as "The Black Whirlies." Whether the news bulletin was real or imaginary, it had smacked me back to reality, had quite literally bummed me out. Adding to my disorientation, my room was triangular in shape.

The next morning I found an ancient terrycloth bathing suit in a closet and walked across the highway to the beach. I remember thinking about a passage in Eldridge Cleaver's *Soul on Ice* in which he described hearing about the shooting of Malcolm X, while watching a movie in prison. He was destroyed by the news but sat through the entire movie, dreading getting the final word on Malcolm's death. That is pretty much how I was feeling. I would hear about the incident with Emily Harris and the thirty shots fired soon enough.

It was 10:30 when I sat down in the sand. I had five hours to kill before my 3:15 flight back to San Diego. Well away from any television or radio, I was not aware that the Los Angeles police and the FBI had picked up the trail of the SLA's Malcolm X Combat Unit and had raided a suspected hideout in Compton two hours before.

The authorities had been led to the run-down bungalow on Eighty-fourth Street by the address on a parking ticket discovered in the van Patty and the Harrises had abandoned in their flight from Mel's. At 8:50 the occupants of the bungalow were told to "come out the front door with your hands up." There was no response. Two tear gas canisters were then fired through the windows, the order was given, and a heavily armed SWAT (Strategic Weapons Assault Team) team stormed the dwelling. It was unoccupied, but a search produced medical supplies, shotgun shells, SLA literature, and some handwritten notes which included backpack weights divided by nine people, a guard duty roster—"Tania: all night to light," said one notation—and what would prove to be a weirdly ironic poem:

Now's the time
We're all alive!
Eat it, Pig
In our minds
The bigger the trigger
The better the target!
The cool
Cool palm
Will smear heavy on the hit.
Sucker pay!
Malcolm
We're here to stay!

They were about to be killed.

From interviews around the neighborhood, police got descriptions of the two vans that had been parked near the residence during the week. This information was relayed to all officers in the field. At 12:20, according to the detailed police report issued two months later two SWAT team members spotted the two vans parked behind a boarded-up apartment building near Fifty-fourth Street, also in Compton. The vehicle identification numbers were punched into police computers and produced two recent registrations in San Francisco. The names on the registrations were aliases and one registration address matched that of the van abandoned the previous day near Mel's. Two hours later a command post was set up in a mobile unit at Compton and Fifty-seventh streets and undercover agents had moved into the neighborhood hoping to pinpoint the location of the SLA.

I read of the shooting at Mel's on the flight down to San Diego. At that point the papers had Angela Atwood laying down the covering fire, and, although the identification of the Harrises was confirmed, it was hard to believe that they were involved. In my mind the SLA was still back in the Bay Area. It seemed impossible that I would cross their path in Los Angeles purely by coincidence.

"Have you heard about the raid?" Betty asked when I walked

in. She had the radio on and reports were coming in about an SLA hideout the police had surrounded on Fifty-fourth Street in Compton. There was also a mention of the abortive raid on Eighty-fourth Street and I temporarily confused the two. I did not realize that at that moment three SWAT teams were taking their positions around a yellow stucco house, now certain that the SLA was inside, but not certain if Patty was with them.

Confirmation of the SLA's exact whereabouts had come from Mrs. Mary Carr, an elderly black woman who had lived in the neighborhood for years. Police had the area sealed off, had evacuated many residents, and were holding back a growing crowd of onlookers and newsmen when Mrs. Carr walked up to a patrolman and told him that a black man, a white man, and several white women were holed up in her daughter's house on Fifty-fourth Street. She identified Cinque, Willie, and the rest of the SLA women from photographs and said they were heavily armed. The patrolman relayed this information to his commanding officer, and the three SWAT teams took their positions to the front and rear of the dwelling.

The small house Mrs. Carr described on Fifty-fourth Street was more of a neighborhood hangout than a private residence, and four people were still hanging out, drinking, and carrying on, when Cinque had knocked on the door around 4:00 A.M. the night before. "I saw the lights and heard the music," he is quoted as saying, "and figured black folks lived here." He bought his way in for $100, but it is not clear which of the two women who answered the door took the money. Although at least a dozen people came and went during the following day (going out for sandwiches and beer, visiting neighbors, children going and coming from school), what happened inside that house, from the moment Cinque and his five comrades began unloading their vans of weaponry, to the sound of shattering glass when the first tear gas canister crashed through the front windows, is sketchy at best. Some of the people who dropped by that day had been drinking heavily and claimed to remember nothing; others told confused, sometimes self-contradictory stories or simply lied outright. But what is clear is that the presence of the SLA did not send the occupants of the house fleeing in fear. Cinque is reputed to have said he and his soldiers just wanted to relax for a while, and that he had come to Los Angeles to see his wife and kids. Whatever the case, he seemed content to doze and just lounge around. But an eventual showdown with police was not far from his mind.

"I know I'm gonna die," he told a visitor, while sipping a bottle of Boone's Farm wine, "and all my people know they will too. But we're gonna take a lot of motherfuckin' pigs with us." Tania, he said, was "real bad," but Bill Harris made a "stupid move," stealing the cartridge belt and "blowing our cover." One of the SLA women—Cinque's "children" as he repeatedly referred to them—is remembered making sandwiches, "acting like the woman of the house," while Willie Wolfe sat on the bed twirling a pistol on his finger and Camilla Hall prepared Molotov cocktails. "She was walking around carrying these two bottles, smiling, following me," said one woman. "She looked like a zombie or something to me—halfway smiling." The woman was something of a zombie herself, later passing out from booze and what she called "nerve pills." When Mary Carr walked in around three o'clock she could not wake the woman nor make the SLA leave. "Us black people gotta stick together," Cinque told her. Entering one of the bedrooms, she came across Camilla and asked what was going on. Camilla just smiled and patted the .45 on her hip. Shortly thereafter Mary Carr left the house with two of her grandchildren in tow.

Meanwhile Cinque and his band were growing increasingly nervous. "There ain't that many insurance men do business around here," he was overheard to say, peeking out the window at an unmarked car. "Trish [Mizmoon], we gotta get outta here. It's getting too hot." But they did not get out. When a nine-year-old boy entered the house moments later, Cinque and his comrades were loading their weapons. "Get in the bathtub if you don't want to get killed," Cinque told him. The boy ran out the back door and down the alley. By five o'clock only three people remained in the house besides the SLA—an eight-year-old boy, a man, and the woman still passed out in the bedroom. The SLA soldiers donned their gas masks and bandoliers and prepared for the siege.

Outside, the three eight-man SWAT teams did the same. They were armed with tear gas guns, shotguns, AR-180 and AR-15 semiautomatic rifles, .243 caliber long rifles, and .38 caliber side-arms. Incredibly, the SLA had them outgunned—four .30 caliber M-1 rifles converted to fully automatic and capable of firing over a thousand rounds in sixty seconds; two semiautomatic rifles; seven 12-gauge shotguns; four automatic pistols; two revolvers; and for all of this well over four thousand rounds of ammunition. They also had two pipebombs with blasting caps and two gallons of gasoline for Molotov cocktails.

At 5:44 P.M. the leader of SWAT team 1 raised his bullhorn. "People in the yellow stucco house with the stone porch, this is the Los Angeles Police Department. Come out with your hands up. Comply immediately and you will not be harmed." A moment, then a small boy walked out the front door, and then a man. Both were hustled off to the side by officers who heard rapid movements coming from inside the house. The surrender order was repeated several times before the first tear gas canister was fired through the window. Seconds later a second canister was fired, this answered by a deafening roar of automatic weapons fire that blew out the front window of the house and bit large chunks of plaster off the dwelling across the street. The SWAT teams answered in kind and the largest domestic firefight in United States history began.

The gun battle raged for over an hour, the SLA firing full force in thirty-second intervals, the SWAT teams laying down "heavy repressive fire" to prevent the terrorists from shooting with accuracy. During this time, eleven separate surrender broadcasts were made, each one drawing another barrage from the house. And although it was quickly assumed that the SLA was equipped with modern army gas masks, the SWAT teams continued pumping gas canisters through the windows, hoping to overload the masks' fil-tration systems and force the terrorists out into the open. At one point a SWAT team leader bellied across the roof of the house next door, but, when he raised up to fire in another canister, he was knocked back by machine gun fire that tore up the edge of the roof in front of him. "Officer wounded," went out the call from a heli-copter hovering overhead. It was acting as a "communication plat-form" above the battle as radio contact between the command post and the SWAT teams was disrupted by radio and television trans-missions from news reporters at the scene.

"You can hear the gunfire in the background," a TV reporter shouted into his microphone. I could—the boom-boom-boom of semiautomatic weapons and the rattle of the SLA machine guns. The reporter ducked behind a car and peeked around the head-lights, the camera lurching and following him, then zooming in on the house as a cop in military gear ran for cover. "It's like Vietnam," the reporter said, then was drowned out by another exchange of gunfire, the chop of a helicopter hovering overhead, and the hoots and yells from the crowd of onlookers as the police pumped more bullets into the house.

I grew steadily sicker as the battle continued, running from the bedroom to the living room, trying to listen to the radio and TV reports at the same time. "It is not certain at this point if Patricia Hearst is inside," said one reporter, and yet others were "reason-ably certain" she was. To hear this matter-of-fact speculation over the pounding gunfire, to see the camera swing to a SWAT team member as he leaned around a wall, his shoulder shuddering as he fired a long burst at the house, and to imagine Patty pinned down, jolted as she was hit, went beyond the unbearable. My mind shut off. I collapsed in a chair and just watched numbly.

"There's smoke coming from the house! The house is on fire!" The camera blurred and jiggled past cops and pavement as the reporter and his cameraman were forced back across the street. "We're being pushed back," he said, "but the house is definitely on fire. I can see smoke rising from the front window."

"They've got somebody out!" Betty called from the living room. I ran in and sank down by the radio.

"We have reports," the broadcaster was saying, "that Patty Hearst is inside the house. Police have taken a black woman into custody who has identified Patty Hearst as one of the SLA mem-bers inside, but this report has not been confirmed by authorities at the scene."

I couldn't stand it any longer. "I've got to go up there," I told Betty. "Let me use your car."

"I'll drive," she said, then ran into the bathroom and returned with two tablets of Valium.

By 6:50 the house at Fifty-fourth Street was totally engulfed in flames. "It's all over!" a SWAT team leader shouted into his bullhorn during a lull in the gunfire. "The house is on fire. Throw your guns out the windows. You will not be harmed!" Seconds later members of SWAT team 2 saw Nancy Ling Perry creeping out of a crawl hole in the back of the house. When she had gotten ten feet, Camilla Hall appeared in the crawl hole behind her, firing a pistol in the direction of the SWAT team. They returned the fire and Camilla dropped to the ground. A moment, then Angela Atwood grabbed Camilla's legs and pulled her body back under the house. Perry turned toward the SWAT team and began firing her revolver. Two police bullets dropped her just as she turned from them. There was no more gunfire coming from the house now, and seconds later the walls and roof collapsed in a fiery explosion. For ten minutes ammunition set off by the incredible heat could be heard popping within the gutted residence, some of it still in the bandoliers worn by the dead SLA soldiers.

Betty and I were doing ninety miles per hour on the San Diego freeway, but had gotten no farther than the outskirts of town before we were pulled over by a highway patrolman. He recognized me and let us go, asking us to try and take it easy. Once he was out of sight Betty pushed the speedometer back up to ninety. Neither of us said a word. When the second patrol car pulled us over I jumped out of the car to explain and found myself in the cop's gunsights. "Back in the car!" he shouted, holding his pistol and flashlight on me. He was an officious bastard. He knew who I was and where I was going but demanded to see every piece of identification Betty and I had. "What're you worried about?" he said. "Your girl friend isn't in there." He half sneered.

"How the fuck do you know?!" I shouted. Betty hushed me

up and urged me back into the car. He didn't give a damn if Patty was alive or dead.

By the time we got to L.A., Betty was certain that Patty was in the house. She had seen kids die in the hospital, but was not sure how well she could handle being with me when I was told that Patty had been killed. Still, she maintained her composure, following the lines of traffic and the crowd of onlookers that led to Fifty-fourth Street. We arrived about the time the coroner's deputies were removing the burnt corpses from the ruins. After making our way to the police perimeter (about a hundred officers were keeping the crowd a block off), I told an officer who I was and asked if there was anything I could do. As he went off in search of Commander Hagan I was shaken by the realization that I might be asked to identify Patty's body.

We were still waiting for Hagan, surrounded by the black residents of the area, when a woman stepped out of the crowd and started haranguing Betty. "White, honky bitch," she shouted. "Tania's found her brown sugar now an' she don't need no more of his shit!" Meaning me.

"Hey, that's Tania's old man," said a man, nudging his friend. "I mean ex-old man. Hey, Slim," he called out, "you think your old lady's in there?"

Betty took me by the arm and moved us away. Moments later Commander Hagan appeared and led us down Fifty-fourth Street past row after row of police motorcycles, large pumper trucks, and squad cars.

I didn't even see the house at first. "There," Hagan said, pointing toward five men who were digging through the charred foundation. That's all that was left of it. No pipes or other metal structures were visible—or at least I didn't see any—and if the house had had a stove and refrigerator they had either melted or had collapsed with the rest of the building. The three houses bordering the rubble were partially burned and the cars behind us had flat tires, shattered windows, and were riddled with wavy patterns of bullet holes from wild automatic-weapons fire. The night air was vibrating with the clatter of a big generator truck used to power enormous mercury vapor lamps. They cast the scene in an eerie, greenish light, diagonally slashed by the long shadow of a charred palm tree that had gone up like some weird pyrotechnic display, a perfect symbol of death in Los Angeles. Technicians and fire department personnel moved through the ruins methodically. The place looked like a movie set. It did not look like much of a place to die.

"There's nothing you can do at this point," Hagan told me. "They took five bodies out of here. The coroner should have his report ready by tomorrow afternoon."

As Betty and I returned to the perimeter, we were approached by a reporter who stuck a microphone in my face. "Tell us what you feel at this moment," he said. Betty and I continued walking back to the car.

For the next hour we drove around aimlessly, blankly, and ended up getting lost in the industrial area of L.A. Finally we stopped at a Denny's restaurant and Betty phoned a friend who lived nearby. We drove to his house in silence, both of us feeling that something was over, that what was done was done. We would find out about Patty tomorrow.

Saturday, May 17
Five charred bodies is all that anyone will say. Got up this morning at 9 and called Commander Hagan to find out there is nothing I can do. Reports will be issued by [coroner] Noguchi between 11 and 12. I have this somewhat optimistic feeling now—perhaps a defense—but little reason for it other than I cannot believe Patty would be willing to stay in a house like that. If she was I have not yet come to grips with it, with this kind of an ending. Strangely, I'm not as agitated now as I have been when some of the tapes came in. It's more a feeling of strangeness, a psychological discorporation. . . .

Just heard over the radio that one of the three women is not Patty. It's becoming a countdown now and I feel like I'm disintegrating.

After I had written that, Betty gave me two more Valium

and I went under. Three hours later she shook me awake. She was smiling. "They've identified the fifth body, and it's not Patty," she said. With that news I started to come back to myself very slowly. We drove into Westwood for something to eat, then headed back to San Diego. Betty's husband, Ridge, had just gotten off twenty-four-hour duty at the hospital when we arrived and he persuaded us to go out to dinner and come down off it all. We ate in a hotel restaurant overlooking the airport and, while I was feeling better, I was obsessed with thoughts of Patty—where she was and with whom, how badly she was crushed by the deaths of the five SLA members, and what would happen next. What happened next came with a phone call at noon the following day.

Sunday, May 19
Just now I feel sick and shaking in a premonitional way. Steve Jenks of the FBI just called from Hillsborough to say that a 6th body has been discovered. All I can do is hope that Patty is with the Harrises. It could be Camilla Hall's body, but the way things have gone from the beginning, this final blow is just the kind of blow I have come to expect. I feel sick now and am forcing myself to write.

Jenks told me that the woman they dragged out of the house said the SLA had prepared for the battle for some time, and it seems they would be determined to take Patty with them.

Yesterday evening we all went to dinner at the top of a downtown hotel and watched the airplanes land. I'm just sitting in the sun now, feeling very strange, feeling limp and nauseated, staring at the very blue sky, watching the clouds go by.

I don't know what prompted the call from Hillsborough, but I assume the Hearsts asked Jenks to phone me the news. In view of that news, and the anguish it must have caused the Hearsts, I was deeply appreciative to them. Like me, the Hearsts had endured "the worst two days of the hundred and four since [Patty] was kidnapped," as John Lester told reporters.

The family had watched the shoot-out on television Friday

night and listened to radio reports throughout Saturday morning. Then came Thomas Noguchi's call that the fifth body had been identified as that of Patricia "Mizmoon" Soltysik. The Hearsts were "tremendously relieved," but their relief was twisted to anguish with the discovery of the sixth body, a white female. Two hours after Jenks called me in San Diego, the Hearsts' phone rang again and Mr. Hearst answered it. Mrs. Hearst watched his face and heard him say, "Oh, thank God." She began to cry, knowing that the sixth body was not Patty's. Shortly thereafter I received a second call from Jenks. After hanging up I sat down in a chair, totally spent of emotions.

At a press conference later that afternoon, Coroner Noguchi issued his report on the deaths of the six SLA soldiers. "They died compulsively," he said. "They chose to stay under the floor as the fire burned out. In all my years as a coroner I've never seen this kind of conduct in the face of flames." The images of death by fire conjured up by Noguchi's autopsy results were both horrifying and astounding. Based upon the concentration of smoke in the singed lungs of Willie Wolfe, Angela Atwood, Mizmoon Soltysik and DeFreeze, it appeared that in their last moments they were actually breathing flames, their gas masks melting on their faces as they burned to death. "Let it be known," Cinque had said on the SLA's first taped communiqué, "that even in death we will win, for the very ashes of this fascist nation will mark our very graves." . . . "They're perfectly willing to die for what they are doing," Patty tried to tell us on that same tape. But except for her no one could really know the strength of their fanaticism. "It was a decision to die," Noguchi told reporters, clearly amazed at the people who had made that decision.

In cold, clinical language the Los Angeles Police Department incorporated Noguchi's findings in a report of its own:

Nancy Ling Perry, age 26, was found in a prone position at the southwest corner of the structure. Found on the decedent was 1) a yellow ring, no stones; 2) remnants of a gas mask; 3) a .30 caliber pistol; 4) a notebook page with handwriting.

. . . Death resulted from two gunshot wounds to the back, one severing the spinal cord and the other penetrating the right lung.

Angela Atwood, age 25, was found lying in a prone position just inside the southwest corner of the burned out structure near the crawl hole. Found on the decedent was 1) remnants of a gas mask; 2) an M-1 automatic rifle; 3) miscellaneous U.S. currency and coins amounting to $1.86; 4) three scraps of paper with handwriting. . . . Death occurred as a result of smoke inhalation and burns. . . .

William Wolfe, age 23, was found inside the southwest corner of the burned out structure to the right of Donald DeFreeze. Found on the decedent was 1) miscellaneous U.S. currency and coins amounting to $127.28; 2) wallet with cards and papers showing identification of a Robert Owen Murphy; 3) one photograph; 4) one peso note; 5) one homemade bomb in a 35 mm film can. . . . Death occurred as a result of smoke inhalation and burns. . . .

Patricia Soltysik, age 24, was found in a kneeling position partially lying across Donald DeFreeze. Found on the decedent was 1) $320.00; 2) three notebook papers with writing; 3) a social security card, a personalized check and a buyer's pass made out to Steven Andrew Weed; 4) one U.C. registration card in the name of Patricia Hearst, cut into two pieces; 6) fifteen rounds of ammunition. . . . Death resulted from a combination of smoke inhalation, burns, and multiple gunshot wounds.

Camilla Hall, age 29, was discovered in a prone position 18 inches east of Angela Atwood. Found on the decedent was 1) $1.95; 2) one knife; 3) one compass; 4) one .38 caliber revolver. . . . The decedent received a gunshot wound in the center of the forehead which caused instantaneous death.

Donald DeFreeze, age 30, was found lying on his side between William Wolfe and Patricia Soltysik, facing an air vent in the foundation. Found on the decedent was 1) 36¢; 2) remnants of charred currency; 3) white metal ring with 13 green stones;

4) four pieces of paper with handwriting; 5) two blasting caps; 6) a .38 snub nose revolver. . . . Death occurred as a result of a self-inflicted gunshot wound to the head. The bullet entered the right temple on a slightly upward trajectory and exited the left temple area. Microscopic examination of this bullet wound indicated the presence of gunpowder in the tissues around the entrance wound in the right temple.

Because the concentration of smoke was the greatest in Cinque's lungs, Noguchi stated that he was probably the last to die, pressing the pistol to his temple and departing this life, as one writer put it, "on a swoon of highest Hitlerian rapture."

"SLA Appears Nearly Destroyed" read the headlines in the next day's newspapers—six dead, two in prison, and three on the run, Patty and the Harrises. With southern California being scoured for them by the authorities, I feared that another confrontation and perhaps a shoot-out might be in store.

Right now I'm just waiting for tomorrow, and then the day after tomorrow. I don't think this thing will go on much longer. . . . I see Patty with the Harrises, but it's hard to guess what's happening in their minds now—whether they are frightened, shattered by the loss of their friends, or are already thinking of revenge. Hopefully they are so blown out that they're considering just giving up. Whatever the case, I hope they take the six deaths in an intelligent way. It was an absolutely mindless and insensible way to die. Not revolutionary or counterrevolutionary, just fucked up romanticism, if I can just figure out what that word means.

I wonder if all six in the group wanted to die that much, or if Cinque pushed his machine gun out the window and made the decision for them. . . .

I am trying to prepare myself for Patty's death, or for her return, but both possibilities are so incomprehensible, so disparate that preparing for them is impossible. But it seems almost certain that it is nearly over.

The next morning, May 21, the Los Angeles district attorney

announced that warrants for Patty and the Harrises had been issued charging them with kidnapping, armed robbery, assault to commit murder, and sixteen other charges. In the face of this, the appeals from the press and the Hearsts for them to surrender seemed futile. One report had them running north, but wherever they were, I figured they would keep running.

At around nine that same evening, Ridge answered a knock at the door to find two FBI agents standing on the porch. They said they had received some anonymous tips about my presence in Los Angeles and wanted to know "in detail" every move I had made in the last six days. "We understand that you purchased two one-way tickets to Australia," one of them told me. I said it wasn't true, but was hard put to explain how I had just happened to be in Los Angeles only a few miles from the shooting at Mel's Sporting Goods. After they left, Ridge and I decided that they must have gotten a call from a shopkeeper who had recognized me while he was selling Ridge a Confederate flag for his uncle in Australia. "If he's typical of their sources," Ridge said, "Patty needn't be too worried about the FBI catching up to her."

The next morning two other FBI agents knocked on the Trimbles' door, but this time to drive me to the U.S. Marshal's office to pick up a summons for me to appear before Browning's grand jury in San Francisco. Afterward they drove me to the airport, where I was confronted by a crowd of newsmen. Someone in the Bureau must have leaked the news of my departure to the media. I had phoned in a reservation under a fictitious name, but when I approached the counter the clerk greeted me with "Hello, Mr. Weed," obviously pleased when a camera crew's light flared up and caught the two of us.

I boarded the plane as soon as possible and took a seat next to a window in the rear. For me there has always been something about flying that lends perspective, that, for the duration of the flight, temporarily transports me away from the events below. I was feeling this, gazing out the window, slightly mesmerized by the rush of the engines, when the pilot came over the intercom. "We are now directly over San Simeon," he said, "and if you look below you can see the famous Hearst castle." The couple across the aisle glanced at me, then looked out the window as the pilot banked the plane to the right and left to give everyone a good view.

Down through twenty thousand feet of airspace the castle sat against the rolling hills like a clean, white ship. It was a beautiful day, the sky blue and the clouds drifting by the window. Looking down at it, I remembered flying over the castle with Patty that October day, circling around it as her aunt and uncle and cousins waved from one of the terraces. I remembered digging through the musty old crates with Patty in one of W.R.'s warehouses, trying on his Stetson hat and later playing tag with her in the Neptune pool. . . . I kept watching the castle, looking back as it receded in the distance and finally disappeared from sight.

11

"SHE SPAT ON OUR ANGUISH," read the lead in a newspaper editorial, and I could understand that bitterness. "We still love you, Patty, and we just want you to come home again," said her sister Anne in a public appeal. I could understand that too, could feel it in myself. But when I got off the plane in San Francisco and made my way through the crowd of newsmen at the terminal gate, it was enough just to have gotten through the last five days and known that Patty was still alive. But that did not, and could not, last very long. I remember walking up the airport concourse with all my books on thought reform and my dog-eared journal, the reporters hustling alongside, when one of them asked: "What do you think about Patty now?" I kept walking, trying to ignore the question because I had no answer for it. At that point I didn't even know what I was feeling, much less what I thought. Aside from the fear of another confrontation between Patty, the Harrises, and the police, I guess I wasn't feeling much of anything. I was just worn out.

For six weeks I had been struggling for answers, trying to come to grips with what had happened to Patty and what I could do to get her out. Starting with my own intuitions and the insights Patty's and my friends could provide, I had involved myself in all those failing strategies—the PIN program, the Debray letter, the press conferences, the appeals to Little and Remiro, and finally the ill-fated prison proposal. All of them were either ignored, rejected, or ridiculed by Patty and the SLA, and people began to wonder why I hadn't given up.

But as the weeks had ground on, and the bank was robbed, and Patty's denunciations had become more venomous, my efforts had gradually become less of a search for that one successful strategy than an attempt to understand how the woman I thought I had known could believe we had forsaken her and could have accepted as pathetically absurd a vision as the one the SLA had to offer. Grasping that vision was a long slow process, working my way up through the various levels of awareness—Hedy Sarne and the Channing Way scene, the BCA, the desperate prison rage of George Jackson, the romantic valor of Che Guevara, the righteousness of the Tupamaros' struggle, and the right-on, hard-ass politics of Popeye Jackson. Very slowly up through all these levels, each one reflecting something about the political being of those eight people who held Patty prisoner and felt that they could change the world with determined love and violence, with "perfect love and perfect hate." I read their notes and studied their poems and began to get inside their heads.

"They've gotten inside *Patty's* head," Wes Davis told me, and another level opened up. Then down to Los Angeles and Lifton and Schein's books on thought reform and coercive persuasion, taken together with Dr. Hacker's insights into the experience of being kidnapped. All against the background of what Patty was, what her family was, what her relationship with me was, I was beginning to understand what had happened. More than anything, I was trying to control the very real pain of uncertainty, rejection, and fear with that understanding, trying to force the theories, insights, and observations in order to explain it all away. And I was almost there, sitting in Dr. Hacker's Beverly Hills office; I thought I was just beginning to get a grasp of it, when gunfire broke out at Mel's Sporting Goods store not ten miles away. I was nowhere when I stood in the crowd at Fifty-fourth Street and Compton twenty-four hours later, watching the forensics squad sifting through the gutted ruins under mercury lights. I was in shock. I stopped writing, stopped thinking, stopped feeling.

"What do you think about Patty now?" the reporter had asked and I kept walking up the concourse.

It was a long time coming off the Compton shoot-out. Only when it appeared that Patty and the Harrises had slipped through the police dragnet did I start to come back to myself; and when I did, I found my mind a stage cleared of everyone but Patty and me. The Harrises didn't register and never had. It was Cinque and Gelina and Fahizah who had summoned up my rage and hatred, and now they were no longer around to overwhelm and complicate my feelings about Patty. But still I was not sure what those feelings were.

I remembered later that week sitting in the witness stand of the SLA grand jury, looking at the photograph Browning had gotten me to sign a month before. "Let the record show," he was saying now, "that the witness, Steven Weed, has circled the area on this photograph purported to be that area representing the alleged mole on Patricia Hearst's face." For the next two hours he and a panel of assistant prosecutors hammered away, asking me questions about Patty's relationship with her parents, about our Berkeley friends, our financial situation, and our politics. He got nowhere. I had no trouble or hesitation in giving a sympathetic portrait of Patty as she was before February 4, but I was thankful his questions had not pressed further.

As I was stepping into the elevator after my testimony, I discovered that Marilyn Baker had somehow managed to squeeze in beside me, the doors bouncing off the camera cords until the rest of the reporters backed off. As we rode down it was quickly apparent that Marilyn's dislike of me had been overshadowed by her revulsion for Patty. What did I think about Patty's trying to kill the people at Mel's Sporting Goods? she wanted to know. "She's just a spoiled brat. Silly Putty, horribly adolescent. What did you ever see in her in the first place?"

I told her it was not the same Patty I had known four months before. I said it calmly, was carefully controlled, but inside a disappointment in Patty was rising up, a resentment that should not have emerged.

"You should call a press conference," Marilyn said, almost demanded, "and announce that you're washing your hands of her, since all she wants to do is play guerrilla."

As offensive as it was, there was something seductive about Marilyn's suggestion, the idea that I could be done with it by merely throwing Patty's insults back at her. After the holocaust on Fifty-fourth Street, which had amounted to something of a national catharsis, this is precisely what the public wanted, a simple answer and a simple reaction: Patty was simply a spoiled brat; Patty had been in on it from the beginning; Patty was under the influence of "mind control." But none of these formulas was sufficient, and while they might have satisfied all those people who had ached for the Hearsts, prayed for Patty, and then felt betrayed by her, they would have resolved nothing for me, nor vented the pressure that was building up again.

"She's under a sentence of destiny," Patrick Tobin told me a few days later. Tobin had been Patty's tour guide on her trip through Europe and for a time had been a cultural mentor of sorts. But it went much deeper than that. He felt a special "fondness" for Patty, loved her, and was deeply saddened by what had happened to a girl, as he described her, with the classical beauty of the Quatrocento, the Perugino-like oval face.

A man of insight and keen, albeit romantic, perceptions, Tobin saw Patty historically. "She's experiencing a traumatic sense of personal expansion," he said, "but in the sensational, egotistical way characteristic of the vulgar side of Hearst greatness." Tobin felt that, like old W.R., Patty had a tendency to substitute will for intellect. "And she certainly knew how to be sarcastic," he said, "to write people off with a few words, as if clank! down came the portcullis, and that was it." Toward the end of the evening, I remember him asking how my male ego was holding up. He shook his head sadly. "Patty certainly must have studied Samson and Delilah," he said.

Baker's simplistic disgust and Tobin's melancholy insights caught me when I was vulnerable and touched a resonant feeling in me. The day before I had awakened literally sick with disgust that Patty could have been so cruel, could turn her back on us so easily and, from what I gathered from Mathews's account, with no apparent remorse. After a couple of hours my disgust had faded out, had been suppressed by will and reasoned reminders that she was really not to blame. But now it was back and I was seized with the irony of my not being able to give up on her, my willingness to do anything and say anything for her, that I had made myself appear clownish. And the April Fool's communiqué announcing her imminent release. Had she been in on that and laughed condescendingly with the others at our floundering? If so, what books, what theories, what memories could forgive her that?

Paul Jacobs, the Old Leftist, looked like a beetle-browed Telly Savalas. He was flat on his back, pulled this way and that by weighted cables, having slipped a disc a couple of days before. "In the old days I was a very physical Young Turk," he grumbled. "Now I destroy my back by leaning down and picking up an empty paper bag." He shook his head and laughed at himself, then winced a little.

I had not seen Jacobs since the early days of the food program, and although I cannot recall exactly why I went to see him this time, it isn't important. I learned something that afternoon.

Jacobs, onetime editor of *Ramparts* magazine, can best be described as a bullet-headed, hard-nosed intellectual. But in his heyday he was a firebrand. Once, when asked what business he was in during the Depression, he answered: "Trying to overthrow the government by force and violence. But business was lousy." That's the kind of man he is. For thirty-five years he was in the forefront of the radical movement and saw dreams of revolution come and go. Jacobs knew that movement inside and out, had perspective on it and a grasp of the power and dedication it inspired. He has a pretty good idea of part of what was happening to Patty.

"What do you think revolutionaries—or self-professed revolutionaries—are doing when they aren't out tossing bombs around?" he asked pointedly. "They're loving each other. Not just casually chatting in their dingy garrets, but loving each other in a new and intense way. They're feeling the strongest sense of camaraderie imaginable. You have to understand that, Steve," he said, "but it's hard if you've never really experienced it. Just as it's hard —perhaps impossible—for the nonbeliever to grasp the 'glow' of religious conversion."

Jacobs shifted up on one elbow and tried to explain this "glow," the powerful sense of community and belonging, the special kind of "us-ness" a radical group can provide. "We had wonderful fantasies about our roles in the Revolution," he told me. "What the Revolution would be like. . . . We saw ourselves as great romantic figures." The discipline of the group, Jacobs then explained, had the effect of resolving personal problems. "I remember the difficulty I had trying to get permission from my cell to marry my wife. . . . Every personal detail of our lives was subject to regulation, and the smallest infraction could bring on a two- or three-hour criticism session, something that was very hard to take. But in a sense our kinship was even stronger for it. I've found it's a bond that has endured through the years."

If that bond could endure, could still soften an articulate skeptic like Jacobs, who looked to have a bit of the Barbary Coast hooligan in him, I had to wonder what kind of force it would have on Patty.

"She's experienced the most profound sense of family and belonging she's ever known," Jacobs said. "That alone is a beautifully fulfilling experience, but one that can be totally entrapping." He winced, then lay back down and nodded toward the foot of his bed. "Tighten that cable a little, will you?" I tightened the cable and rearranged some of the weights. Jacobs looked tired. It was time for me to go. "You've got my head spinning again," I told him when we shook hands. He nodded and smiled. "That's what it's for sometimes."

But my head had not been spinning for the past few days. Rather, it had been making huge sweeps back and forth between two starkly contradictory images of Patty, dragging my emotions along with it. I would listen to Jacobs or read a case history in Lifton and for a while be overcome with a sense of her victimization, a sense of how she'd been overwhelmed. In these moments the image of the way I knew her before would burst in upon my memory, and I'd feel ashamed that I couldn't sustain this sympathy, which, intellectually, I was so certain she deserved. For there was also the woman at Mel's Sporting Goods who'd seemed so proud of her marksmanship, the voice on the last two tapes that cut through all my attempts at understanding.

I was still grappling with these competing images two days later when I walked nervously onto the brightly lit stage and took a seat next to Dick Cavett. The producer of the show had first called me a month or so before, but at that point—when I was running the prison proposal around—a talk show appearance was the furthest thing from my mind. But then, shortly after the shoot-out, he called again, this time with a hook. Three well-known kidnapping victims—Reg Murphy, Burke Elbrick, and J. Paul Getty III, along with Brian Jenkins, an authority on kidnapping, had already agreed to take part. I did have something I wanted to say now: a criticism of the Los Angeles massacre, and a plea to the public and law enforcement not to turn against Patty.

Moving some of the press people back off the stage, the director consulted the TV monitor, then cued us, and the show began. For the next half hour I struggled to talk with Cavett about something I had not fully resolved for myself. Fortunately we stuck mostly to abstractions, the theories and examples I could by that time produce with facility. But then toward the end Cavett had almost apologetically asked: "Do you mind if I ask you . . . something I think everyone would like to know . . . do you feel you still love Patty?" Unable to give an unqualified answer, the best I could do was to be jokingly evasive: "I expect that ten years from now people will still be asking me that question . . . ," implying that I thought the question a stupid one.

The studio guards thought they could rush me out of the building after the show, but the reporters were two steps ahead of us. After a couple of detours to various exits, all well covered by the press, one of the guards pushed open an emergency door for me and succeeded in setting off a fire alarm for the entire ABC building. I dashed out and raced down an alley toward a cab as two contingents from the press converged on me. "Do you think Patty wants to turn herself in?" one of the reporters shouted as I ducked into the cab. I told the driver to take off, step on it or some such thing, but he merely gave me a puzzled look, said something that sounded like Polish, and pulled away leisurely, the reporters running alongside. One of them got his hand in the window just as I was rolling it up and got stuck. I rolled it down, threw a couple of dollars over the front seat, jumped out at a stoplight, sprinted down Central Park West, and scrambled over a wall. I lost the last few diehard reporters somewhere in the park but kept running, suddenly feeling strangely liberated, just pounding down the pavement, cutting across the grass, and hearing occasional rustlings in the bushes from startled gays or muggers as I ran by. I felt almost free, as though I were outrunning the confusion; or at least for a while I did.

When I entered the apartment of some friends I was staying

with, I was winded and sweating. I sat down in a heap and idly glanced through some notes I had prepared for the show, then came across a question written in a feminine hand, scribbled down while I was on stage—"Do you still love her?" It was impossible to tell if the writer was joking with me at Cavett's obviousness, or if she had sensed in my evasiveness that I didn't really have an answer. After reading the question again I went to the window and watched the traffic on Seventy-second Street, trying to think of what I'd do with the next week.

Although the answer seems obvious to me now, at the time all I could have said was, "Sometimes yes, when I *think* she's a victim; sometimes no, when I *feel* she *is* just a *spoiled brat;* but mostly in between, when I don't know what to think or how I feel about her." That night I went to the window and watched the traffic come and go on West Seventy-second Street. Again I was feeling in between, right down the middle.

Robert Lifton's Cape Cod house blended naturally with the setting, a weathered, gray building, surrounded by pines and backed by sand dunes and beyond them the sea. It had been with an eye toward visiting him that I had accepted Dick Cavett's offer to come to New York. The day after the show, I had called Lifton and, two days later, had appeared at his door around noon.

When I arrived, Lifton was working in a small cottage, separated from the main house. At first I was nervous; I felt awkward and worried that I was imposing, but he quickly put me at ease. A tall, dark-haired man in his early forties, Lifton was plainspoken, direct, and sympathetic. Of the books I had read on thought reform, it had been his that had affected me the most, with their detailed case histories and their humanist, philosophical touch. I felt he, if anyone, could help me put Patty's behavior in perspective. He drew a cup of coffee from a large aluminum canister next to his desk and we began to talk. That talk lasted until midnight.

He began with a simple question: "What clicked inside you when you first began to realize that she had actually gone over? The first intuitions of this kind of shift of opinion can often hold a key," Lifton explained.

I thought back to two weeks before when I heard Tom Mathews's account of being kidnapped by Patty, how it had finally forced me to accept the change. But I knew that it was three weeks earlier, in the week after the "Sexist-Ageist Pig" tape of April 24, when my fears and obsessions really started. "There was no one intuition of fact that brought it about," I told Lifton after a moment of reflection. "It was just an accumulation of things."

For the next two hours we explored that accumulation, the conversation moving back and forth between us, articulating and bringing into focus my experience and intuitions of the SLA's political inspirations, its group psychology, Patty's perceptions of betrayal, my readings and talks with Dr. Hacker, and, in general, my growing ability to have an imaginative grasp of the reality of what Patty had seen and experienced for the first two months of the kidnapping. As we talked, we moved from Lifton's work cottage and walked along the beach. It was a beautiful day, clear and blue; the surroundings reduced to elemental beauty of sky and sea and sand. After the traffic jams, the crowds, and blaring horns of New York City, it was a perfect place for me to put things together. Walking, pausing to stare at a gull or to gaze off across the water at a distant sailboat, all the jagged pieces of information and memories, all the shards of emotion, began to fall into place for me. I told Lifton of my vivid memory of having been stung in late April by a long interview with Joe Remiro in *The Phoenix*, stung by the strength of his conviction and the reality of his perspective. The phantom of the SLA began to become human, and when I went to see Wes Davis on April 29, all of this had been building up and it did not take much to trigger a change. "Almost overnight I became obsessed with the thought that my unquestioned confidence in Patty's loyalty had really been nothing but stubbornness and blindness," I told Lifton, "that I had been the husband who had been the last to know. My memories of how happy she had been . . . she seemed too well moored in her life for me to think anything else."

"In the life and death ethos anything becomes possible," I remember Lifton's saying. "To be immersed in death as Patty has been is often to lose a certain hold on life and to be especially vulnerable to new ways of redefining oneself in terms of that experience. This need to change can be particularly strong if in addition the environment is one that can produce guilt and guilt-anxiety in the victim."

I had at first resisted this last factor, trying to explain how unencumbered Patty was with the anxious little complexes of inadequacy and shame that trouble most people to some degree—how basic, healthy, and confident she was in this respect. But as we talked, I began to think of other things, to remember how much importance she placed on people's rights, her feelings of sympathy with the underdog. "Everyone has existential and social guilt that can be tapped to some degree," Lifton said. "A susceptibility to the repeated and unanimous opinion that he is wrong, or selfish, or simply inadequate as a human being. And the self-deprecating effects of this guilt and shame can readily undermine the self-image and in turn bring about important changes in attitude."

We talked about the crucial importance of the self-image, the constant human struggle for self-definition, and about Lifton's observations that in most of the people he had studied who had been through the coercive reform process in China, it was possible to identify childhood and adolescent strains which emerged during the reform process. Conversion often touches childhood motifs, early aspirations, relationships to parents and authority figures, and, perhaps most important, what has been the "submerged metaphor," which represents the personal solution to the postadolescent identity crisis. "It's this self-symbol of adult identity that often helps determine the particular form a later conversion will take," Lifton said. He wanted to know if these considerations might have some applicability to Patty's case, and I found that the examples came to mind almost of themselves:

her long-standing need to have independence from her family, the strong desire for "specialness" that motivated her choice of friends and pursuits, and, in line with that, her "seeking wisdom and identification with teachers—Heather, Othello, and finally me. "I like it when you teach me things," I remember her saying, when I'd point out something to her. But sometimes it was easy to forget that Patty was just nineteen years old, not completely resolved in some of the things that Lifton was talking about. How she used to wish we had met ten years later. "You've done all those things, been to all those places," I remembered her saying, "and I haven't done anything."

Later that evening over dinner in the nearby town of Wellfleet, Lifton and I talked about the nature of Patty's change and the prospects for the future. I suggested that, despite all we had talked about, I still had an easier time seeing her change more as *rebellion* than as *conversion*—more *personal* than *political*. For the politics we had heard from her on the tape had sounded so clichéd, imitative, superficial, politically naive, going no deeper than catchwords and flap quotations from George Jackson. But Lifton cautioned me about trying to distinguish the personal from the political, pointing out that from the first moment the people of the SLA began to talk to her, it was in political language and with political interpretations. "Patty undoubtedly sees her change as more political than personal or, more accurately, has organized her personal realignments in political terms," Lifton remarked. "The increase in colorlessness in her voice, the almost symbolic denunciations of you and her family would support that view. And in all the ways that you and the Hearsts let her down, she was able to find political lessons."

It was not difficult for me to provide examples. Patty had seen her father act out of concern for his wealth, her mother act out of concern for her privilege; in the way I had spoken of her as "a girl cruelly used," and, even more importantly, in parts of the life we had led together before, the SLA had found ample proof to show Patty that I was irredeemably sexist and paternalistic. Lifton and I talked about the pleasant little roles Patty and I would fall into perhaps too often—me, the teacher/father, the "grouchy old man," as she would sometimes call me, and her, the child/student, with her coloring book and "Sesame Street." "There is a power to the Women's Movement," Lifton said, "and the SLA's ability to develop in Patty the idea that, next to you, she had been a passive nonentity was probably the single most important cause of her turning away from you." And there were other things, incidents, pieces of conversations, that took on a new light as we talked: my materialistic interest in antiques, even my encouraging a détente with her parents, and pointing out that taking a job with a Hearst magazine would not be the worst thing in the world. It must have begun to seem, in retrospect, like a false escape to Patty from the suffocation of her family. "Please don't make me go back there," I remembered Patty pleading when I agreed with her parents that it might be wise for her to go "home" to recuperate from a knee operation she was going to have. "Please don't make me go back." There was real anguish in her voice that I just did not take seriously.

A few hours later, Lifton and I were sitting quietly in his den sipping coffee. It was midnight and our discussion had come to an end. Outside, an offshore wind was blowing. We could hear it in the trees.

"I do not want to leave you without a word of encouragement," Lifton said after a moment. "If the milieu that brought about her change was removed, as it seems it already partly has been, I don't think it likely that she will sustain her present state of mind very long. Sooner or later she will come into contact with modifying influences, and while it is not reasonable to expect her to be able to return to where she was before, we can hope that a valuable integration of all her experiences will eventually take place. The modern psychological style is one of flux and flow; she is still young and it's not too late for her. Perhaps that's not too much comfort to you now," he said, "but at least I think we've answered some things today."

For twelve hours we had been working our way through all the layers, exploring the interconnections between what had seemed like contradictions, binding them with dialogue, talking them out,

335

and finally resolving them. We had not arrived at any startling revelations or simple answers. Rather, the dialogue itself was the answer, or at least for me it was. And while there was comfort in feeling the knots and the confusion dissolve into a wider perspective, I felt quietly melancholy. It was as if I had had to go through it all again, to circle around and return to where I had begun, to what I had always felt, in order to understand it for the first time. And what I had always felt, but could not give in to, was the tragedy of the whole affair. I remember lying awake in that hospital bed, trying to tell myself that people get over these things. But coming through that was the feeling that what had happened to Patty and me was just too damaging, too monstrous to absorb and return to our life as it was. I had been right in that, but wrong in my assumption, my hope that Patty's strength of character, her "spunk" as her father called it, would be directed against her captors. The people who held her captive and lived with her for two months had been able to get behind that strength to her vulnerability and dependence, and she had turned away from us.

Toward the end of the evening I remember thinking out loud, telling Lifton that, given who Patty was and what had happened to her, there was really no other path she could have taken. "I think that's the definition of tragedy," he said.

The next morning Lifton was back at work in his study, and I decided not to bother him. I put on my trunks, walked across the sand dunes to the beach, and took off on a long, good run. Afterward I lay down in the sand and hardly thought at all.

On June 7, three weeks after the Fifty-fourth Street shoot-out, Patty and the Harrises issued what was to be the SLA's last communiqué. I was staying with friends outside of Newport, Rhode Island, at the time and read it in the newspaper.

Whether or not they were shattered by the death of their friends, Bill and Emily Harris's final word was little more than a replay of earlier communiqués—full of self-righteous rhetoric about fascism and revolutions, denunciations of "pig agents," and strains of fanatical mysticism. "Our past as middle-class White

Amerikans," said Emily, "was meaningless. It was truly wasted potential, so filled with desperate pessimism that we could feel the emptiness of Capitalistic Amerika even before we could understand it. . . . [Now] our lives are real because we see the truth and the future. . . ."

But Patty's statement was different. For the first time she described the love and respect she had come to feel for those six people who had at first held her prisoner, had threatened her, and then had become comrades before dying in the holocaust of Fifty-fourth Street.

Greetings to the people. This is Tania. I want to talk about the way I knew our six murdered comrades.

Cujo [Willie Wolfe] was the gentlest, most beautiful man I've ever known. We loved each other so much, and his love for the people was so deep that he was willing to give his life for them. . . . Neither Cujo or I had ever loved an individual the way we loved each other. . . . I was ripped off when the pigs murdered Cujo. . . . The pigs probably have the little old man monkey that Cujo wore around his neck. He gave me the little stone face one night. . . .

Gelina [Angela Atwood] was beautiful. Fire and joy. . . . She wrote poetry—some of it on the walls of Golden Gate, all of it in the L.A. pig files now—that expresses how she felt. . . . We laughed and cried together. She taught me how to fight the enemy within, through her constant struggle with bourgeois conditioning. . . .

Gabi [Camilla Hall] practiced until her shotgun was an extension of her right and left arms, an impulse, a tool of survival. She loved to touch people with a strong, not delicate, embrace. Gabi taught me the patience and discipline necessary for survival and victory. . . .

Zoya [Mizmoon] wanted to give meaning to her name, and on her birthday (the day of the shoot-out) she did. Zoya, female guerrilla, perfect love and perfect hate reflected in stone-cold eyes. . . .

Fahizah [Nancy Ling Perry] was a beautiful sister who didn't talk much, but who was the teacher of many by her righteous example. She, more than any other, had come to understand and conquer the putrid disease of bourgeois mentality. Fahizah taught me the perils of hesitation. She was wise, and bad, and I'll always love her.

Cinque loved the people with tenderness and respect. Cin knew that to live was to shoot straight. [He] was in a race with time, believing that every minute must be another step forward in the fight to save the children. He taught me virtually everything imaginable, but wasn't liberal with us. He'd kick our asses if we didn't hop over a fence fast enough or keep our asses down while practicing. Most importantly, he taught me how to show my love for the people. . . . On February 4 [the night of her kidnapping] Cinque Mtume saved my life. . . .

It's hard to explain what it was like watching our comrades die, murdered by pig incendiary grenades. A battalion of pigs facing a fire-team of guerrillas, and the only way they could defeat them was to burn them alive. It made me mad to see the pigs looking at our comrade's weapons, to see them holding Cujo's .45 and his watch, which was still ticking. He would have laughed at that. There is no surrender. No one in that house was suicidal—just determined and full of love. . . . One day, just before making the last tape, Cujo and I were talking about the way my parents were fucking me over. He said that his parents were still his parents because they had never betrayed him. . . .

I died in that fire on Fifty-fourth Street, but out of the ashes I was reborn. I renounced my class privilege when Cin and Cujo gave me the name Tania. While I have no death wish, I have never been afraid of death. For this reason, the brainwash/duress theory of the pig Hearsts has always amused me. Life is very precious to me, but I have no delusions that going to prison will keep me alive. . . . Patria o muerte, venceremos. . . .

I was both hurt and a little sickened by what Patty said, but those feelings did not last very long. There was nothing new to grapple with now, nothing to unravel, no more questions to ask. More than anything, I felt a hollowness inside of me, a sense of the terrible loss, the terrible waste of it all. I knew that was just something I would have to feel for a while, but something that would pass in time. . . .

Three months later, before leaving for England, I was digging through some of my old things when I came across a postcard Patty had sent me while staying with Heather two summers before.

My Darling—
This is a view from the Quantocks, but it's really so much more beautiful. When you look down from the hills the countryside looks like a quilt with the little fields and villages making up the patchwork. This is a wonderful place. You'd really love it. We'll have to come back here someday and do some heavy duty walking (truckin').

I have been spending most of my time with Heather and her two month old grandson. He's so cute. He laughs all the time. . . . Well, he does whimper a bit when he's hungry or tired, but he really is a good little baby. If he had webbed toes he'd be perfect.

Do you miss me? I know you do by your asking me why I haven't written in so long ("I haven't had a letter in about five days!!"). Your letters always make me smile as I read. I miss you terribly. See you soon, Sweetie.

I love you,

Patty

Heather was waiting on the platform when my train pulled into the station in Shropshire. Although we had never met before, we knew each other immediately, embraced like two old friends, then loaded my suitcase in her Morris Minor and sputtered three miles down a narrow lane to her "black and white" Elizabethan cottage set cleanly in a valley next to a stream. Earlier I had called her from Bristol. "Do you want to eat American or English?" she asked cheerfully. "English, of course," I said, and English it was. After showing me through her house, which was beautifully done up with antique oaken furniture, a great old grandfather clock ticking away in a corner—Heather referred to it as "he"—handmade quilts on the beds upstairs, small-paned windows, and delicate knickknacks everywhere, she sat me down to a meal "simply reeking of England"—steak and kidney pie, potatoes from her garden, and strawberry trifle for dessert. "I'm a bit of a fanatic about gardening," she said, then told me how Patty had sent her some clippings from *Sunset* magazine to give her some ideas for laying it out. "Whenever I needed anything done for me in California, Patty was the one I could always depend on. A real get-up-and-go girl I used to call her."

I stayed with Heather for two weeks, and it was easy to see why Patty had been so taken with her. A handsome gray-haired woman with soft blue eyes and a fine mixture of gentility, charm, and earthiness, Heather was truly a lady, a "self-sufficient woman who's been everywhere," as Patty had described her. She was also something of a scholar of English history. During the days she took me around to all the sights, the two of us walking through Catherine of Aragon's stone castle, poking around an ancient, moss-covered abbey set back in the hills, and having toasted tea cakes at the Alfoxton Lodge, once the residence of Wordsworth. Patty had stayed there for a few days on her visit, Heather told me. "She charmed all the old ladies down on holidays. The little Indian waiter still asks about her."

Heather and I spent a lot of time just talking about Patty, sitting by the fire in the evenings, walking through her garden or down along the stream in the afternoons. I remember our laughing about what a "hellcat" Patty could be at times, how she would hiss at me and paw the air in my direction when I would remind her of something she should be doing. "Yes, rather snarly at times." Heather smiled. "But I have to say it was quite cute."

That was really the tone of our visit. Each of us had come to understand what had happened to Patty, but by then it was more with a sense of wonderment than grief. "She could be so scorching about anything she considered spurious," Heather remarked, smiling and shaking her head, "and now she seems to be gulping it down in great draughts." But of course there were also quiet, wistful moments when a special memory would touch us. One evening I remember sitting by the fire while Heather was in the kitchen making us some tea. When she brought it in she told me what she was thinking about.

"One night," she said, "it was rather late and Patty knocked quietly on my door to show me a love poem she had been reading. I·believe it was by D. H. Lawrence," she said, then related how Patty had sat on the edge of her bed and read the poem to her. " 'That's how you must feel about Rex,' she told me when she was finished." Heather smiled. "She was so sweet and sensitive. An extraordinary girl. She fawned over Jamie, my grandson, and I do believe that even at the age of three months he was actually flirting with her."

A few nights later Heather and I were visited by a fine old country handyman named Malcolm, who brought along some of his elderflower wine "to nip at." He was a character right out of Dickens, short thick limbs, rather portly, "preserved in amber" as Heather described him. For the next few hours Malcolm kept us convulsed with laughter, his speech dotted with old sayings and Elizabethan phraseology. He would hunch forward in his chair, talking with great deliberation, a deadpan expression, and gesturing with his thick hands as he described coming upon some Terry Thomas types out on a fox hunt. "I say there, old chap, have you seen the hounds?" he mimicked them. "No, but I seen some dogs. . . . If you want to see a fool in the country"—he chuckled—"you'd better bring him with you." It was a fine evening, mellowed by Malcolm's wine, warmed by his stories and the small fire.

After Malcolm left, remarking that "the terrible thing 'bout tanglefoot wine is that your upstairs keeps working, but your legs don't," Heather's and my thoughts returned to Patty. I remember her making an observation that had started to occur to me at Cape

Cod with Lifton. "The whole thing has the dimensions of the Greek tragedy, doesn't it?" she said. "The way Patty was singled out, the way she was—her name, her age, her character that was both strong and vulnerable. It could only have happened just the way it did to Patty.

"And all the rest of you, too, struck where it was hardest for you. Poor Mr. Hearst, who could always pick up the telephone to get anything done, finding himself for the first time in his life powerless. Mrs. Hearst, who'd always had privacy and a good name, forced to see her family exposed and dissected in every nerve and fiber. And you, with your pride in thoughtful detachment, finding yourself at an utter loss to understand." Heather then paused a moment. "I just hope that Patty is digesting her situation," she said quietly. Another moment, then she asked, "Do you *feel* you'll ever see her again?"

I told her that I hoped so, that perhaps someday when she had gained some perspective on what had happened, not just to her, but to all of us, we might have the chance to see each other again and simply talk.

By then I could, and can, answer another question, the one scribbled into my notebook that night in New York. . . . Two years ago Patty and I were about to be married. We were in love, we had everything to look forward to, and then in those terrible seconds on the night of February 4 we were torn apart without time for words or even looks between us. That is how it ended. We never had the chance to begin a life together as man and wife, nor did we ever experience the bitterness and resentment that comes when love begins to fade and a relationship begins to fail. Because of this, it is impossible for me to think back to our days in Wyntoon, our evenings watching the stars from the tree house, and all the other times we had together without feeling warm and wistful about them. In that sense, yes, I still love Patty. But it's much like the love for someone who has died or been lost. Regardless of the grueling months of the kidnapping and whatever might happen in the future, none of it can destroy or erase those times we had together, this commitment to the past. They are something permanent, enduring.

Just now, thinking back to our days in Berkeley, I remember walking to campus one afternoon and seeing her coming toward me, the same, choppy, determined little step bouncing her along. Her face was downcast, preoccupied with thoughts about a paper due, perhaps, or another book to read. She didn't see me leaning against a tree, watching her, smiling at her. Then, when she was only a few steps away, she looked up and there was this wide smile, half-surprised, half-self-mocking, her hands stretching out as if to say, "You caught me. Here I am."